FUNDAMENTALS OF POLITICAL SOCIOLOGY

Fundamentals of Political Sociology

N.M. Sood

SUMIT ENTERPRISES
New Delhi-110 002 (India)

First Published 2011

ISBN 978-81-8420-274-8

Published by:

SUMIT ENTERPRISES
4649B/21, Ansari Road, Darya Ganj
New Delhi-110 002
Phone: 011-23279353, 9810217567
E-mail: sumit_enterprises2007@yahoo.co.in

PRINTED IN INDIA

Published by Sri Lokesh Kumar for Sumit Enterprises, New Delhi-110002, Typeset by Abhijeet Typesetters, Printed at Nev Prabhat Printing Press, Tronicacity (UP)

Contents

dom [illegible]
soci [illegible]
in tod [illegible]
became [illegible]
In [illegible]
then [illegible]
decl [illegible]
the [illegible]
alle [illegible]
socia [illegible]
sociol [illegible]
majo [illegible]
theo [illegible]
Plura [illegible]
inter [illegible]
a sh [illegible]
look [illegible]
sem [illegible]
the [illegible]
recog [illegible]
wea [illegible]
Sch [illegible]
recog [illegible]
clas [illegible]
patt [illegible]
in the [illegible]
Thus [illegible]

Preface

Political Sociology is the study of political power and domination in social relationships, and looks at how major social trends can affect the political scenario of a country. But in today's fast changing world especially in India, politics has become dirty word, where strange fellows share the same bed. In pre-Independence India, many political leader sacrificed their life for the welfare of nation. The history is full of heroic deeds of innumerable political leaders who bear all pains for the Independence of India and other countries.

Political sociology looks at how major social trends can affect the political process, as well as exploring how various social forces work together to change political policies. Political sociologists apply several theories to substantive issues. Three major theoretical frameworks are pluralism, elite or managerial theory and class analysis which overlaps with Marxist analysis. Pluralism sees politics primarily as a contest among competing interest groups. Elite or managerial theory is sometimes called a state-centred approach. It explains what the state does by looking at constraints from organizational structure, semiautonomous state managers, and interests that arise from the state as a unique, power concentrating organization.

The Indian Constitution and political community have given recognition to the grave condition of resourcelessness of the weakest sections of Indian society through the system of 'Scheduled' castes and 'Scheduled' tribes. In other words, while recognizing the heuristic value of 'caste', 'gender', 'tribe' and 'class' as separate analytical and sociological categories, this paper suggests that caste, tribe and class merge into each other in the domain of absolute as well as chronic poverty in India. This clarification is important as there are a large number of instances of 'caste into class' and 'class into caste' as well as tribe-caste convergence in terms of economic conditions. But they do not negate the fact that for the last several decades there is marginal difference in the caste status of the absolutely poor classes and there is very limited evidence of economic prosperity ('creamy layer') among the depressed castes and tribes particularly in the rural domain of the Indian economy.

Besides, it presents a combination of the analytical and critical approaches to the study of political sociology. Tracing the evolution of political sociology in India and abroad as a specialized field of study, it discusses the major issues of the discipline. An essential reading for the students of social sciences in general and of sociology and political science in particular.

—Editor

1

Concepts of Political Sociology

Political sociology is the study of the relations between state and society. The discipline draws on comparative history to analyse socio-political trends. A typical research question in this area might be: "Why do so few American citizens choose to vote?" The field developed from the work of Max Weber, Barrington Moore, Jr., and Moisey Ostrogorsky.

Theory

There are four main areas of research focus in contemporary political sociology:

1. The socio-political formation of the modern state.
2. "Who rules"? How social inequality between groups (class, race, gender, etc.) influences politics.
3. How public personalities, social movements and trends outside of the formal institutions of political power affect politics, and
4. Power relationships within and between social groups (e.g. families, workplaces, bureaucracy, media, etc). Contemporary theorists include Robert A. Dahl, Seymour Martin Lipset, Theda Skocpol, Luc Boltanski and Nicos Poulantzas.

Political sociology looks at how major social trends can affect the political process, as well as exploring how various social forces work together to change political policies. Political sociologists apply several theories to substantive issues. Three major theoretical frameworks are pluralism, elite or managerial theory and class analysis which overlaps with Marxist analysis. Pluralism sees politics primarily as a contest among competing interest groups. Elite or managerial theory is sometimes called a state-centred approach. It explains what the state does by looking at constraints from organizational structure, semiautonomous state managers, and interests that arise from the state as a unique, power concentrating organization. A leading representative is Theda Skocpol.

Social class theory analysis emphasizes the political power of capitalist elites. The theory emerged from Marxism in the 1850s based primarily on the premise of economic exploitation of one class by another. It split into two parts: one is the power structure or instrumentalist approach, another is the structuralist approach. The power structure approach focuses on Who Rules? and its most well-known representative is G. William Domhoff. The structuralist approach emphasizes how the very way a capitalist economy operates only allows and encourages the state to do some things but not others. Its best known representative was Nicos Poulantzas. Important innovations in the field come from the French Pragmatism and particularly from the Political and Moral Sociology elaborated by Luc Boltanski and Laurent Thevenot.

Political sociology also concerns the play of power and personality, for instance, the impact of globalization upon identity: "The fragmentation and pluralization of values and life-styles, with the growth of mass media and consumerism and decline of stable occupations and communities, all means that previously taken for granted social identities have become *politicized.*"

POLITICAL SOCIALISATION

Political socialization is a concept concerning the "study of the developmental processes by which children and adolescents acquire political cognition, attitudes and behaviors".

Agents of Socialization

These Agents of Socialization all influence in one degree or another an individual's political opinions: Family, Media, Friends, Teachers, Religion, Race, Gender, Age, Geography, etc. These factors and many others that people are introduced to as they are growing up will affect their political views throughout the rest of their lives. Most political opinions are formed during childhood. Many Political Ideas are passed down from Parents to young Adults through them expressing their beliefs.

Factors

The agents a child surrounds him/herself with during childhood are crucial to the child's development of future voting behaviors. Some of these agents include:

Family: Glass et al. (1986) recognizes family (1) as a primary influence in the development of a child's political orientation, mainly due to constant relationship between parents and child

Child's party	*Parent=Dem*	*Parent=Ind*	*Parent=Rep*
Democrat	45%	25%	30%
Independent	27%	53%	36%
Republican	7%	10%	83%

Schools: Most influential of all agents, after the family, due to the child's extended exposure to a variety of political beliefs, such as friends and teachers, both respected sources of information for students.

Mass Media: Becker et al. (1975) argue that the media (2) functions as a political information-giver to adolescents and young children.

Religion: Religious tradition can have a strong effect on someones political views. For example, Protestants tend to be more conservative.

Political Parties: Scholars such as Campbell (1960) note that political parties (3) have very little direct influence on a child due to a contrast of social factors such as age, context, power, etc.

POLITICAL SPECTRUM

A political spectrum (plural spectra) is a way of modelling different political positions by placing them upon one or more geometric axes symbolizing independent political dimensions. Most long-standing spectra include a right wing and left wing, which originally referred to seating arrangements in the 18th century French parliament. According to the simplest left-right axis, communism and socialism are usually regarded internationally as being on the left, opposite fascism and conservatism on the right. Liberalism can mean different things in different contexts, sometimes on the left, sometimes on the right.

However, researchers have frequently noted that a single left-right axis is insufficient in describing the existing variation in political beliefs, and often include other axes. Though the descriptive words at polar opposites may vary, often in popular biaxial spectra the axes are split between cultural issues and economic issues, each scaling from some form of individualism (or government for the freedom of the individual) to some form of communitarianism (or government for the welfare of the community). In this context, the left is often considered individualist (or libertarian) on social/cultural issues and communitarian (or populist) on economic issues, while the right is often considered communitarian (or populist) on social/ cultural issues and individualist (or libertarian) on economic issues.

HISTORICAL ORIGIN OF THE TERMS

The terms *Right* and *Left* refer to political affiliations which originated early in the French Revolutionary era of 1789-1796, and referred originally to the seating arrangements in the various legislative bodies of France. The aristocracy sat on the right of the Speaker (traditionally the seat of honour) and the commoners sat on the Left, hence the terms Right-wing politics and Left-wing politics.

Originally, the defining point on the ideological spectrum was the *ancien regime* ("old order"). "The Right" thus implied support for aristocratic or royal interests, and the church, while "The Left" implied support for republicanism, secularism and civil liberties. Because the political franchise at the start of the revolution was relatively narrow, the original "Left" represented mainly the interests of the bourgeoisie, the rising capitalist class. At that time, support for laissez-faire capitalism and Free markets were counted as being on the left; today in most Western countries these views would be characterized as being on the Right. As the franchise expanded over the next several years, it became clear that there was something to the left of that original "Left": the precursors of socialism and communism, advocating the interests of workers and peasants.

Academic Investigation

For almost a century, social scientists have considered the problem of how best to describe political variation; a sample of their results is given below.

Early Research

In 1950, Leonard W. Ferguson carried out an analysis of political values using ten scales measuring attitudes toward:

- Birth control
- Capital punishment
- Censorship
- Communism
- Evolution
- Law
- Patriotism
- Theism
- Treatment of criminals
- War.

Submitting the results to factor analysis, he was able to identify three factors, which he named *Religionism*, *Humanitarianism*, and *Nationalism*.

Leonard Ferguson's *Religionism* was defined by belief in God and negative attitudes toward evolution and birth control; *Humanitarianism* was related to attitudes opposing the harsh treatment of criminals, capital punishment, and war; and *Nationalism* described variation in opinions on censorship, law, patriotism, and communism.

This system was derived empirically; rather than devising a political model on purely theoretical grounds and testing it, Ferguson's research was exploratory. Although replication of the *Nationalism* factor was inconsistent, the finding of *Religionism* and *Humanitarianism* had a number of replications by Ferguson and others.

Eysenck's Research

Shortly afterward, Hans Eysenck began researching political attitudes in Great Britain. He believed that there was something existentially similar about the National Socialists or Nazis on the one hand, and the Communists on the other, despite their opposite positions on the left-right axis.

As Hans Eysenck described in his 1956 book *Sense and Nonsense in Psychology*, Eysenck compiled a list of political statements found in newspapers and political tracts and asked subjects to rate their agreement or disagreement with each.

Submitting this value questionnaire to the same process of factor analysis used by Ferguson, Eysenck found two factors, which he named "Radicalism" (R-factor) and "Tender-Mindedess" (T-factor). Eysenck's R-factor is easily identified as the classical "left-right" dimension, although the T-factor is less intuitive; high-scorers favoured pacifism, racial equality, religious education, and restrictions on abortion, while low-scorers had attitudes more friendly to militarism, harsh punishment, easier divorce laws, and companionate marriage.

Despite the difference in methodology, location, and theory, the results attained by Eysenck and Ferguson matched; simply rotating Eysenck's two factors 45 degrees renders the same factors of *Religionism* and *Humanitarianism* identified by Ferguson in America.

Hans J. Eysenck was an outspoken opponent of what he perceived as the authoritarian abuses of the left and right, and accordingly he believed that, with this T axis, he had found the link between nazism and communism: according to Eysenck's research findings, members of both ideologies were tough-minded. Central to Eysenck's thesis was the claim that tender-minded ideologies were democratic and friendly to human freedoms, while tough-minded ideologies were aggressive and authoritarian.

Although he was a longstanding opponent of nazism, having left Nazi Germany to live in Britain, Eysenck was not shy in attacking communism, noting the anti-Semitic prejudices of the Russian communist government, the luxurious lifestyles of the USSR's leaders despite their talk about equality and the poverty of their people, and the Orwellian "doublethink" of

East Germany's naming itself the *German Democratic Republic* despite being "one of the most undemocratic regimes in the world today." Accordingly, he carried out studies on Nazism and communist groups, finding members of both groups to be more dominant, and more aggressive, than control groups.

At the time, Han J. Eysenck's conception of 'tough-mindedness' was criticized for a number of reasons.

- Firstly, virtually no values were found to load only on the tough/tender dimension.
- Secondly, his interpretation of tough-mindedness as a manifestation of "authoritarian" versus tender-minded "democratic" values was incompatible with the Frankfurt school's single-axis model, which conceptualized authoritarianism as being a fundamental manifestation of conservatism, and many researchers took issue with the idea of "left-wing authoritarianism."
- Thirdly, the theory which Eysenck developed to explain individual variation in the observed dimensions, relating tough-mindedness to Extroversion and Psychoticism, returned ambiguous research results.
- Lastly, Eysenck's finding that nazists and communists were more tough-minded than members of mainstream political movements was criticised on technical grounds by Milton Rokeach.

Despite the problems of Hans J. Eysenck's model, his dimensions of R and T were found by factor analyses of values in Germany and Sweden, France, and Japan.

One interesting result Eysenck noted in his 1956 work was that in the United States and Great Britain, most of the political variance was subsumed by the left/right axis, while in France, the T-axis was larger, and in the Middle East, the only dimension to be found was the T-axis: "Among mid-Eastern Arabs it has been found that while the tough-minded/tender-minded dimension is still clearly expressed in the relationships observed between different attitudes, there is nothing that corresponds to the radical-conservative continuum."

Rokeach's Research

Dissatisfied with Hans J. Eysenck's work, Milton Rokeach

developed his own two-axis model of political values in 1973, basing this on the ideas of *freedom* and *equality*, which he described in his book, *The Nature of Human Values.*

Milton Rokeach claimed that the defining difference between the left and right was that the left stressed the importance of equality more than the right. Despite his criticisms of Eysenck's tough-tender axis, Rokeach also postulated a basic similarity between communism and nazism, claiming that these groups would not value freedom as greatly as more conventional social democrats, democratic socialists and capitalists would, and he wrote that "the two value model presented here most resembles Eysenck's hypothesis."

To test this model, Milton Rokeach and his colleagues used content analysis on works exemplifying nazism (written by Adolf Hitler), communism (written by V.I. Lenin), capitalism (by Barry Goldwater) and socialism (written by various socialist authors).

Multiple raters made frequency counts of sentences containing synonyms for a number of values identified by Rokeach, including freedom and equality, and Rokeach analyzed these results by comparing the relative frequency rankings of all the values for each of the four texts:

In excerpts from...

- Socialists (socialism)-Freedom ranked 1st, Equality ranked 2nd
- Hitler (nazism)-Freedom ranked 16th, Equality ranked 17th
- Goldwater (capitalism)-Freedom ranked 1st, Equality ranked 16th
- Lenin (communism)-Freedom ranked 17th, Equality ranked 1st.

Later studies using samples of American ideologues and American presidential inaugural addresses were consistent with this model.

Later Research

In further research, Hans J. Eysenck refined his methodology to include more questions on economic issues. Doing this, he revealed a split in the left-right axis between social policy and economic policy, with a previously undiscovered dimension of *socialism-capitalism* (S-factor). While factorially distinct from Eysenck's previous R factor, the S-factor did positively correlate with the R-factor, indicating that a basic left-right or right-left tendency underlies both social values and economic values, although S tapped more into items discussing economic inequality and big business, while R is known to relate more to the treatment of criminals, and to sexual issues and military issues. An online quiz tests users on the three Eysenckian political dimensions.

A recent analysis of survey data using principal component analysis was carried out in 2003 in the UK; the results of this study yielded the same two dimensions as found by Eysenck's original research: the familiar "left-right" R-dimension that mixes economic issues and social issues, and a second T-dimension that is described as "pragmatism vs idealism."

Another replication came from Dr. Ronald Inglehart's research into national opinions based on the World Values Survey, although Inglehart's research described the values of *countries* rather than individuals or groups of individuals within nations. Inglehart's two-factor solution took the form of Ferguson's original Religionism and Humanitarianism dimensions; Inglehart labelled them "secularism-traditionalism," which covered issues of tradition and religion, like patriotism, abortion, euthanasia and the importance of obeying the law and authority figures, and "survivalism-self expression," which measured issues like everyday conduct and dress, acceptance of diversity (including foreigners) and innovation, and attitudes towards people with specific controversial lifestyles such as homosexuality and vegetarianism, as well as willingness to partake in political activism.

Other Proposed Dimensions

Numerous alternatives exist, usually developed by those that feel their views are not fairly represented on the traditional right-left spectrum.

One alternative spectrum offered by the conservative *American Federalist Journal* accounts for only the degree of political control without consideration for any other social or political variable, and thus places totalitarianism (total government control i.e. fascism (corporatism) and communism at one extreme and anarchism (no government at all) at the other extreme.

In 1998, political author Virginia Postrel, in her book *The Future and Its Enemies*, offered another single axis spectrum that measures one's view of the future; on one extreme are those who allegedly fear the future and wish to control it: *stasists*, and on the other hand are those who want the future to unfold naturally and without attempts to plan and control: *dynamists*. The distinction corresponds to the utopian versus dystopian spectrum used in some theoretical assessments of liberalism, and the book's title is borrowed from the work of the anti-utopian classic-liberal theorist Karl Popper.

Other Proposed Axes Include

- Focus of political concern: *Communitarianism* vs. *Individualism*. This axis is often considered perpendicular to the left-right axis in popular multi-axis charts (often rendered "populism" vs. "libertarianism"), but is a legitimate axis in itself, comparing a focus on the community vs. a focus on the individual. This language is preferred to the prejudiced language of "totalitarianism" (anti-freedom) vs. "libertarianism" (pro-freedom), because one can have a political focus on the community without being totalitarian and undemocratic. Christian Democracy is a political philosophy that would be counted as communitarian on this axis, but is not totalitarian or undemocratic.
- Role of the church: *Clericalism* vs. *Anti-clericalism*. This axis is less significant in the United States (where views of the role of religion tend to be subsumed into the general left-right axis) than in Europe (where clericalism versus anti-clericalism is much less correlated with the left-right spectrum).
- Urban vs. rural: This axis may be the most useful and significant today in European as well as Australian politics and Canadian politics. The urban vs. rural axis was equally prominent in the United States' political

past, but its importance is debatable at present. In the late 18th century and early 19th century in the United States, it would have been described as the conflict between Hamiltonian Federalists and Jeffersonian Democrats.

- Foreign policy: *interventionism* (the nation should exert power abroad to implement its policy) vs. *non-interventionism* (the nation should keep to its own affairs); similarly, *multilateralism* (coordination of policies with other countries) vs. *isolationism* and *unilateralism*
- Relations with individual states or groups of states may also be vital to party politics. During the Cold War, parties often had to choose a position on a scale between pro-American and pro-Soviet Union, although this could at times closely match a left-right spectrum. At other times in history relations with other powerful states has been important. In early Canadian history relations with Great Britain were a central theme, although this was not "foreign policy" but a debate over the proper place of Canada within the British Empire.
- International action: *Multilateralism* (states should cooperate and compromise) versus *Unilateralism* (states have a strong, even unconditional, right to make their own decisions).
- Political violence: *pacifism* (political views should not be imposed by violent force) vs. *militancy* (violence is a legitimate or necessary means of political expression). In North America, particularly in the United States, holders of these views are often referred to as "doves" and "hawks", respectively.
- Foreign trade: *globalization* (world economic markets should become integrated and interdependent) vs. *autarky* (the nation or polity should strive for economic independence). During the early history of the Commonwealth of Australia, this was the major political continuum. At that time it was called *Free trade* vs. *Protectionism*.
- Trade freedom vs. trade equity: *Free trade* (businesses

should be able trade across borders without regulations) vs. *Fair trade* (international trade should be regulated on behalf of social justice).

- Diversity: *multi-culturalism* (the nation should represent a diversity of cultural ideas) vs. *assimilationism* or *nationalism* (the nation should primarily represent, or forge, a majority culture).
- Participation: *Democracy* (rule of the majority, or mob rule) vs. *Aristocracy* (rule by the enlightened) vs. *Tyranny* (total degradation of Aristocracy, ancient Greek philosophers such as Plato and Aristotle recognized tyranny as a state in which the tyrant is ruled by utter passion, and not reason like the philosopher, resulting in the tyrant pursuing his own desires rather than the common good.)
- Freedom: *Positive liberty* (having *rights* which impose an obligation on others) vs. *Negative liberty* (having *rights* which prohibit interference by others).
- Social power: *Totalitarianism* vs. *Anarchism* (Control vs. No Control) Analyzes the fundamental political interaction between people, and between individuals and their environment. Often posits the existence of a 'moderate' system as existing between the two extremes.
- Change: *radicals* (who believe in rapid change) and *progressives* (who believe in measured, incremental change) vs. *conservatives* (who believe in minimal or cautious change) vs. *reactionaries* (who believe in changing things to a previous state).
- Origin of state authority: *popular sovereignty* (the state as a creation of the people, with enumerated, delegated powers) vs. various forms of *absolutism* and *organic state* philosophy (the state as an original and essential authority) vs. the view held in *anarcho-primitivism* that "Civilization originates in conquest abroad and repression at home."

OTHER MULTI-AXIS MODELS

Nolan: Economic Freedom, Personal Freedom

The Nolan chart was created by libertarian David Nolan.

This chart shows what he considers as "economic freedom" (issues like taxation, free trade and free enterprise) on the horizontal axis and what he considers as "personal freedom" (issues like drug legalization, abortion and the draft) on the vertical axis. This puts left-wingers in the left quadrant, libertarians in the top, right-wingers in the right, and communitarians (whom Nolan originally named populists) in the bottom. It is possible to consider the Nolan chart to be an Eysenck model that has been rotated 45 degrees. The popular "diamond" presentation of the Nolan chart makes this particular comparison readily apparent.

The traditional left-right spectrum forms a diagonal across the Nolan chart, with communism and fascism both in the ultra-populist corner, an assignment hotly disputed by more liberal-minded communists who do not advocate state control over matters of personal freedom. There is some discrepancies between various forms of the model. In some, the bottom section is labelled with neutral, non-pejorative terms (such as 'communitarian') whereas others use emotional, loaded terms such as 'statist', 'authoritarian', or 'totalitarian'.

The Nolan chart has been re-oriented and visually represented in many forms since David Nolan first created it, and has been the inspiration for an endless array of political self-quizzes, perhaps the most famous of these being the World's Smallest Political Quiz, which places one on the Diamond Chart. As of 2005 this quiz is being used in 420 schools. It can be found in at least a dozen popular textbooks that feature the Quiz as part of their enhanced digital content. In August 2000 Portrait of America did a telephone survey that was done using the same questions and scale. More recently, The Institute for Humane Studies has created Politopia, a similar quiz. Interestingly, the Institute found that most applicants fell into the lower, populist section.

Three Axis Variants of Nolan Chart

There are two three-axis models based on the Nolan Chart. The Friesian Institute has suggested a model that combines the economic liberty and personal liberty axes with positive liberty, creating a cube. The Vosem Chart splits the economic axis of the Nolan chart into two axes, corporate economics (zaxis) and individual economics (y-axis), which combine with the civil liberty axis (x-axis) to form a cube.

Political Compass

The political compass largely follows the Eysenck method with the two-axes representing economic issues as right-vs-left and issues of freedom as authoritarian-vs-liberal. One can determine their position on the political compass through a online quiz by the same name.

Greenberg & Jonas: Left-right, Ideological Rigidity

In a 2003 *Psychological Bulletin* paper, Jeff Greenberg and Eva Jonas posit a model comprising the standard left-right axis and an axis representing ideological rigidity. For Greenberg and Jonas, ideological rigidity has "much in common with the related concepts of dogmatism and authoritarianism" and is characterized by "believing in strong leaders and submission, preferring one's own in-group, ethnocentrism and nationalism, aggression against dissidents, and control with the help of police and military."

Greenberg and Jonas posit that high ideological rigidity can be motivated by "particularly strong needs to reduce fear and uncertainty" and is a primary shared characteristic of "people who subscribe to any extreme government or ideology, whether it is right-wing or left-wing."

UK Inferred Model: Left-right, Political Pragmatism

While multiple axes on the political spectrum had been postulated for a while, statistical analysis of survey data using principal component analysis to verify the theory and establish their existence, number and meaning was not done until recently. A 2003 study in the UK yielded two significant eigenvectors (that is, groups of questions that tend to be answered consistently), one less well-constrained than the other. Creator Chris Lightfoot examined the survey questions and tried to assign a meaning to the axes: one is like the familiar "left-right" axis that mixes economic and social issues, and the other indicates a degree of "political pragmatism". The outcome of that study is that the UK political spectrum is most sensibly described with two axes.

Pournelle: Liberty-control, Irrationalism-rationalism

This very distinct two-axis model was created by Jerry Pournelle. The Pournelle chart has liberty (a dimension similar to the diagonal of the Nolan chart, with those on the left seeking liberty and those on the right focusing control, farthest right being state worship, farthest left being the idea of a state as the "ultimate evil") perpendicular to rationalism, defined here as the belief in planned social progress, with those higher up believing that there are problems with society that can be rationally solved, and those lower down skeptical of such approaches.

Inglehart: Tradition-secular, Self Expression-survivalist

In its January 4, 2003 issue, *The Economist* discussed a chart, proposed by Dr. Ronald Inglehart and supported by the World Values Survey (associated with the University of Michigan), to plot cultural ideology onto two dimensions. On the y-axis it covered issues of tradition and religion, like patriotism, abortion, euthanasia and the importance of obeying the law and authority figures. At the bottom of the chart is the *traditionalist* position on issues like these (with loyalty to country and family and respect for life considered important), while at the top is the *secular* position.

The x-axis deals with self-expression, issues like everyday conduct and dress, acceptance of diversity (including foreigners) and innovation, and attitudes towards people with specific controversial lifestyles such as vegetarianism, as well as willingness to partake in political activism. At the right of the chart is the open *self-expressionist* position, while at the left is its opposite position, which Dr. Inglehart calls *survivalist*. This chart not only has the power to map the values of individuals, but also to compare the values of people in different countries. Placed on this chart, EU countries in continental Europe come out on the top right, Anglophone countries on the middle right, Latin American countries on the bottom right, African, Middle Eastern and South Asian countries on the bottom left, and ex-Communist countries on the top left.

Mitchell: Eight Ways to Run the Country

In his book *Eight Ways to Run the Country: A New and Revealing Look at Left and Right* Brian Patrick Mitchell identifies four main political traditions in Anglo-American history:

- republican constitutionalism
- libertarian individualism
- progressive democracy
- plutocratic nationalism.

These four have given rise to eight distinct political perspectives:

- communitarian
- progressive
- radical
- individualist
- paleolibertarian
- paleoconservative
- theoconservative
- neoconservative.

A potential ninth perspective, in midst of the eight, is populism, which is vaguely defined and situation dependent, having no fixed character other than opposition to the prevailing power. These perspectives vary according to their regard for kratos (the use of force) and arche (the recognition of rank). Mitchell roots his distinction of arche and kratos in the West's historical experience of church and state, crediting the collapse of the Christian consensus on church and state with the appearance of the four main traditions. Mitchell's vertical axis is a scale of kratos/akrateia; his horizontal axis is a scale of archy/anarchy. Anarchy, for Mitchell, is not the absence of government, but the rejection of rank. Thus there can be both anti-government anarchists (left-libertarians, whom Mitchell calls libertarian individualists) and pro-government anarchists (Mitchell's progressive democrats, who use government against social hierarchies such as patriarchy). Mitchell also distinguishes between left-wing anarchists and right-wing anarchists, whom Mitchell renames "akratists."

2

Political Participation

Participation is both an activity and an attitude. As an activity it is a social activity. Someone taking a morning walk is not participating in anything. Someone taking part in a 100-meter race does. Someone staying in a neighbourhood for a long time without knowing any of one's neighbours is not having a participant attitude. What then is political participation? Of course, we mean a kind of political activity and a kind of political attitude. Since the 50's however it has attracted widespread attention and there seems to be a general agreement among the Political Scientists on the value and necessity of further political participation. But this apparent agreement conceals major disputes both at the levels of political theory and practical politics.

Before we explore these we should begin with the concept of political participation itself. The concept of political participation has been popularised in Political Science by the Behaviouralists. Of course arguments in favour of greater political participation had been advanced by republican and democratic theorists from Rousseau onwards and are still in use by contemporary political theorists. The behaviouralist paradigm rides on a liberal view of politics.

Classically, such a view draws a distinction between state and individual on the one hand and public and private on the other; it also leans on the side of the latter categories. Accordingly, when participation is seen as an attitude, it is taken as an individual's favourable orientation to the state or government. That was the basis on which Americans were seen as having a 'participant political culture'. The systematic use of culture and political culture as social science concepts dates only from 1950s. Here the political culture is seen as a shorthand expression to denote the set of values within which a political system operates. It is something between the state of public opinion and an individual's personality characteristics.

FORMS OF POLITICAL PARTICIPATION

The concept of political participation accommodates the following main forms of political participation:

1) voting in local or national elections;
2) voting in referendums;
3) canvassing or otherwise campaigning in elections;
4) active membership of a political party;
5) active membership of a pressure group;
6) taking part in political demonstrations, industrial strikes with political objectives, rent strikes in public housing, and similar activities aimed at changing public policy;
7) various forms of civil disobedience, such as refusing to pay taxes or obey a conscription order;
8) membership of government advisory committees;
9) membership of consumers' councils for publicly owned industries;
10) client involvement in the implementation of social policies;
11) various forms of community action, such as those concerned with housing or environmental issues in the locality.

If we take into account the broad concept of political participation, we can probably increase the list by adding such forms as:

1) Performing social duties such as jury service and military duties;
2) Town/village meetings and public debate on controversial issues;
3) Various forms of codetermination, such as student-faculty committees in the universities and government advisory committees;

4) Shared project management involving full-scale partnership, delegation or empowerment such as benefit-sharing arrangements or developmental projects;
5) New social movements seeking and promoting personal and collective identity, such as women's movement and movements for ethno-cultural identities.

On the whole there are several levels and forms at which and through which people may participate politically, as involved objects of a process of economic and political transformation set in motion by someone else, as expected beneficiaries of a programme with preset parameters, as politically co-opted legitimisers of a policy or as people trying to determine their own choices and direction independent of the state.

POLITICAL PARTICIPATION AND INDIAN DEMOCRACY

There has indeed been an upsurge in political participation in India with increasing competitiveness of the political parties, increased voter turnout, emergence of new forms of participation such as new social movements, institutions of grassroots politics, local level democracy and political assertions of the historically disadvantaged castes and ethno-regional groups. Apparently this represents a healthy trend towards further deepening of Indian democracy. Do we have a participant culture now in India? Though higher political mobilisation and higher electoral participation do not by themselves contribute to a participant culture, there has been a significant change of popular orientation form dependence on regular administration and traditional authority-symbols of society to people's representatives in everyday life, whether for certificates, aids or arbitration. But this upsurge in participation needs to be understood in the complexity of Indian process of democratisation. It is doubtful as to how much space has been created for a rational individual who exercises his/her sovereign power of citizenship in the electoral arena. This doubt arises not from the non-fulfillment of the basic requirements of procedural democracy like Universal Adult Franchise, rule of law and fundamental rights but from constraints on meaningful rational participation of the individual in democratic process. First, with numerous small parties that are not properly institutionalized and under total control of charismatic leaders, and some big parties showing no interest in promoting institutionalization, the individuals participate with severe constraints because parties are still in the centre of Indian democratic process. Second, several developments tend to constrain voters' right in recent years, such as the aborted attempt to make the qualifications and holdings of the election-candidates

transparent, increasing use of electronic voting machines which make it impossible for a voter to 'waste' his or her vote and thereby express disapproval about the candidates. Third, instead of social cleavages being neutralised by political cleavages the latter tend to be grafted on the former in India due to unprincipled mobilisation leading to a 'crisis of governability'.

This type of mobilisation and politicisation of masses by parties may have made Indian democracy not more deepening but 'more inclusive'. But the trouble with this inclusiveness is that the terms of inclusion are not always inclusive or modern but often exclusive and promote a step furthering the 'effective creolisation of the modern ideas, ideals and institutions of democratic politics in a non-European setting' (Yadav, 1998). Finally, the institutional space for non-electoral modes of efficacious political activity has not grown to a degree found in European settings. On the whole however political parties have proved to be the most effective agents of political participation in India. Indian democratic experience has witnessed new forms of political participation in recent years and a rise in the quantity of political participation-though the exact nature and significance of that for Indian democracy can be disputed.

POLITICAL ELITES

A power elite, in political and sociological theory, is a small group of people who control a disproportionate amount of wealth, privilege, and access to decision-making of global consequence. The term was coined by Charles Wright Mills in his 1956 book, *The Power Elite*, which describes the relationship between individuals at the pinnacles of political, military, and economic institutions, noting that these people share a common world view. The power elite is described as consisting of members of the corporate community, academia, politicians, media editors, military service personnel, and high-profile journalists. Individuals identified as belonging to the power elite include David Rockefeller, Averell Harriman and Robert McNamara.

Mills argues in his book that the US power elite consists of members of society characterized by consensus building and the homogenization of viewpoints. This power elite has historically dominated the three major sectors of US society: economy, government, and military. Elites circulate from one sector to another, consolidating their power as they go.

Social Structure

The power elite are the leadership of the upper class, able to shape the economy through their simultaneous access to both state and corporate power. Unlike the ruling class, a social formation based on heritage and social ties, the power elite is characterized by the organizational structure through which its wealth is acquired. According to Mills, the power elite is "the managerial reorganization of the propertied classes into the more or less unified stratum of the corporate rich." Domhoff further clarified the differences in the two terms: "The upper class as a whole does not do the ruling. Instead, class rule is manifested through the activities of a wide variety of organizations and institutions... Leaders within the upper class join with high-level employees in the organizations they control to make up what will be called the power elite."

Mills wrote that the power elite refers to "those political, economic, and military circles, which as an intricate set of overlapping small but dominant groups share decisions having at least national consequences. Insofar as national events are decided, the power elite are those who decide them." According to Mills, the governing elite in the US primarly draws its members from three areas: (i) the highest political leaders (including the president) and a handful of key cabinet members and close advisers; (ii) major corporate owners and directors; and (iii) high ranking military officers. The elite occupies what Mills terms the top command posts of society.

Such positions give their holders enormous authority over governmental, financial, educational, social, civic, and cultural institutions. A small group is thus able to make decisions and take actions that touch everyone.

POLITICAL ALIENATION

Political alienation is the distance perceived by individuals between their government and themselves. Political alienation describes a certain select group of people who happen to hold general views about local and federal governments. These views and or beliefs are distinguished between feelings about specific officials within government and feelings about the institutions and laws themselves. Political alienation is a specified force of nature which affects operational and conceptual thoughts about political systems. political alienation is adversely related to political efficacy. Political alienation also relates to peoples distrust of government.

Political Communication

Political communication is a field of communications that is concerned with politics. Communication often influences political decisions and vice versa.

Fields and Areas of Study

The field of political communication concern 2 main areas:

- Election campaigns-Political communications involved in campaigning for elections.
- Government operations-This role is usually fulfilled by a Ministry of Communications, Information Technology or similar political entity. Such an entity is in charge of maintaining communication legislation and would be responsible for setting telecommunications policy and regulations as well as issuing broadcasting licenses, comments press releases, etc...

According to James Chesebro, there are five critical approaches to contemporary Political communications:

1. Machiavellian-i.e. power relationships
2. Iconic-symbols are important
3. Ritualistic-Redundant and superficial nature of political acts-manipulation of symbols.
4. Confirmation-political aspects looked at as people we endorse

5. Dramatistic-politics is symbolically constructed. (Kenneth Burke).

POLITICAL LEGITIMACY AND EFFECTIVENESS

Effectiveness legitimacy is the degree to which goals are accomplished, the speed with which they are attained, and the efficiency of resources expended to reach them. In other words, the legitimacy of governing institutions depends on their capacity "to achieve the citizens' goals and solve their problems effectively and efficiently" (Schimmelfennig 1996, 3.1.). Efficiency "has a legitimizing effect" and is an integral part of effectiveness, yet effectiveness is more fundamental than efficiency, since assessing the efficiency of an outcome requires that the outcome first be achieved. The effectiveness dimension is thus output oriented and pertains to the results of policies, rules, and decisions. The concept of "output legitimacy" encompasses the aspects of legitimacy based on effectiveness or efficiency, where effectiveness refers to the problem solving capacity of governing institutions, and efficiency refers to their ability to solve problems without wasting resources (Risse 2004; Schimmelfennig 1996). Output legitimacy refers to the degree of problem solving effectiveness, the efficacy of decisions and solutions (Charnovitz 2006, 367), and the acceptance created by the successful implementation of these solutions (Zürn 2000, 184). Governing institutions obtain effectiveness legitimacy by ultimately achieving their objectives and making efficient use of resources to do so.

Effectiveness is essential to overall legitimacy because governance could be transparent, accountable, participatory, representative, appropriate, lawful, and fair, but if it is ineffective at achieving obligatory objectives then none of this really matters. Governance that achieves nothing is a useless waste of resources. People expect results from governing institutions, and these institutions are established and ultimately exist to address the collective objectives of society. The essence of effectiveness legitimacy is that governing institutions efficiently and competently achieve their prescribed tasks and duties.

Effectiveness is a unique dimension of legitimacy because the concept of achieving societal objectives is not easily incorporated within the other dimensions of legitimacy. One could perhaps include the achievement of objectives as a third aspect of appropriateness, after the Behavioural and structural aspects, arguing the position that it is appropriate for governance to achieve assigned tasks efficiently and effectively. Yet the idea of getting the job done does not fit well with the essence of appropriateness, and having three aspects of appropriateness legitimacy would make that dimension conceptually difficult and unnecessarily complicated. One could also potentially include effectiveness and efficiency within the representation dimension, arguing that citizen interests and desires are not adequately represented unless the goals of governance are ultimately achieved. Yet this deviates from the core meaning of representation. Representation legitimacy firstly emphasizes that the interests and desires of citizens are represented in governance, not that there are actually achieved, and secondly that the composition of representatives reflect the population in general, which says nothing about achieving collective objectives. Moreover, in a democratic polity with numerous conflicting interests it is not uncommon for the desires of some groups to go unachieved without representation legitimacy being diminished. One could argue that it is the majority desires that matter, and effectiveness could be tied to the achievement of majority goals. Yet the representation of majority desires remains different from their achievement, and effectiveness would remain a poor fit within representation. There is very little overlap between effectiveness and the other dimensions of legitimacy, but a theory of political legitimacy that overlooked the essential aspect of getting the work of governance completed would be deficient, and thus effectiveness is included as a separate dimension.

BUREAUCRACY

Bureaucracy is the combined organizational structure, procedures, protocols, and set of regulations in place to manage activity, usually in large organizations. As opposed to adhocracy, it is often represented by standardized procedure (rule-following) that guides the execution of most or all processes within the body; formal division of powers; hierarchy; and relationships, intended to anticipate needs and improve efficiency.

A bureaucracy traditionally does not create policy but, rather, enacts it. Law, policy, and regulation normally originates from a leadership, which creates the bureaucracy to implement them. In practice, the interpretation and execution of policy, etc. can lead to informal influence-but not necessarily. A bureaucracy is directly responsible to the leadership that creates it, such as a government executive or board of directors. Conversely, the leadership is usually responsible to an electorate, shareholders, membership or whoever is intended to benefit. As a matter of practicality, the bureaucracy is where the individual will interface with an organization such as a government etc., rather than directly with its leadership. Generally, larger organizations result in a greater distancing of the individual from the leadership, which can be consequential or intentional by design.

Bureaucracy is a concept in sociology and political science referring to the way that the administrative execution and enforcement of legal rules are socially organized. Four structural concepts are central to any definition of bureaucracy:

1. a well-defined division of administrative labour among persons and offices,
2. a personnel system with consistent patterns of recruitment and stable linear careers,
3. a hierarchy among offices, such that the authority and status are differentially distributed among actors, and
4. formal and informal networks that connect organizational actors to one another through flows of information and patterns of cooperation.

Examples of everyday bureaucracies include governments, armed forces, corporations, non-governmental organizations (NGOs), intergovernmental organizations (IGOs), hospitals, courts, ministries, social clubs, sports leagues, professional associations and academic institutions.

Origins

While the concept as such existed at least from the early forms of nationhood in ancient times, the word "bureaucracy" itself stems from the word "bureau", used from the early 18th century in Western Europe not just to refer to a writing desk, but to an office, i.e., a workplace, where officials worked. The original French meaning of the word *bureau* was the baize used to cover desks. The term bureaucracy came into use shortly before the French Revolution of 1789, and from there rapidly spread to other countries. The Greek suffix-*kratia* or *kratos*-means "power" or "rule".

Development

Perhaps the early example of a bureaucrat is the scribe, who first arose as a professional on the early cities of Sumer. The Sumerian script was so complicated that it required specialists who had trained for their entire lives in the discipline of writing to manipulate it. These scribes could wield significant power, as they had a total monopoly on the keeping of records and creation of inscriptions on monuments to kings.

In later, larger empires like Achaemenid Persia, bureaucracies quickly expanded as government expanded and increased its functions. In the Persian Empire, the central government was divided into administrative provinces led by satraps. The satraps were appointed by the Shah to control the provinces. In addition, a general and a royal secretary were stationed in each province to supervise troop recruitment and keep records, respectively. The Achaemenid Great Kings also sent royal inspectors to tour the empire and report on local conditions.

The most modernesque of all ancient bureaucracies, however, was the Chinese bureaucracy. During the chaos of the Spring and Autumn Period and the Warring States Period, Confucius recognized the need for a stable system of administrators to lend good governance even when the leaders were inept. Chinese bureaucracy, first implemented during the Qin dynasty but under more Confucian lines under the Han, calls for the appointment of bureaucratic positions based on merit via a system of examinations. Although the power of the Chinese bureaucrats waxed and waned throughout China's long history, the imperial examination system lasted as late as 1905, and modern China still employs a formidable bureaucracy in its daily workings.

Modern bureaucracies arose as the government of states grew larger during the modern period, and especially following the Industrial Revolution. As the authors David Osborne and Ted Gaebler point out "It is hard to imagine today, but a hundred years ago bureaucracy meant something positive. It connoted a rational, efficient method of organization – something to take the place of the arbitrary exercise of power by authoritarian regimes. Bureaucracy brought the same logic to government work that the assembly line brought to the factory. With the hierarchical authority and functional a specialization, they made possible the efficient undertaking of large complex tasks."

Tax collectors, perhaps the most disliked of all bureaucrats, became increasingly necessary as states began to take in more and more revenue, while the role of administrators increased as the functions of government multiplied. Along with this expansion, though, came the recognition of the corruption and nepotism often inherent within the managerial system, leading to civil service reform on a large scale in many countries towards the end of the 19th century.

Types of Bureaucratic Agencies

Examining different agencies from a management point of view, they differ in two main ways: whether or not the activities of the operators can be observed, and whether the results of those activities can be observed. The first factor deals with outputs, or what the agency does on a day to day basis. The second factor deals with outcomes, or the overall results of agency work. The extreme cases where outputs and outcomes are either simple or difficult to observe yields four different kinds of agencies: production, procedural, craft, and coping.

- Production organizations are those in which both outputs and outcomes are observable. Examples include the Social Security Administration, United States Postal Service, and IRS. In production organizations, managers can observe the outputs of officials, and can (for example in the IRS) measure the amount of money collected in taxes, and estimate with accuracy how much more tax money will be produced by increasing the level of auditing activity.
- Procedural organizations are those where outputs can be observed, but outcomes are unclear or not observable.

Examples include the Occupational Safety and Health Administration, and the United States armed forces during peace time. OSHA may observe the actions of health inspectors, but may not be able to measure how these individual actions add up to improved safety and health in the workplace. In the armed forces during peacetime, all aspects of training and deployment can be observed, but it cannot be measured how these activities deter aggression, or prepare for a future (unknown) conflict.

- Craft organizations are those where outputs are hard to observe, but outcomes are fairly easy to evaluate. Examples include the armed services at war, who may operate under a fog of war, but whose battle outcomes can be easily measured. Another example is the United States Department of Labour and their "Wage and Hour Division". While the outputs of individual inspectors in the field are difficult to measure, overall outcomes of negotiated compliance agreements and referrals to federal attorneys for legal action are easily measurable.
- Coping organizations are those where neither outputs nor outcomes are observable. Typical examples include Police Departments, and the United States Department of State. Some of the activities of diplomats and policeman cannot be observed or measured (e.g. sensitive conversations with foreign leaders, and interactions with citizens on the street), and the outcomes are also difficult to judge (e.g. changes in foreign perceptions of US interests, and the level of order on a policeman's beat)

An agency's type substantially impacts its approach to its mission, (i.e. the degree to which its members are devoted to accomplishing the agency's stated mission) and to compliance with the law and existing policy.

Views on the Concept

In a letter of July 1, 1790, the German Baron von Grimm declared: "We are obsessed by the idea of regulation, and our Masters of Requests refuse to understand that there is an infinity of things in a great state with which a government should not concern itself." Jean Claude Marie Vincent de

Gournay sometimes used to say, "We have an illness in France which bids fair to play havoc with us; this illness is called *bureaumania*." Sometimes he used to refer to a fourth or fifth form of government under the heading of "bureaucracy". In another letter of July 15, 1765 Baron Grimm wrote also, "The real spirit of the laws in France is that bureaucracy of which the late Monsieur de Gournay used to complain so greatly; here the offices, clerks, secretaries, inspectors and *intendants* are not appointed to benefit the public interest, indeed the public interest appears to have been established so that offices might exist."

This quote refers to a traditional controversy about bureaucracy, namely the perversion of means and ends so that means become ends in themselves, and the greater good is lost sight of; as a corollary, the substitution of *sectional* interests for the *general* interest. The suggestion here is that, left uncontrolled, the bureaucracy will become increasingly self-serving and corrupt, rather than serving society. Indeed, the cynical Parkinson's Law suggests that bureaucracies grow independent of their function.

Karl Marx

In Karl Marx's and Friedrich Engels's theory of historical materialism, the historical origin of bureaucracy is to be found in *four* sources: religion, the formation of the state, commerce, and technology.

Thus, the earliest bureaucracies consisted of castes of *religious* clergy, officials and scribes operating various rituals, and armed functionaries specifically delegated to keep order. In the historical transition from primitive egalitarian communities to a civil society divided into social classes and estates, beginning from about 10,000 years ago, authority is increasingly centralized in, and enforced by a state apparatus existing separately from society. This state formulates, imposes and enforces laws, and levies taxes, giving rise to an officialdom enacting these functions. Thus, the state mediates in conflicts among the people and keeps those conflicts within acceptable bounds; it also organizes the defence of territory. Most importantly, the right of ordinary people to carry and use weapons of force becomes increasingly restricted; in civil society, forcing other people to do things becomes increasingly the legal right of the state authorities only.

But the growth of trade and commerce adds a new, distinctive dimension to bureaucracy, insofar as it requires the keeping of accounts and the processing/recording of transactions, as well as the enforcement of legal rules governing trade. If resources are increasingly distributed by prices in markets, this requires extensive and complex systems of record-keeping, management and calculation, conforming to legal standards. Eventually, this means that the total amount of work involved in commercial administration outgrows the total amount of work involved in government administration. In modern capitalist society, private sector bureaucracy is *larger* than government bureaucracy, if measured by the number of administrative workers in the division of labour as a whole. Some corporations nowadays have a turnover larger than the national income of whole countries, with large administrations supervising operations.

A fourth source of bureaucracy Marxists have commented on inheres in the technologies of mass production, which require many standardized routines and procedures to be performed. Even if mechanization replaces people with machinery, people are still necessary to design, control, supervise and operate the machinery. The technologies chosen may not be the ones that are best for everybody, but which create *incomes* for a particular class of people or maintain their power. This type of bureaucracy is nowadays often called a technocracy, which owes its power to control over specialized technical knowledge or control over critical information.

In Marx's theory, bureaucracy rarely creates new wealth by itself, but rather controls, co-ordinates and governs the production, distribution and consumption of wealth. The bureaucracy as a social stratum derives its income from the appropriation of part of the social surplus product of human labour. Wealth is appropriated by the bureaucracy by law through fees, taxes, levies, tributes, licensing etc.

Bureaucracy is therefore always a *cost* to society, but this cost may be accepted insofar as it makes social order possible, and maintains it by enforcing the rule of law. Nevertheless there are constant conflicts about this cost, because it has the big effect on the distribution of incomes; all producers will try to get the maximum return from what they produce, and minimize administrative costs. Typically, in epochs of strong economic growth, bureaucracies proliferate; when economic growth declines, a fight breaks out to cut back bureaucratic costs.

Whether or not a bureaucracy as a social stratum can become a genuine ruling class depends greatly on the prevailing property relations and the mode of production of wealth. In capitalist society, the state typically lacks an independent economic base, finances many activities on credit, and is heavily dependent on levying taxes as a source of income. Therefore, its power is limited by the costs which private owners of the productive assets will tolerate. If, however, the state owns the means of production itself, defended by military power, the state bureaucracy can become much more powerful, and act as a ruling class or power elite. Because in that case, it directly controls the sources of new wealth, and manages or distributes the social product. This is the subject of Marxist theories of bureaucratic collectivism.

Marx himself however never theorized this possibility in detail, and it has been the subject of much controversy among Marxists. The core organizational issue in these disputes concerns the degree to which the *administrative* allocation of resources by government authorities and the *market* allocation of resources can achieve the social goal of creating a more free, just and prosperous society. Which decisions should be made by whom, at what level, so that an optimal allocation of resources results? This is just as much a moral-political issue as an economic issue.

Central to the Marxian concept of socialism is the idea of workers' self-management, which assumes the internalization of a morality and self-discipline among people that would make bureaucratic supervision and control redundant, together with a drastic reorganization of the division of labour in society. Bureaucracies emerge to mediate conflicts of interest on the basis of laws, but if those conflicts of interest disappear (because resources are allocated directly in a fair way), bureaucracies would also be redundant. Marx's critics are however skeptical of the feasibility of this kind of socialism, given the continuing need for administration and the rule of law, as well as the propensity of people to put their own self-interest before the communal interest. That is, the argument is that self-interest and the communal interest might *never* coincide, or, at any rate, can always diverge significantly.

Max Weber

Max Weber has probably been one of the most influential users of the word in its social science sense. He is well-known for his study of bureaucratization of society; many aspects of modern public administration go back to him; a classic, hierarchically organized civil service of the continental type is — if perhaps mistakenly — called *Weberian civil service* several different years between 1818 and 1860, prior to Weber's birth in 1864.

Weber described the ideal type bureaucracy in positive terms, considering it to be a more rational and efficient form of organization than the alternatives that preceded it, which he characterized as *charismatic domination* and *traditional domination.*

According to his terminology, bureaucracy is part of legal domination. However, he also emphasized that bureaucracy becomes inefficient when a decision must be adopted to an individual case.

According to Weber, the attributes of modern bureaucracy include its impersonality, concentration of the means of administration, a levelling effect on social and economic differences and implementation of a system of authority that is practically indestructible.

Weber's analysis of bureaucracy concerns:

- the historical and administrative reasons for the process of bureaucratization (especially in the Western civilisation)
- the impact of the rule of law upon the functioning of bureaucratic organisations
- the typical personal orientation and occupational position of a bureaucratic officials as a status group
- the most important attributes and consequences of bureaucracy in the modern world.

A bureaucratic organization is governed by the following seven principles:

1. official business is conducted on a continuous basis
2. official business is conducted with strict accordance to the following rules:
   - the duty of each official to do certain types of work is delimited in terms of impersonal criteria
   - the official is given the authority necessary to carry out his assigned functions
   - the means of coercion at his disposal are strictly limited and conditions of their use strictly defined
3. every official's responsibilities and authority are part of a vertical hierarchy of authority, with respective rights of supervision and appeal
4. officials do not own the resources necessary for the performance of their assigned functions but are accountable for their use of these resources
5. official and private business and income are strictly separated
6. offices cannot be appropriated by their incumbents (inherited, sold, etc.)
7. official business is conducted on the basis of written documents.

A bureaucratic official:

- is personally free and appointed to his position on the basis of conduct
- exercises the authority delegated to him in accordance with impersonal rules, and his or her loyalty is enlisted on behalf of the faithful execution of his official duties
- appointment and job placement are dependent upon his or her technical qualifications
- administrative work is a full-time occupation
- work is rewarded by a regular salary and prospects of advancement in a lifetime career.

An official must exercise his or her judgment and his or her skills, but his or her duty is to place these at the service of a higher authority; ultimately he/she is responsible only for the impartial execution of assigned tasks and must sacrifice his or her personal judgment if it runs counter to his or her official duties. Weber's work has been continued by many, like Robert Michels with his Iron Law of Oligarchy.

Criticism

As Max Weber himself noted, real bureaucracy will be less optimal and effective than his ideal type model. Each of Weber's seven principles can degenerate:

- Competences can be unclear and used contrary to the spirit of the law; sometimes a decision itself may be considered more important than its effect;
- Nepotism, corruption, political infighting and other degenerations can counter the rule of impersonality and can create a recruitment and promotion system not based on meritocracy but rather on oligarchy;

Even a non-degenerated bureaucracy can be affected by common problems:

- Overspecialization, making individual officials not aware of larger consequences of their actions
- Rigidity and inertia of procedures, making decision-making slow or even impossible when facing some unusual case, and similarly delaying change, evolution and adaptation of old procedures to new circumstances;
- A phenomenon of *group thinking*-zealotry, loyalty and lack of critical thinking regarding the organisation which is *perfect* and *always correct* by definition, making the organisation unable to change and realise its own mistakes and limitations;
- Disregard for dissenting opinions, even when such views suit the available data better than the opinion of the majority;
- A phenomenon of *Catch-22* (named after a famous book by Joseph Heller)-as bureaucracy creates more and more rules and procedures, their complexity rises and coordination diminishes, facilitating creation of contradictory and recursive rules, as described by the saying "the bureaucracy is expanding to meet the needs of the expanding bureaucracy".

- Not allowing people to use common sense, as everything must be as is written by the law.

In the most common examples bureaucracy can lead to the treatment of individual human beings as impersonal objects. This process has been criticised by many philosophers and writers (Aldous Huxley, George Orwell, Hannah Arendt) and satirized in the comic strip *Dilbert, TV* show *The Office*, Franz Kafka's novels *The Trial* and *The Castle*, Douglas Adams' story *The Hitchhiker's Guide to the Galaxy*, and the films *Brazil* and *Office Space.*

Michel Crozier

Michel Crozier wrote The Bureaucratic Phenomenon (1964) as a re-examination of Weber's (1922) concept of the efficient ideal bureaucracy in the light of the way that bureaucratic organizations had actually developed.

Whereas for Weber, bureaucracy was the ultimate expression of a trend toward the efficient, rational organization, Crozier examined bureaucracy as a form of organization that evokes:

> *"... the slowness, the ponderousness, the routine, the complication of procedures and the maladapted responses of the bureaucratic organization to the needs which they should satisfy" (Crozier, 1964)*

He examined a number of culturally specific examples of bureaucratic organizations in an attempt to understand why bureaucracies so often became dysfunctional.

After reviewing the different ways in which the term is used, Crozier describes the sense in which he uses the term bureaucracy thus:

> *"A bureaucratic organization is an organization that can not correct its behaviour by learning from its errors" (Crozier, 1964)*

Adding:

> *"... not only a system that does not correct its behaviour in view of its errors; it is also too rigid to adjust, without crises, to the transformations that the accelerated evolution of the industrial society makes more and more imperative" (Crozier, 1964).*

In essence, Crozier presents an argument against the Tayloristic notion of 'the one best way' to organize an activity and Weber's view of bureaucracy as the ultimate expression of rationality and efficiency. He notes that in 1964 'advanced organizations' had already:

> *"... been obliged to discard completely the notion of the one best way [and] are beginning to understand that the illusion of perfect rationality has to long persisted, weakening the possibilities of action by insisting on rigorous logic and immediate coherence" (Crozier, 1964).*

From his analysis of his case studies, he develops a theory of bureaucratic dysfunction based on his observations. Although he later extends his ideas to cover other settings, the two main cases on which he bases his theory are both located in France: "The Clerical Agency" and "The Industrial Monopoly". Crozier chose these examples not only because he was French, but also because he claims that socially and culturally France has developed in such a way that it created organizations that closely resembled the Weberian notion of an ideal bureaucracy.

His theory is based on the observation that in situations where almost every outcome has been decided in advance according to a set of impersonal and predefined rules and regulations, the only way in which people are able to gain some control over their lives is to exploit 'zones of uncertainty' where the outcomes are not already known.

For Crozier, organizations are not autonomous entities but social constructs that are: "... man made and socially created [and] the indirect result of the power struggles within the organization" (Crozier, 1964).

Attacking both the rationalists and the human relations school for ignoring the role that such power struggles play in the shaping of an organization he argues that organizational relations are in fact a series of strategic games where the protagonists attempt either to exploit any areas of discretion for their own ends, or to prevent others from gaining an advantage: *"Each group fights to preserve and enlarge the area upon which it has some discretion, attempts to limit its dependence upon other groups and accept such dependence only insofar as it is a safeguard... [preferring] retreatisim if there is no other choice but submission" (Crozier, 1964).*

The result of this is that goals are subverted and the organization becomes locked into a series of inward looking power struggles. Thus, paradoxically, the result of attempting to design an efficient organization that runs on rational and impersonal lines is to create a situation where the opposite to is true.

Theory of Bureaucratic Dysfunction

Crozier argues that:

> *"... the bureaucratic system of organization is primarily characterized by the existence of a series of relatively stable vicious circles that stem from centralisation and impersonality" (Crozier, 1964).*

He outlines four such 'vicious circles' that he observed in the organizations he studied.

The development of impersonal rules

In an attempt to be rational and egalitarian, bureaucracies attempt to come up with a set of abstract impersonal rules to cover all possible events. Crozier gives the example of the concours (competitive examinations) which mean that, one the exams are passed, promotion become simply a matter of seniority and avoiding damaging conflicts. The result, he argues, is that hierarchical relationships decline in importance or disappear completely which means that higher level in the bureaucracy have effectively lost the power to govern the lower levels.

The Centralization of Decisions

If one wishes to maintain the impersonal nature of decision making, it is necessary to ensure that decision are made at a level where those who make them are protected from the influence of those who are affected by them. The effect of this is that problems are resolved by people who have no direct knowledge of the problems they are called upon to solve, and so, priority is given to the resolution of internal political problems instead. In this case, the power to influence events over which one has direct experience is lost and it is passed to some impartial central body.

The Isolation of Strata and Group Pressure within Strata

The suppression of the possibility of exercising discretion among superiors and the removal of opportunities for bargaining from subordinates results in an organization that consists of a series of isolated strata. The notional equality within the strata becomes the only defence for the individual against demands form other parts of the organization and allows groups some degree of control over their own domain. The result is very strong per group pressure to conform to the norms of the strata regardless of individual beliefs or the wider goals of the organization.

The Development of Parallel Power Relationships

It is impossible to account for every eventuality, even by the constant addition of impersonal rules and the progressive centralisation of decision making; consequently, individuals or groups that control the remaining zones of uncertainty, wield a considerable amount of power. This can lead to the creation of parallel power structures that give certain groups or individuals in certain situations, disproportionate power in an otherwise regulated and egalitarian organization. Once again, this can lead to decisions being made based on factors separate from the overall goals of the organization.

American Usage

...[A]dministration in the United States must be at all points sensitive to public opinion. A body of thoroughly trained officials serving during good behaviour we must have in any case: that is a plain business necessity. But the apprehension that such a body will be anything un-American clears away the moment it is asked. What is to constitute good behaviour? For that question obviously carries its own answer on its head. Steady, hearty allegiance to the policy of the government they serve will constitute good behaviour. That policy will have no taint of officialism about it. It will not be the creation of permanent officials, but of statesmen whose responsibility to public opinion will be direct and inevitable. Bureaucracy can exist only where the whole service of the state is removed from the common political life of the people, its chiefs as well as its rank and file. Its motives, its objects, its policy, its standards, must be bureaucratic.

Popular dictionary definitions reflect a popular dislike for bureaucracy. *The American Heritage Dictionary'*, after two traditional definitions of the word, the third and last definition of bureaucracy reads in part: "numerous offices and adherence to inflexible rules of operation;... any unwieldy administration." According to *Webster's New world Dictionary of the American Language*, one of the definitions reads in part "bureaucracy is governmental officialism or inflexible routine."

Roget's Thesaurus gives among the synonyms for *bureaucracy*: "officialism", "officiousness", and "red tape".

American science fiction writer Jerry Pournelle has proposed a theory he refers to as "Pournelle's Iron Law of Bureaucracy", which states:

> *"In any bureaucracy, the people devoted to the benefit of the bureaucracy itself always get in control and those dedicated to the goals the bureaucracy is supposed to accomplish have less and less influence, and sometimes are eliminated entirely."*

This robust tendency is purported to operate to the effect that:

> *"...in any bureaucratic organization there will be two kinds of people: those who work to further the actual goals of the organization, and those who work for the organization itself. Examples in education would be teachers who work and sacrifice to teach children, vs. union representative who work to protect any teacher including the most incompetent. The Iron Law states that in all cases, the second type of person will always gain control of the organization, and will always write the rules under which the organization functions."*

Austrian School Analysis

The analysis of bureaucracy by the Austrian school reflects its characteristic focus on economics, and emphasizes the distinction between bureaucratic management and profit management.

Current Academic Debates

Modern academic research has debated the extent to which elected officials can control their bureaucratic agents. Because bureaucrats have more information than elected officials about what they are doing and what they should be doing, bureaucrats might have the ability to implement policies or regulations that go against the public interest. In the American context, these concerns led to the "Congressional abdication" hypotheses—the claim that Congress had abdicated its authority over public policy to appointed bureaucrats.

Theodore Lowi initiated this debate by concluding in a 1979 book that the U.S. Congress does not exercise effective oversight of bureaucratic agencies. Instead, policies are made by "iron triangles", consisting of interest groups, appointed bureaucrats, and Congressional subcommittees (who, according to Lowi, were likely to have more extreme views than the Congress as a whole). It is thought that since 1979 interest groups have taken a large role and now do not only effect bureaucracy, but also the money in congress. The idea of "iron triangles" has since evolved to "iron hexagons" and then to a "hollow sphere."

The relationships between the Legislatures, the Interest Groups, Bureaucrats, and the general public all have an effect on each other. Without one of these pieces the entire structure would completely change. This relationship is considered "mu", or such that not one single piece can describe or control the entire process. The public votes in the legislatures and the interest groups provide information, but the legislature and bureaucrats also have an effect on the interest groups and the public. The entire system is codependent on each other.

William Niskanen's earlier (1971) 'budget-maximizing' model complemented Lowi's claims; where Lowi claimed that Congress (and legislatures more generally) failed to exercise oversight, Niskanen argued that rational bureaucrats will always and everywhere seek to increase their budgets, thereby contributing strongly to state growth. Niskanen went on to serve on the U.S. Council of Economic Advisors under President Reagan, and his model provided a strong underpinning for the worldwide move towards cutbacks of public spending and the introduction of privatization in the 1980s and '90s.

Two branches of theorizing have arisen in response to these claims. The first focuses on bureaucratic motivations; Niskanen's universalist approach was critiqued by a range of pluralist authors who argued that officials' motivations are more public interest-orientated than Niskanen allowed. The bureau-shaping model (put forward by Patrick Dunleavy) also argues against Niskanen that rational bureaucrats should only maximize the part of their budget that they spend on their own agency's operations or give to contractors or powerful interest groups (that are able to organize a flowback of benefits to senior officials). For instance, rational officials will get no benefit from paying out larger welfare checks to millions of poor people, since the bureaucrats' own utilities are not improved. Consequently we should expect bureaucracies to significantly maximize budgets in areas like police forces and defence, but not in areas like welfare state spending.

A second branch of responses has focused more on Lowi's claims, asking whether legislatures (and usually the American Congress in particular) can control bureaucrats. This empirical research is motivated by a normative concern: If we wish to believe that we live in a democracy, then it must be true that appointed bureaucrats cannot act contrary to elected officials' interests. (This claim is itself debatable; if we fully trusted elected officials, we would not spend so much time implementing constitutional checks and balances.)

Within this second branch, scholars have published numerous studies debating the circumstances under which elected officials can control bureaucratic outputs. Most of these studies examine the American case, though their findings have been generalized elsewhere as well. These studies argue that legislatures have a variety of oversight means at their disposal, and they use many of them regularly. These oversight mechanisms have been classified into two types: "Police patrols" (actively auditing agencies and looking for misbehavior) and "fire alarms" (imposing open administrative procedures on bureaucrats to make it easier for adversely affected groups to detect bureaucratic malfeasance and bring it to the legislature's attention). A third concept of self-interested bureaucracy and its effect on the production of public goods has been forwarded by Faizul Latif Chowdhury. In contrast to Niskanen and

Dunleavy, who primarily focused on the self-interested behaviour of only the top-level bureaucrats involved in policy making, Chowdhury in his thesis submitted to the London School of Economics in 1997 drew attention to the impact of the low level civil servants whose rent-seeking behaviour pushes up the cost of production of public goods. Particularly, it was shown with reference to the tax officials how rent-seeking by them causes loss in government revenue. Chowdhury's model of rent-seeking bureaucracy captures the case of administrative corruption whereby public money is directly expropriated by public servants in general.

FORMS OF GOVERNMENT

The following list groups major political systems in alphabetical order. The various subtype political systems are listed below the main system.

Authoritarian (The Rule of the Few)

- o Aristocracy
- o Communist state
- o Consent
- o Corporatism
- o Despotism
- o Democracy
- o Diarchy
- o Dictatorship;
  - Military dictatorship
  - Stratocracy
  - Enlightened absolutism.
- o Kleptocracy
- o Monarchy;
  - Absolute monarchy
  - Constitutional monarchy
  - Despotism
  - Duchy
  - Grand Duchy
  - Enlightened absolutism
  - Elective monarchy

- Hereditary monarchy
- Popular monarchy
- Principality
- New Monarchs
- Self-proclaimed monarchy.

o Plutocracy;

- Timocracy.

o Police state

o Theocracy

o Tyranny.

Anarchy (Absence of Organized Government)

o Ochlocracy

o Tribalism.

Anarchism (Government of Consent, Not Coercion)

o Anarchist communism

o Libertarian socialism

o Libertarian municipalism

o Anarcho-syndicalism

o Green anarchism

o Isocracy

o Local Government

o Minarchism.

Democracy (The Rule of the Many)

o Consociationalism

o Deliberative democracy

o Democratic socialism

o Dictatorship of the proletariat

o Direct democracy

o Futarchy

o Participatory democracy

o Representative democracy;

- Parliamentary system
- Consensus government

- Westminster system.
- Polyarchy
- Presidential system
- Semi-presidential system.

o Republicanism.

- Constitutional republic
- Parliamentary republic
- Slaterisum

o Totalitarian democracy.

By Approach to Regional Autonomy

This list focuses on differing approaches that political systems take to the distribution of sovereignty, and the autonomy of regions within the state.

- Sovereignty located exclusively at the centre;
  - o Empire
  - o Unitary state.
- Sovereignty located at the centre and in peripheral areas;
  - o Federation and Federal republic
  - o Confederation.
- Diverging degrees of sovereignty;
  - o Asymmetrical federalism
  - o Federacy
  - o Associated state
  - o Devolved state-sovereignty can be abolished without changing the constitution.

By Political Franchise

This list shows a division based on differences in political franchise (*suffrage*).

- Autocracy-rule by one
- Oligarchy-rule by minority
- Democracy-rule by majority
- Republic-rule by law
- Anarchism-rule by no one.

3

Political Sociology and Social Movements

THE ARCHEOLOGY OF A RUPTURE

Today the problem of mobilization is so central to the study of contentious politics and social movements that few appear able to conceive of a different question or ask why the field took the shape it did. Before the rise of current approaches, research on political movements was driven by three broad traditions, all of which were deeply curious about the relationship between social structure and politics. The oldest tradition was class analysis, ultimately Marxist in origin, and was committed to understanding the roots of radical politics in class conflicts inherent in different modes of production. A second tradition was based on the variety of role theory exemplified by Robert Merton and others, which usually took the form of explanations based on role strain, status inconsistency, and relative deprivation. A third tradition, ultimately Durkheimian in origin, was rooted in the structural-functionalism of Talcott Parsons and his students.

An early exemplar of class analysis is Seymour Martin Lipset's first book, *Agrarian Socialism* (1950), which sought to explain the anomalous rise of a rural political movement with ostensibly socialist aims in the Canadian wheat belt. The analysis looked closely at the characteristics of wheat agriculture on the North American prairie, the close-knit nature of rural communities, and the inherent conflict between producers and middlemen in commercialized smallholding agriculture. Lipset wanted to understand why radical politics was so rare in North America by studying this deviant case, and he closely analyzed the reasons why this radical, seemingly anticapitalist movement moderated its ideology and policies once it achieved regional political power and nationalized key commercial sectors.

A later exemplar in this tradition is Jeffery Paige's *Agrarian Revolution* (1975), which was ultimately motivated to explain the origins of the tenacious revolutionary movement in Vietnam that so preoccupied American politics at that time. Building on Stinchcombe's (1961) typology of rural enterprise, Paige offered an elegant theory that linked variations in the ideologies and aims of rural political movements— whether they were reformist or radical, socialist or nationalist—to the varied features of agricultural enterprise in regions that exported products on world markets. Both Lipset and Paige had something to say about the organizational capacity of the groups involved, but their primary interest was in explaining not how these groups mobilized, but why these movements adopted varied aims and ideologies. Other examples of work in this tradition include Calhoun (1982), McNall (1988), Schwartz (1976), and Scott (1976), all of which traced degrees of political radicalism to features of economic organization and communities in historical context.

Davies (1962) and Gurr (1970) exemplified the relative deprivation tradition. The core idea is that it is not overall levels of hardship that drive groups to engage in rebellion, but their deprivation relative to socially conditioned expectations. Although rarely explicit, this tradition was ultimately rooted in conceptions derived from role theory, which viewed social structures as constellations of overlapping, socially constructed roles with assigned statuses, normative expectations, and varying degrees of socially structured role strain (Merton 1968a,b). One version of the theory is that individuals who experience status inconsistency or frustrated upward mobility are the most likely to become radicalized. Another version is that those groups who experience a decline in status relative to others—either because of another group's rise or their own decline—are the most likely to become radicalized. The key mechanism in these theories is psychological frustration, which breeds aggression and makes individuals likely recruits for extremist movements. For both Davies and Gurr, protest and radical politics were conceived as political violence, in contrast to more quiescent forms of routine politics. Other prominent examples are Kornhauser's (1959) analysis of mass society as the foundation of totalitarian movements, Gusfield's (1955, 1963) analysis of the temperance movement as a form of status politics, and Lipset's (1959a,b, 1960) later essays on right-wing extremism and working-class authoritarianism.

The core idea of the Parsonian tradition was the familiar Durkheimian notion that a wellintegrated and stable society is ultimately based on a moral order in which normative expectations, based on widely held values, are in a state of equilibrium with the existing division of labor. As societies grow and change, social structures become more differentiated and specialized, necessitating adaptive changes in norms and laws that regulate the inevitable conflict that change brings. Rapidly changing societies are singularly prone to disruption, and the individuals who are most affected by rapid change experience forms of social and psychological strain that make them more likely to join radical movements, whether secular or religious. One emblematic contribution to this tradition was Smelser's (1959) study of workingclass radicalism in the English industrial revolution, which attributed it (contra Marx) to the disruption of working-class families. His later theory of collective behaviour (Smelser 1962) traced qualitative variations in the aims and ideologies of social movements to the extent to which a society's moral order was disrupted by change. The idea spread widely in the form of modernization theory into the field of comparative politics, where it became central to explanations of revolution in developing countries (Huntington 1968, Johnson 1966).

These traditions shared three essential features. First, they all sought to relate variations in features of social structure to the character of social movements. Second, they all were ultimately interested in explaining variations in political orientations—why movements are liberal or radical, reformist or revolutionary, peaceful or violent—not the capacity of groups to mobilize. Third, they all offered fairly specific predictions about the structural circumstances under which different forms of politics would emerge.

These traditions differed in equally fundamental ways. Their conceptions of social structure were very different, as were the mechanisms thought to link social position to political behaviour. Class analysis and subsequent analyses of economic enterprise and community structure offered a concrete conception of social structure in which a rational awareness of economic and political interest—sometimes reinforced by moral ideas embedded in community traditions—played a central role. Relative deprivation and collective behaviour theories offered more abstract conceptions of social structure indicated by aggregate social trends in which social marginality, psychological disorientation, and frustration played a central role, but they shared a common goal of relating features of social contexts to the qualitative character of political movements. Whereas all three of these traditions have been largely relegated to the prehistory of research on social movements and contentious politics, they all spawned theories that had the now-rare virtue of yielding reasonably clear empirical implications. The observation that each of these traditions repeatedly failed to predict the outbreak of the kinds of movements they were designed to explain contributed heavily to their eclipse.

Class analysis, especially in its original Marxist form, had long been dogged by its overprediction of radical working-class movements and the remarkable rarity of the revolutions in the circumstances that Marx and the early Marxists had expected. This had already bred forms of neo-Marxism that emphasized the functions of the capitalist state (Miliband 1969), the production of consciousness in the labor process (Burawoy 1979, 1984), or the extension of elite ideological hegemony over subordinate classes (Thompson 1966). The history of radical movements also made many observers keenly aware of the role of organized repression and violence employed by the forces of order. The reputation of such figures as Lenin, Trotsky, and Mao as innovative strategists who could turn unfavorable circumstances into revolutionary situations suggested that the analysis of organization, strategy, and the balance of forces in political environments were the ultimate determinants of the strength and success of radical movements. Theories of relative deprivation and Parsonian theories of collective behaviour suffered from a similar problem. The evidence adduced to confirm them was often impressionistic, yet the clarity with which they were stated invited quantitative tests of their predictions. Efforts by skeptics to test their underlying propositions often failed to confirm their predictions (e.g., Paige 1971). The most ambitious early study to undermine the reigning theories was Tilly's (1964) dogged empirical pursuit of the social origins of the Vend´ee counterrevolution in western France in the 1790s. To test explanations derived from two competing sociological traditions, Tilly looked intensively at the transformation of western France's social structure on the eve of the revolution. Class analysis, represented by the French historians who interpreted their revolution in classic Marxist terms, portrayed the counterrevolution as the reaction of social classes rooted in precapitalist modes of production: nobility and peasants in noncommercialized agriculture. Modernization theory, in contrast, predicted that the counterrevolution would have occurred in those communities most disrupted by the penetration of capitalist economic relations.

Tilly found that neither theory fit the evidence he collected from archival sources about the region's economic development and community organization. The counterrevolution did not emerge in the regions most transformed by capitalism, as predicted by modernization theory, nor did it originate in the regions least transformed, as predicted by Marxist class analysis. More importantly, the groups that led the insurgency and participated most actively in it were not those that either theory would predict. There was, in fact, no consistent group pattern to the conflict at all: Each of the major social groups in the region, including the merchants and urban bourgeoisie who were thought to be most favorable to the bourgeois French revolution, were divided against one another and found themselves on both sides of a new political cleavage. The driving wedge was the requirement that the Catholic clergy take a loyalty oath to the new revolutionary government and repudiate papal authority. The local clergy were split by this demand, and those who refused were driven into opposition, taking many of their parishioners with them—splitting the social structure along what Tilly called "vertical lines" that did not obey the logic of either class analysis or modernization theory.

This research convinced Tilly that it was ultimately more short-term processes of mobilization that shaped the formation of political movements. In subsequent empirical work, which pioneered the application of quantitative techniques to historical data on collective action, he and several collaborators tested propositions derived from relative deprivation theory and collective behaviour-modernization theory, finding that these theories failed to predict rates of collective violence or collective protest, and that rates of collective protest failed to covary with other measures of social disruption. Other work examined the evolution of the size, duration, and frequency of strikes in France that showed them to be highly influenced by the scale of economic enterprise, the rates of unionization, and the timing of national political events. All of these pointed to a more political focus on the organizations and processes that influence group mobilization.

MOBILIZATION STUDIES

Others who were dissatisfied with the portrayal of political protest as an expression of emotional frustration and violent impulses had already offered a different view. For them, protest was a political activity that was as rational and goaldirected as routine politics. Gamson (1968) characterized the relative deprivation and collective behaviour traditions as one-sidedly concerned with problems of social control from the perspective of authorities, and neglectful of problems of authority, influence, and conflict from the perspective of those in subordinate positions. He drew on long-standing political science traditions in the analysis of influence, interest groups, and political parties and on sociological conflict theory and elite theory to argue a different proposition: "Discontent is viewed as an opportunity or a danger for particular subgroups, not as a problem of social control. It is important because of its consequences for mobilization of political influence". Gamson (1975) followed with an empirical study of American protest groups that focused on their strategies and organizational forms, relating them to their levels of success. One important departure was his treatment of unruliness (including violence) as a strategy designed to further a group's goals, not as an emotional reaction to frustration.

Tilly (1978) later contributed to this emerging resource mobilization perspective by defining a new focus on how discontented groups mobilized for political action. Tilly introduced ideas about repression and facilitation by the state and other powerful actors that were extended further by McAdam (1982) in his study of the American civil rights movement. McAdam placed even greater emphasis on the broader political environment within which insurgent groups mobilized, and labelled his approach the political process perspective. Another important contribution that paralleled McAdam's was Skocpol's (1979) state-centered analysis of revolution, which shifted attention even more into the political environment. Skocpol argued that mass mobilizing revolutionary movements achieve their aims only when they occur in conjunction with a state that has alienated the ruling class and that is pressured to the point of crisis by the international system. These works were all decisive departures from earlier traditions and defined a new field that focused on the mobilization of groups—their ability to organize, recruit adherents, deploy strategy, gain strength, and achieve their aims—within the limits of existing political opportunities.

One concise and influential early statement of this perspective was by McCarthy & Zald (1977), whoarticulated what they called the new "extreme" assumption, quoting Turner & Killian (1972): "There is always enough discontent in any society to supply the grass-roots support for a movement if the movement is effectively organized and has at its disposal the power and resources of some established elite group." They added, "For some purposes we go even further: grievances and discontent may be defined, created, and manipulated by issue entrepreneurs and associations." McCarthy & Zald emphasized that this was a partial theory; it ignored the social conditions that generated political motivations.

These contributions initiated a pronounced paradigm shift in political sociology in which the study of social movements and contentious politics diverged from the field's foundations into the subfield that exists today (Jenkins 1983). In a way that very few appear to have recognized, the emerging resource mobilization tradition did not simply offer a different perspective on social movements; it changed the question that was being asked, radically narrowing the intellectual horizons of the field. The puzzle that had long preoccupied political sociology rapidly receded from view—how to explain the political orientation of mobilized groups and the aims and contents of movements.

Along with the decline of interest in this question was a parallel decline in curiosity about the relationship between social structure and politics, something that defined the sociological tradition. Social structure, if invoked, was important only to the extent that it promoted or impeded the capacity of groups to mobilize. Questions about the political character of group aims were implicitly set aside as a separate matter—preconditions (viewed narrowly as unspecified grievances) that provided the raw material for mobilization, but were outside the scope of the theoretical problem. Analytically speaking, the action was in the process of mobilization, not in the formation of political orientations. The leading exponents of this perspective excelled at describing the changes in social structure and political institutions that were the backdrop for major episodes of political contention. These accounts, however, simply provided a historical backdrop for the main event: an analysis of the means through which groups mobilized and movements grew. The theory focused on processes of mobilization, not the formation of political orientations. The puzzle was not why a mobilized group adopted the political orientation it did—that, presumably, was given by historical circumstances— but how it was able successfully to mobilize and emerge. We have ended up with a subfield that aims to explain the conditions under which a movement—of any type—can grow and succeed, but we no longer have explanations to offer about variation in the substantive content of a movement—the type of politics that it represents.

The shift in the definition of the problem was heavily influenced by other disciplines— borrowings from political science and reactions to challenges from economics. The unacknowledged intellectual foundation of the resource mobilization perspective is the American political science tradition of interest group theory that viewed politics as a continual contest for influence by groups with different levels of power. This tradition offered a more palatable view of political conflict and protest as part of the normal influence processes of a pluralistic society. However, unlike the sociological tradition, it had never shown interest in the formation of political orientations or why they might vary. In the distinctive American political science tradition that traced its ancestry to Arthur Bentley's (1908) treatise on politics as a constant struggle by interest groups, the emphasis was on how groups pursued their interests and used existing political opportunities to achieve their aims. The existence of groups with conflicting interests was assumed as a given starting point of these theories; the central problematic was how political institutions channeled the clash of interests to produce political outcomes. This focus on political process and lack of curiosity about the formation of political orientations is the enduring and largely unrecognized contribution of American political science to the resource mobilization and political process perspectives in sociology.

This tendency was strongly reinforced by the field of economics: Olson's (1965) powerful critique of the group political theories that inspired resource mobilization theory. From a rational choice perspective, Olson revealed a serious logical flaw in group theory—the conflation of individual with group interest. He pointed out that logically it would not be in individuals' interests to contribute to collective action if they could benefit from group gains without personally bearing the costs of collective action. For Olson, this free rider problem was at the core of the puzzle of collective action. Therefore the central challenge of any theory of collective action was to specify the selective incentives for individuals to contribute to group goals.

Olson's solutions to the collective action problem—and those of the intellectual traditions in economics and political science that his ideas spawned—were limited primarily to the rational calculation of individual benefits and costs. This was viewed as a direct challenge to the discipline of sociology, and resource mobilization theorists responded with a wide range of alternative solutions to the collective action problem (another term for the problem of mobilization). In many ways the field of social movements and contentious politics has been a prolonged effort to establish a sociological alternative to the more parsimonious theories of economics. The increasing insistence on the subjective dimensions of mobilization— collective action frames, the formation of collective identities, the role of emotions—is essentially motivated by a feeling that the initial emphases on organization, networks, and political opportunity structures were not sufficiently different from rational choice models to offer a fully sociological alternative.

Another shaping influence was methodological: The outcomes of mobilization are observable and readily quantifiable. Counts of events, rates of protest, the formation and membership of unions, political parties, movement newspapers, and the scale of protests were all readily measurable and analyzable with increasingly sophisticated multivariate techniques. The shift of attention to mobilization coincided with the rise of systematic quantitative research in political sociology. Those who were interested in testing theoretical propositions and demonstrating the utility of their theories of mobilization had strong incentives to focus on this set of outcomes.

For more than two decades debates in this subfield have been about the role of organization, political opportunity, resources, strategy, collective identity, cognitive frames, and emotions, all of them defined as complementary or competing approaches to understanding group mobilization. Since the mid-1990s one of the primary intellectual activities in the field has been to negotiate competing claims and formulate integrative syntheses among the different perspectives. The extraordinary variety of answers to questions about recruitment and commitment to social movements and to their broader societal reception gives the appearance of intellectual breadth and vitality. All of this breadth and vitality, however, has remained within the narrowed boundaries of the defining question—how groups mobilize, or why social movements emerge.

ALTERNATIVE DIRECTIONS

While the puzzle of political orientation has largely dropped out of theoretical discourse in the subfield of social movements, it is still pursued by students of political sociology in related fields: ethnicity and nationalism, revolution, and labor unions, and in a range of historical and comparative case studies. For obvious reasons it is a central concern in the recently revived interest in political violence and terrorism. Although these studies often address subjects that can be conceived of as social movements, they have been largely ignored in that subfield because they address a question that is no longer part of its central focus. As we shall see, however, the emphasis on mobilization has influenced many of these studies as well, and political orientation is often treated as a byproduct of successful group mobilization.

Mobilization is a centrally important process in movement emergence and growth, but this is not the same thing as explaining why a movement adopts a certain kind of political orientation. To take an extreme example, suicide bombing may be a tactic suited to certain kinds of political opportunity structures, but this begs the question of how populations of potential suicide bombers are formed and how, once recruited, they are molded into agents of destruction. Is there a systematic relationship between the political orientation of movements and the characteristics of their adherents, their social experiences prior to joining a movement, or their experiences afterwards as members of a social movement organization?

These questions inevitably lead us back to a sustained examination of the relationship between social structure and politics, by reviving the field's former curiosity about the social lives of movement participants and nonparticipants alike. The range of possible conceptions of social structure is very broad. The older generation of structural analyses did not come close to exhausting the range of potentially useful ones. Social structure can be conceived concretely or abstractly, as an empirical description of a historically situated setting, or as an aggregate measure of some dimension of social life. It can be conceived in terms of categories such as status, class, gender, or occupation, or as relationships such as kinship, authority, social networks, community, or small-group interaction. It can be considered at the macro level of national polities, at the meso level of organizations or communities, or at the micro level of small groups. There are few prior constraints on those who want to understand the social sources of political orientation.

Moreover, social structures need not be conceived as static. Most of the early studies of political movements were premised on gradual or abrupt changes in social structure. The collective behaviour tradition identified individuals who were most affected by disruptive social change as likely recruits for protest movements, but the idea was not limited to them. Arguments about the moral economy of traditional communities—for example, peasant villages in subsistence economies (Scott 1976) or craft organization in early industrial economies (Calhoun 1982)—traced the origins of radical movements to the decline of communities and the violation of their moral codes. These studies balanced a concern to explain political orientation (anticapitalist radicalism) and organizational capacity (densely networkedcommunity ties). They also balanced recognition of the ways that compelling economic interests interacted with, and were reinforced by, outrage at the violation of culturally rooted moral codes— a defense of tradition that ironically was transmuted into anticapitalist radicalism.

To examine possible links between social structure and politics does not mean that one will find them. One of the primary reasons for examining social structural sources of political orientations is to uncover circumstances where the expected relationships fail to appear. Cases in which the posited social structures fail to explain are just as useful as the reverse, and provide new intellectual puzzles. The only convincing way to develop alternatives to structural explanations is to show how they can account for outcomes where a structural explanation falters.

Several studies have already addressed these issues, although they fit uneasily with the dominant focus on mobilization. Perhaps the most familiar is Gould's research on social networks and political mobilization. Networks in social movement research are primarily understood as mechanisms of micromobilization through which individuals are recruited into movement organizations or episodes of collective action (McAdam 1986, McAdam & Paulsen 1993). Gould's work focuses on mobilization, but his careful reconstruction of the role of networks in the revolutionary insurgencies of nineteenth century Paris and the 1794 Whiskey Rebellion in western Pennsylvania were not motivated to explain how insurgents mobilized. Gould's actual problem—similar to Tilly's in *The Vend´ee* (1964)—was to accurately identify the interests and collective identities of the participants by delineating the social networks through which they mobilized. His core finding, which contradicted the assumptions of generations of historical scholarship, was that the revolutionary mobilization behind the Paris Commune of 1871 was based on neighbourhood networks and community solidarities, not the working-class identities that had defined insurgent mobilization in 1848. Gould's conclusions were as much about the identities and motives of the participants as they were about their capacity to mobilize (Gould 1991, 1993, 1995). Similarly, his network analysis of the Whiskey Rebellion was motivated to understand its actual social basis, which he identified as a cross-class insurgency led by local elites who were cut out of federal patronage networks that were expanding westward beyond the Appalachian Mountains (Gould 1996). Gould's aim in both these studies was to show how the interests and identities of participants in revolutionary mobilizations were defined by evolving social networks. A second set of examples looked closely at the social foundations of well-known political movements and found that prevailing structural explanations failed to accurately identify the interests and identities of the participants. Tilly's analysis of the Vend´ee counterrevolution—discussed above—is an outstanding early example. He described a process in which Catholic clergy were forced to renounce loyalty to the pope or lose their parishes, a demand that split the priests and in turn divided all the major social groups in the community. This was a short-term process of identity formation touched off by rapid changes in political institutions—and deep splits in the community that were not predicted by the preexisting social structure or by its long-term changes as capitalism advanced. Tilly's findings had profound implications for theories about the relationship between social structure and politics—implications, we have already seen, that he did not subsequently pursue.

Remarkably similar processes are described in Walder's (2006, 2009) analysis of the formation of student Red Guard factions during China's Cultural Revolution of 1966–1968. He found that none of the interest group or network explanations long employed to account for Red Guard factionalism withstood close examination, and found instead a pattern in which university political networks were split and their occupants turned against one another by forced choices similar to those in revolutionary France described by Tilly.

Another example is Traugott's (1980, 1985) analysis of the class origins of the Parisian working-class insurgents of 1848 and of the militia that suppressed them. Contrary to Marx's analysis of these events and subsequent Marxist historiography, Traugott found that the actors on both sides of the barricades came from virtually identical working-class backgrounds, and both initially had revolutionary orientations. The political orientations of the two sides diverged over a year during which they participated in differently organized militias, only one of which was able to build cohesion and solidarity among its members. Similarly, Markoff and Shapiro have shown empirically that levels of conflict in the aims of different social classes varied by context in revolutionary France, and that outcomes were the process of repeated political interactions through time that fully represented the original aims of none of the participants. The common thread in these studies is a curiosity about the relationship between social structure and politics and unexpected findings that pointed the authors to short-term processes that altered the political orientations and outcomes that were otherwise presumed to come from social structure.

A third group of examples are from studies of ethnic mobilization, a field that has led a largely separate existence from social movement research, overlapping with it only occasionally. A central problem in this field is to explain why ethnic identity becomes salient as a cause of conflict—instead of class, occupation, or some other collective identity. This makes it difficult to limit the question narrowly to that of mobilization or to ignore the social structural sources of identity and conflict. One strand of theory explains ethnic antagonism as a product of competition in labor markets. Another attributes persistent ethnic identity to a cultural division of labor in which immigrant, language, or religious groups are concentrated in occupational niches. Research in this area tests the implications of competing theories in explaining ethnic political mobilization. It is more common in this subfield to balance a concern with identity formation with that of group mobilization. Olzak, for example, has examined competing theories about the labor market and other social origins of ethnic antagonism, and she has examined the problem of mobilization as conceived in social movements research.

Afourth example is studies of labor unions— a field that has often sought to explain levels of labor militancy or the prevalence of radical or reformist ideologies in trade unions. Perhaps the clearest example is Kimeldorf's (1989) comparison of longshoremen's unions on the East and West coasts of the United States. In the West they were dominated by communists, whereas in the New York region they were dominated by labor rackets and organized crime. Kimeldorf's explanation was a rare melding of social structural and political process explanations. It included both a careful analysis of the varied structure and organization of the industries on the two coasts and differences in the origins and composition of their labor forces and of the varied political opportunity structures of New York and San Francisco at the time the unions formed. Finally, some have sought to explain political orientation by reference to the structure of the national polity—but not through the familiar concept of political opportunity structure. Swanson (1960) argued that the dominant religious ideas in a society varied with the extent to which it had a unitary authority structure. He applied this classification scheme (Swanson 1971) to the outcomes of the rebellions that accompanied the Protestant Reformation in Europe, and claimed a close correspondence between prior regime type and Protestant versus Catholic outcomes (Swanson 1967). Subsequent authors tried to identify theoretical mechanisms behind some of these associations (Paige 1974) or challenged Swanson's findings (Wuthnow 1985). Bergesen (1977) applied these ideas to the explanation of political witch hunts. In a different vein, Hechter drew a distinction between indirect and direct rule by the center of a national polity to explain the paradoxical eruption of nationalist movements in modern nation-states. Nationalist movements emerge as a reaction to central government attempts to shift from indirect to direct rule over ethnically distinct regions (Hechter 2000). Similarly, the shift from class politics to cultural politics in capitalist democracies is a reaction to the intrusion of welfare state legislation and direct administration into areas of social life formerly left to families and local communities (Hechter 2004). All of these studies explore the social structural sources of political orientations, and all of them consider phenomena that can readily be translated into generic questions about social movements. Their lessons have been largely lost on theories about social movements because these theories have been concerned with a separate question—mobilization. There nonetheless exists a foundation for a more systematic effort to understand the social roots of movement political orientations, should this once again become a major intellectual concern.

POLITICAL ORIENTATION AS BY-PRODUCT

One obvious approach to the question of movement political orientation falls completely within the field's current intellectual limits: that it is explained by relative organizational capacity, strategic advantage, or the structure of political opportunities. This approach sees political orientation as a by-product of successful mobilization within a given political environment.

The kind of movement that emerges depends on which groups have organizational capacity, and which movements grow depends on the structure of political opportunities in relation to other groups' political preferences. Political process models imply that opportunity structures shape the orientations of movements by selectively repressing groups with certain political orientations and facilitating the actions of others. A familiar example is the U.S. civil rights movement in the 1950s and 1960s. McAdam (1982) emphasized the broad appeal of nonviolent, church-based activism in building national support for the movement outside the South and the weakening of support for the movement after the rise of more threatening expressions of activism such as the Black Panthers and urban rioting. Militant organizations and tactics led to police repression and white backlash, whereas moderate and nonviolent strategies generated sympathy and external support. McAdam was primarily interested in the effects of strategies on the overall fate of the struggle for civil rights; he was not attempting to explain the specific political orientations of the various submovements that were working toward civil rights for African Americans. However, the overall impact of these circumstances can be conceived as a kind of environmental selection that shaped the orientations of a movement by permitting some kinds of movement organizations to grow and suppressing others. Similar observations have been offered about repressive and violent regimes and otherwise treacherous political environments. In such circumstances secretive movements that work underground and exercise strong internal discipline have a competitive advantage over organizations that are open, loosely organized, and less hierarchical. To operate successfully in such circumstances a movement often adopts a radical ideology, uses violence as a strategy, and deals harshly with internal dissent. Movements that do not are more easily suppressed, clearing the field for organizations with a more radical and authoritarian cast. A corollary of this idea is that the more disciplined and violent movement organizations have a competitive advantage over rival movement organizations that are less disciplined, more open, and democratic.

This is the agenda implied by McAdam (1996) when he called for explaining "movement form" by reference to political opportunity structures, especially those outside of liberal democratic settings. Boudreau (1996) argued that political opportunity structures have steered democratic movements onto a revolutionary course in a variety of authoritarian regimes. Almeida (2008), analyzing waves of protest over eight decades in El Salvador, argued that a shift to state-sponsored repression pushes democratic movements into revolutionary and violent forms of resistance. White (1989) argued that the turn to violence of the Irish Republican Army was more a response to government repression than an expression of the intensity of group grievances. This approach to explaining the features of political movements views political orientation as a byproduct of group mobilization or a response to the structure of political opportunities.

Recent attempts to address the neglected question of collective violence have followed a similar path. Tilly (2003) offered an explanation that remains firmly within the intellectual tradition that he helped establish, in effect an elaboration of the "polity model" sketched in his early work (Tilly 1978). Violence here is seen as a product of the organization of the regime and the strategies and organizational capacities of the two sides. The explanation featured a new emphasis on the social mechanisms that are activated as part of these contextualized conflicts—a theme elaborated in separate work (McAdam et al. 2001). The mechanisms invoked represent a more careful elaboration of elements of familiar mobilization processes. Goodwin's (2006) theory of insurgent movement terrorism against noncombatant populations differs from Tilly's approach primarily by reintroducing social structural elements into the perceptions and calculations of movement leaders. He views terror as a product of movement strategy, in particular judgments by movement leaders about the support that these populations offer either to the targeted states or to the movement itself. Elements of social structure are introduced in the form of barriers to interaction and cooperation between movements and populations that might be presented by language, religious differences, and territorial segregation. They are not introduced to explain the motivations and perceptions of those leading or participating in the movement itself; motives and organization are a given starting point of the analysis.

Whereas much of the recent literature on revolutions resonates strongly with the main themes of the political process perspective, the study of that subject has moved steadily away from its former preoccupation with political movements. Essentially, the study of revolution declared its independence from the study of social movements several decades ago. In the Marxist, relative deprivation, and Parsonian traditions, revolution was conceived as a straightforward outcome of the strength of the social forces fueling the movements that toppled regimes. Skocpol's (1979) state-centered analysis liberated the study of revolution from these earlier voluntarist perspectives and, extending the logic of political process models, shifted attention to the capacity of states to respond to challenges from below. The central insight is that revolution is not a straightforward outcome of the political orientation of mobilized populations, but a contingent outcome of a state's organizational capacity, its relationship to other powerful social groups, and influences that operate in the international political system. Therefore, whether a democratic, nationalist, or revolutionary socialist movement thrives and achieves success depends on a configuration of political circumstances and historical legacies that are beyond the control of mobilized populations. In this tradition the study of revolution can readily be translated into a question of state capacity and regime survival (Goldstone 1991). The study of revolution, then, is inherently concerned with explaining how certain political orientations triumph as macrohistorical events, but it has shifted its attention away from the formation of movement political orientations and even more toward political process and political opportunity than many studies of social movements.

These by-product explanations of political orientation are already familiar, although they have received much less explicit and systematic attention than the process of mobilization. It remains to be seen whether they will be intellectually satisfying except in the context of questions about the strategic choices of movements that are a given starting point in an analysis. Not all social circumstances, and not all mobilized groups, have an equal capacity to generate any given political orientation. The limits of byproduct explanations will become evident only when laid against alternatives that investigate the social structural sources of movements— and vice versa.

MOVEMENT ORGANIZATIONS

Social movement organizations are a familiar subject in the political process perspective because they are the key actor in mobilization processes. They vary in ways that contribute to or impede a movement's success, as past research has emphasized. They also embody and enforce political orientations, and they differ in ways that affect their ability to alter and shape the political beliefs of their adherents. Some are easy to join, and others make it very difficult. Some are easy to leave, and others make it very difficult. Some movement organizations are able to command only a portion of a member's time and effort; others are able to command very large portions. Some are geographically or socially isolated and provide for most of their members' needs (guerilla bands, underground revolutionary organizations, sect-like groups); others are little more than clubs in an open and liberal environment. It follows that the potential impact of social movement organizations and their leaders on the views and level of commitment of their members varies considerably. The more effective the mechanisms that enforce group olidarity, the greater will be the group's impact on its members (Hechter 1987). The evolution of the political orientation of social movements and their impact on their members was once a major preoccupation of political sociology. The famous early example was Michels's (1915) analysis of how the growth and success of radical labor parties turned them into oligarchies that adopted more moderate and reformist political aims. Lipset et al. (1956) showed how the generation of what would later be called social capital in the organization of the typesetting trade created a strong social basis for union democracy rather than oligarchy. Others examined the powerful pull that small sect-like ideological groups have on the mentalities and discipline of their members, ideas that strongly paralleled processes in religious sects (Lofland 1966). This older interest has been revived in recent studies of new religious movements and sect-like socialist parties (Lalich 2004).

It has been widely noted in recent publications that participation in a social movement has a powerful effect on an individual's subsequent life course (McAdam 1989, Yang 2000). This implies that one should look more closely at the point at which these changes take place, during the movement itself. What actual impact do social movement organizations have on the political orientations of members, how is this impact achieved, and through what mechanisms? The more fundamental question this approach raises is to what extent social movement organizations collect like-minded individuals, mobilizing them for objectives that they all understand and about which they all essentially agree beforehand. Alternatively, to what extent do they attract individuals with vague and unformed ideas and commitments and shape and transform their political outlooks and into something very different from where they began? These questions may revive interest in one of the most important and enduring questions in political sociology: why organizations designed to liberate populations from oppression sometimes create new and more intensive forms of oppression.

4

Political Sociology of Poverty

Political sociology of poverty requires an analysis of the relationship between the political, economic and socio-cultural actors, institutions and processes in the context of poverty. It assumes that poverty is a complex and cumulative consequence of power relations over a period of time between groups within a region and between regions in the modern world system.

This paper on political sociology of poverty in India is based upon the assumption that

a) the caste system and economic inequality complement each other in the case of the poorer sections of Indian society,

b) Indian society has experienced complexities in identification of class system due to the manifold gradations of social rank, which have evolved in the form of caste and tribe along with quasireligious settings of deprivation,

c) the colonial and post-colonial polity have been organized around the recognition of nebulous coexistence of 'caste' and 'class' principles in the approach of state and political community towards the weaker sections of the society.

The Indian Constitution and political community have given recognition to the grave condition of resourcelessness of the weakest sections of Indian society through the system of 'Scheduled' castes and 'Scheduled' tribes. In other words, while recognizing the heuristic value of 'caste', 'gender', 'tribe' and 'class' as separate analytical and sociological categories, this paper suggests that caste, tribe and class merge into each other in the domain of absolute as well as chronic poverty in India. This clarification is important as there are a large number of instances of 'caste into class' and 'class into caste' as well as tribe-caste convergence in terms of economic conditions. But they do not negate the fact that for the last several decades there is marginal difference in the caste status of the absolutely poor classes and there is very limited evidence of economic prosperity ('creamy layer') among the depressed castes and tribes particularly in the rural domain of the Indian economy.

HISTORICAL CONTEXT

Any attempt to comprehend the Indian experience of poverty eradication through construction of welfare state and political mobilization in the last five decades needs to recognize that India is a post-colonial society where a) the colonial heritage in the statecraft, and b) the legacy of anti-imperialist national movement in the political community and political culture, play critical roles. This relationship between the 'colonial past' and the 'democratic present' is very significant for understanding the changing nature and orientation of the state and society in the context of poverty in India since independence in 1947.

It is also necessary to remember the differences between the rise of democratic polity in Europe and the emergence of welfare state in India. To quote Jawaharlal Nehru, a pioneer of democratic socialism during the anti-colonial movement between 1920s and 1940s and the first Prime Minister of free India from 1947 to 1964, "In Western countries, full blooded democracy with adult suffrage came to the people very late, in the Twentieth Century". They had in the meantime profited from the Industrial Revolution. They got the resources before they gained democracy so that when the demands came for better living conditions they had the resources to fulfil them. In India, we have full-blooded democracy but not the resources.

The results of the Indian endeavour of poverty eradication are not satisfactory in international terms. But the specific and comparative aspects of India help us in contextualising the Indian project of nation building through planning for a poverty free welfare state and a socialistic society between 1950 and the end of the millennium. They also provide insights about the international standing of India in the community of nation-states, where the largest democracy of the world is found to be lagging behind Sri Lanka, China and Indonesia. The Indian political process is being shaped by continuous interaction between the imperatives of interest group dynamics, democratization, decolonization and nation-building. These four factors provide the basis for legitimacy of the post-colonial state. They also give content to the concepts of 'public welfare' and 'national interest'. As a consequence, there were several changes in the state and society relationship in India during this period, which have caused i) decline of politics and rise of economics, ii) rise of dominant caste coalitions and decline of upper caste hegemony, iii) erosion of national constitutional consensus and rise of centrifugal movements, iv) stress on decentralization along with weakening of the process of centerformation including planning, v) rise of movements of erstwhile marginalized categories of people e.g. women, depressed classes like Dalits and Scheduled Tribes, ethnic groups, etc., vi) rise of 'region' instead of 'nation' as the operational category of the party system, vii) weakening of the middle class political culture as well as rise of crime-politics nexus with patronage from the neo-rich classes, and viii) rolling back of the welfare state under the pressure of global forces of liberalization.

The relationship between poverty, politics and state has continued to play a significant role in the political sociology of independent India as it did during the colonial era. The issue of poverty came onto the State's Agenda through different processes after the end of colonial period. First there was a constitutional process which was a consequence of the nationalist discourse where "Community Development" and decolonization were presented as two sides of the same coin. It created an appropriate focus in the making of the constitution of independent India.

Secondly, there came a developmentalist phase which gained importance during the drive for promoting capacity building among the rural cultivators through "Land Reform" in the 1950s. The idea of 'poor peasant' became unacceptable in the discourse of development under the Congress Raj. Of course, it failed to include the landless labourers in its conceptualization of recasting the rural power structure through 'land reforms'.

Then came the phase of nation wide rural agitations in the 1960s. The newly created propertied peasants started asking for increase in state's patronage and, the pauperised peasants urged for radical transformations to ensure jobs, wages, dignity and justice. The states' responses were crystallized as the "Green Revolution". Finally, India became market oriented in the 1980s as state-centric initiatives became counter productive at worst and ineffective at best. There was a new faith in market mediated system management among the propertied sections of Indian peasantry as well as the urban propertied classes. It was termed "the era of liberalization". Rolling back of the state did show some results in the first few years. But the bifurcation of the propertied and the pauperised was reinforced by the end of the 1990's. Thus there are new indications of pressures about continuity of chronic poverty and creation of 'new poor' in the context of liberalization. In fact, it may be appropriate to suggest that after the 'first generation reforms' or 'structural adjustments' and the consequential rolling back of the state, there is resurfacing of poverty in rural and urban sectors resulting in unrest and conflicts. This rediscovery of poverty is accompanied by refocusing of the political agenda of the India political sectors including political parties, trade unions, peasant bodies and other major components of the power pyramid in India.

THE CONSTITUTIONAL CONTENT

The conceptualization of poverty free welfare state in India has been accomplished in two phases-i) the period of national movement for freedom from foreign rule, and ii) the making of Indian Constitution through a constituent assembly. The Indian national movement was able to focus the attention of the masses on growing poverty and the recurrence of famine which was due to defective policies of the colonial government. It was the view of leading public men like Dadabhai Naoroji (1825-1917), M. G. Ranade (1842-1901) and R. C. Dutt (1848-1909) that the solution to the social and economic backwardness of India could not be found through the British Government's policy of laissez-faire, but that only a national government which actively promoted development by direct government action could bring about improvement in living standards. The resolutions of the Indian National Congress from 1929 onwards emphasized the need "to make revolutionary changes in the present economic structure of the society and to remove grave inequalities in order to remove poverty and ameliorate the condition of the masses". The resolution of 1931 underlined that "political freedom must include real economic freedom of the starving millions" and elaborated the fundamental rights which should be included in the Constitution of free India to provide a basis for it. It was followed by the formation of a National Planning Committee with Jawaharlal Nehru as Chairman in 1937 on the initiative of Subhash Chandra Bose as the President of Indian National Congress. A complementary process of conceptualization was contributed by the constant debate about the nature and priorities of the state in post-colonial India among the Gandhians, socialists, communists, radical humanists and other ideological groups in the national movement. The charter of demands and agitations by various class organizations of peasants and industrial workers provided the guidelines for the approach of the national movement to poverty and its eradication from villages and towns of India. In fact the decisive push to the colonial rule came with large scale peasant mobilization in the last decades of the freedom movement.

The concept of welfare state became the lodestar of the Constituent Assembly of India. It made its impact on the thinking of the leading lights of the Assembly who wanted to secure 'justice – social, economic and political' for all citizens of the Republic. They were clear that without social and economic democracy, political democracy had no meaning in a poor country like India. The Preamble, Fundamental Rights (Articles 12 to 35), Directive Principles of State Policy (Articles 36 to 51), and the special provisions for Scheduled Castes and Tribes and Backward Classes (Articles 330 to 342) are significant dimensions of the Indian constitution from this perspective. They have created the imperatives for progress from political democracy to social and economic democracy which means "working for a certain measure of well-being for all".

The Preamble of the Constitution commits the state to the development of a free society based on the dignity of the individual in which there would be equality of status, opportunity and justice. The state has to endeavour towards harmonization of interests between individuals, groups, and between individuals and groups on one hand and interests of the community on the other. The Preamble places justice above the other principles of liberty, equality and fraternity. The values embedded in the Preamble are elaborated in the Fundamental Rights and the Directive Principles. The Fundamental Rights have covered all the traditional civil ar political rights included in the Universal Declaration of Human Rights. There are six broad categories of the fundamental rights:

i. The right to equality (Articles 1, 15,16,17, and 18)
ii. The right to freedom (Articles 19 and 21)
iii. The right against exploitation (Articles 23 and 24);
iv. The right to freedom of conscience and free profession, practice and propagation of religion (Articles 25 to 28);
v. The right to minorities to conserve their culture, (Articles 29 and 30); and
vi. The right to constitutional remedies for the enforcement of all these Fundamental Rights (Article 32).

The Directive Principles of State Policy are basically inspired by the concept of a welfare state. Article 37 declares that the Directive Principles are "fundamental in the governance of the country" and that "it shall be the duty of the State to apply these principles in making laws". However these are non-justiciable. Article 38 defined the aim as follows; "The State shall strive to promote the welfare of the people by securing and protecting as effectively as it may a social order in which justice – social, economic and political, shall inform all the institutions of the national life". In Article 39, stress was laid on the right to adequate means of livelihood, equally for men and women; equal pay for equal work for both men and women; conditions of work ensuring health and strength, protection of children and youth against exploitation and against moral and material abandonment. It is also laid down that the state should ensure that 'the ownership and control of the material resources of the community are so distributed as best to subserve the common good'; and that the 'operation of the economic system does not result in the concentration of wealth and means of production to the common detriment'.

Furthermore, the duty is enjoined on the State that 'it should, within the limits of its economic capacity and development, make effective provision for securing the right to work, to education and to public assistance in cases of unemployment, old age, sickness and disablement, and in other cases of undeserved want' (Article 41). The state should also provide for 'securing just and human conditions of work and for maternity relief'; and 'security to all workers-agricultural, industrial and otherwise-a living wage, conditions of work ensuring a decent standard of life and full enjoyment of leisure and social and cultural opportunities' (Articles 42 and 43).

Particular stress is laid on special assistance to the weaker sections of the people, including the Scheduled Castes and the Scheduled Tribes and the other weaker sections with a view to promoting their educational and economic interests and to protecting them from social injustice and exploitation. With regard to rural economy, Articles 40 and 48 enjoin the application of modern scientific methods to agriculture and animal husbandry and the implementation of programmes and improvements through self-governing Panchayats. Promotion of cottage industries on an individual and cooperative basis is mentioned in Article 43.

Article 45 fixed a definite time limit during which the State would endeavour to provide free and compulsory education for all children until the age of fourteen years from the commencement of this Constitution. The above principles were given a more precise direction when Parliament accepted the socialist pattern of society as the objective of social and economic policy in December 1954. In 1976, the 42nd Amendment Act added certain new directives to the Constitution of India:

a) that children are given opportunities and facilities to develop in a healthy manner and in conditions of freedom and dignity;

b) that the operation of the legal system promoted justice on a basis of equal opportunity, and in particular the State provided free legal aid in cases of economic and other disabilities;

c) that the participation of workers in management of industries is secured; and

d) that the environment is protected and improved and the forests and wild life are safeguarded.

ANTI-POVERTY MOBILIZATIONS AND THEIR RESULTS

The direction of post-colonial polity in India was evolved during the three Five Year Plans between 1951 and 1965 in the context of peasant mobilization and other protest movements. Self-reliance was the basic goal of the Nehruvian agenda under the hegemony of the Congress Party. It is important to recognize that the response to the peasant movements in the Fifties by the nascent post-colonial state and the hegemonic ruling party, Congress, was:

a) to eliminate intermediaries for creating a broad based proprietary class in the village who took interest in promoting agricultural production;
b) to facilitate infrastructure facilities through a variety of inputs and concessions;
c) to ensure minimum price support through purchase of agricultural products by public sector corporations.

The impact of these reforms created two opposite results –

i) it promoted the expansion of owner-cultivator class which came from upper and upper-middle strata of the caste system; and
ii) it created insecurity among tenants, agrarian workers, and semibonded tillers due to increased pressure of market forces upon the agricultural sector.

Agriculture was changing into a 'market oriented, cash based, and profit claiming occupation, causing deterioration of the situation of the poorer strata in rural India. In short, there was emergence of commercialization, monetization and market/profit oriented production due to the state's plans and programmes between 1950 and 1965. The number of agricultural proletariat-(who belonged to the 'lowest' castes and the Scheduled Tribes) grew at an exponential rate. But the strategy of "incremental democratic modernization" encountered a series of problems from 1963 onwards, which made the Nehruvian approach obsolete in many spheres of State policies. A new set of national issues regarding food scarcity, increase in prices, national defence, foreign dependence, economic stagnation, and regional inequalities generated a cumulative stress between 1963 and 1967. As a consequence a new agenda called Ten Point Programme came into being. The dilemma of dependent accumulation and declining dominance of the Congress Party created a shift in India's direction of development. The slogan of "Jai Jawan-Jai Kisan" (victory to the soldiers-victory to the peasants) symbolized the new thrusts of the State. The 'sixties saw a wave of disenchantment with the entire planning process'. There was visible growth of discontent in the late sixties (Kumar, 1989).

Between anti-Congressism and Naxalism, there was a great range of activism and mobilization all over rural and urban India. This coincided with the 4th Five Year Plan and the 5th Lok Sabha elections. Despite the intelligence and experience, Indian planning had gotten into a rut. The results were disappointing. It was time, therefore, for the planners to ask themselves whether the things they had been trying to do were really correct. Thus the period of the 4th Five Year Plan was marked by political weakness and economic anxieties. The poorer sections of the society and the pro-poor political formations were making impressive moves for collective action. It was the era of second wave of land conflicts after the late nineteen forties and early fifties. The second wave of rural mobilization in the sixties contained two distinct groups of rural masses. There was a movement launched by the newly emerged proprietary classes constituted by rich farmers and middle peasant proprietors. The communists called them 'Kulaks' which was an exaggeration of their economic capacity. They were also named 'Bullock Capitalists'. Their mobilization was aimed at securing increased patronage from the state. They did not come into conflict with the interests of the industrial and commercial urban proprietary classes. It was led by peasant based regional political formations which came into existence in 1960s in several provinces of India. Many of them got amalgamated into a national political party, Bharatiya Lok Dal, led by Charan Singh in 1974.

Another movement was launched by the agrarian poor with increasing prominence of the agricultural workers. The movements of the rural poor in the 1960s and 70s were centred around a combination of economic, social and political issues. Economically, they were in need of security of employment, minimum wages, rights over a certain share of the produce, distribution of surplus lands, and reduction and liquidation of debts. Socially, they were agitated about violation of legally acquired rights, gender discrimination, violence and humiliation by upper caste/class men and public officials. Politically, they were attempting to resist repression and terror of the upper and middle castes who had recently turned into land owning classes in rural India. They found a nexus of the newly emerging proprietors and the nascent post-colonial state. They also felt that the state was paying more attention to the proprietary classes as it considered them as the agents of development. They were led by the left wing parties like Communist Party, Communist Party (Marxist), Socialist Party and Communist Party (Marxist-Leninist).

The rural poor in the 1960s comprised of a) pauperized peasants, b) agrarian workers belonging mostly to the depressed castes and tribes and other marginal groups, and c) a large section of women. Their struggles gave rise to uncomfortable questions regarding the usefulness of the socio-economic framework of developmental planning adopted after independence. They exposed the limits of the development policies as they had failed to improve the condition of the poor even after three Five Year Plans, and a generation long political stability in the form of Congress rule. They brought the nation 'face to face' with the continuity of unimaginable forms of exploitation and oppression of the rural poor. It was an indictment of the post-colonial state and its patronage to newly propertied castes and communities in the name of development and nation building since 1950s. Above all it proved that there is a 'dialectical interconnection' between the various sectors of the society and polity.

POLITICS OF POVERTY ERADICATION

The issue of poverty became a central question during 1964-71. It was triggered by the Lohia-Nehru-Nanda debates in Lok Sabha in 1964 about the nature of poverty and its extent. It became recognized as a political imperative of democratic governance as a large number of people were still trapped in economic settings which forced them to live below the levels of subsistence. It was legitimized by the slogan of Garibi Hatao (eliminate poverty) by the Congress Party under the leadership of Indira Gandhi who routed most of the anti-Congress political parties in the general elections of 1971-72. It appeared that after a long wait, the moment had arrived for fulfilling the dreams of Swaraj by creating an egalitarian social order based upon economic self-reliance and democratic social transformations.

It is another matter that the electoral mandate was not translated into effective socio-economic steps due to a variety of reasons – domestic as well as international. Low savings, limited investment, sluggish industry, a steep rise in the money supply and a sharp decline in agricultural production were the prominent features of economic administration. The problems were further complicated by international 'price revolution' and a phase of 'stagflation' in the world economy. In 1973-74, inflation had turned everything topsy-turvy. It was coupled with the crisis of leadership within the Congress Party at the Central and the provincial levels. The situation gave rise to multiple political pressures, student-youth movements and working class protests which culminated in a national movement against the failures of the government in terms of checking corruption, controlling price rise, creating employment, and providing relief to the poor. It was led by Jayaprakash Narayan, one of the founders of democratic socialism in India (who later devoted himself to the cause of Sarvodaya or Gandhian reconstruction of the Indian society, economy and polity to promote welfare of all) and was supported by socialists and others.

After a phase of indifference and tolerance, the ruling party declared the State of Emergency due to the intensity of internal protests. At the same time, it had to adopt a 20-Point programme of welfare measures to show that even in a situation of crisis, the government is committed to continue the process of relief and welfare.

Inspite of these adversities, the change in the orientation of the political community and the policy makers in the early 1970s, was remarkable. According to C.T. Kurien (1979), "When a small group in the Planning Commission proposed in 1962 that the central concern of our planning has to be the removal of poverty as early as possible, it was a novel and consequently very suspicious idea. But within a decade it had become not only the accepted economic dogma, but also a highly articulated political programme". The new mood was reflected in the Fifth Five Year Plan. For example, Towards An Approach to the Fifth Plan (1974-79) proclaimed "there would seem to be a conspicuous element of historic inevitability in a direct approach to reducing poverty becoming the main thrust of the Fifth Five Year Plan. The Plan is being formulated by a government that has massive mandate from the people, both in the Parliamentary elections of 1971 and the state elections of 1972, on the basis of a programme whose centre piece is Garibi Hatao. The homogeneity of the Governments at the Centre and most of the states during the formulation and early years of the Fifth Plan is guaranteed. This should enable bold and imaginative proposals being put through on the basis of an enlightened national consensus" (Kurien, 1978).

Thus, the Fifth Five Year Plan was a landmark due to its special thrust on creating the maximum possible dent on the low end poverty while ensuring that the country moves one more step in the direction of economic independence. It was also remarkable due to its recognition that the Indian economy had reached a stage where larger availability of resources makes it possible to launch a direct attack on – a) unemployment, b) under-employment, and c) poverty. It clearly admitted that the twin causes of poverty are i) underdevelopment, and ii) inequality and it is inadmissible to ignore or underplay either factor. Therefore, it pointed out that the problem of poverty couldn't be overcome within the foreseeable future by efforts in one direction only.

India entered the phase of liberalization in 1980s under Prime Minister Rajiv Gandhi and the process continued inspite of change in leadership at the level of the Prime Minister. The year 1991 was the beginning of an explicit phase of rolling back of the state due to the imperatives of liberalization. Relatively higher growth was recorded during 1980-2000 and particularly during 1990s which was a decade of structural economic reforms. It also showed decline in poverty and improvement in health and literacy levels of the people of India. But India continues to suffer from high levels of illiteracy, high rate of infant mortality, high incidence of disease, disability, and malnutrition even after half a century of freedom and democracy. Allocations for health and education have been only 4.1 percent of the GDP (1996-97) which was lower than several developing post-colonial countries like Malaysia and Sri Lanka.

The sociological consequences of the liberalization-globalisation drive have been summarized by Yogendra Singh (2002) as state versus market dilemma. He argues that the extent to which the power of market increases and expands, the significance of the state as a supreme political institution, undergoes major alterations. Idealistically, some protagonists of the market even anticipate the end of the notion of sovereignty. For societies such as India, where nation-building has still not reached the level of integrative maturity, such fears of the end of sovereignty or a threat to it due to unhindered play of the global market force cause not only acute anxiety but also pose a challenge (Y. Singh, 2002).

POVERTY AND CONFLICT LINES: CLASS, CASTE AND TRIBES

Analysis of poverty-politics relationship needs understanding of power dynamics and conflict patterns because inequality of access to resources generates processes of conflict in the context of interests between the included, the marginal and the excluded sections of any society. The conflicts make reform and strategies and processes of poverty elimination imperative. This requires a multi-dimensional understanding of the interconnectivity of the spheres of state, market and community and the interrelatedness of the local, regional/ national, and global domains. All these need special attention in exploring the challenges of chronic poverty.

Poverty and the poor are always associated with (a) resourcelessness, (b) choicelessness, (c) insecurity and (d) deprivation which creates incapacities in the pursuit of dignified life in a given society for a person, household, group or community. Furthermore, those suffering chronic poverty also suffer several simultaneous disadvantages including gender, age, caste, ethnicity, location, etc. According to A.R. Desai

(1986) a new class configuration has emerged as a direct consequence of the conjunction of peasant mobilization and government measures over the last few decades. It contains the following categories of rural population: a) *Rich Farmers and Land lords* owning 15 acres and more, possessing 50 per cent of the total land and constituting 7 per cent of the population, b) *Middle Farmers* – with 5 to 15 acres of land, possessing 30 per cent of the total land and constituting 19 per cent of the population, c) *Poor Farmers* owning between 1 and 5 acres, possessing 17 per cent of the total land and constituting 30 per cent of rural population, and d) *Agricultural Labour* without land or owning less than 1 acre of land, possessing about 2 per cent of the total land and constituting 44 per cent of the population. The national picture also suggested presence of five categories on the basis of household income with 10, 19, 12, 192 and 420 million persons in them (Stern, 1993).

The population below poverty line (1993-94) has two major features: i) Overwhelming presence of the Scheduled Castes and Scheduled Tribes population, ii) Assam, Bihar, Madhya Pradesh, Maharashtra, Orissa and Uttar Pradesh were found to be above the national figures of population below poverty line where as West Bengal, Tamil Nadu and Karnataka were within the proximity of national figure (35.9 per cent).

The relation between the resourcelessness of the chronic poor and settings of conflict is rooted in the quest for security and dignity through ending of choicelessness of the chronic poor in a variety of ways. Such households, loaded with a complex set of disadvantages and assetlessness, are usually involved in subsistence type of activities which get them poor returns. Since their earnings are meager, they survive on small amounts of borrowed money or they are forced to suffer from hunger.

They are mostly unable to change the power relationships and there are no mechanisms of grievance redressal. The powerful local forces, in conjunction with the corruptible sections of the state apparatus, manipulate and misappropriate the common resources and pubic funds which create further helplessness and frustration. It has been termed as 'web of poverty' with centrality of continuous alienation of the people trapped in it and occasional confrontation in the society. This could lead to social tension, despair or a combination of both (Sharma, 2000).

The increasing visibility of a "fault line of deprivation and conflict" is a consequence of such a setting in India today. It is visible in a number of districts of Uttar Pradesh (13), Bihar (26), Orissa (10), Jharkhand (10), Chattisgarh (4), Madhya Pradesh (16), Andhra Pradesh (4), Assam (3), Tripura (1) and Arunachal Pradesh (3) (India Today, 2003). In the terminology of bureaucracy and media, these states have a number of districts which are conflict prone due to the effective presence of "Naxalites", "Senas" (private armies), externally aided "extremists", and separatists. Despite the variation of labels, all of them indicate presence of deepening social conflicts around issues of deprivation and poverty. It is another matter that the pattern, form and objectives of mobilization of discontent are defined by: a) social cleavages, and b) the political conditions of the states.

At the same time, the growth of economic, social and cultural disequilibria, rooted in chronic poverty and resourcelessness is a cause of national concern. It affects governability as well as social and economic development. It also promotes increasing togetherness between poverty and political violence, which causes legitimization of crises and invites use of police force to control its proliferation. If the state gets tough, it creates "martyrs" and myths. If the state remains tolerant and mild it faces escalation of violence and disruption of law and order. The feeling of political and economic exclusion invites entrepreneurs of violence. Therefore, the advocates of violence enjoy such settings where a large number of persons are found to be living on the margins of the economy and society. How do we institutionalize the process of conflict resolution, in a volatile setting of chronic poverty and social deprivations ? There is gradual decay of the state apparatus at the micro and meso levels in around 76 districts of India where under-development and poverty provide conducive setting for growth of organised violence. The "fault line" and its growing visibility needs further study.

The issue of chronic poverty and conflict is associated with the persistence of insecurity in the life setting of a person, household, group, or community (UNDP, 1999). Human security suggests that people can exercise their choices in pursuit of secure and dignified existence in society safely and freely. It has two main aspects; a) safety from chronic threats such as hunger, disease and repression, and b) protection from sudden and hurtful disruptions in the patterns of daily life whether in homes, in jobs or in communities. According to the United Nations approach, the many threats to human security, differing for individuals at different times, fall into seven categories:

i. Economic insecurity,
ii. Food insecurity,
iii. Health insecurity,
iv. Personal insecurity,
v. Environmental insecurity,
vi. Community and cultural insecurity,
vii. Political insecurity.

These insecurities and threats can affect people everywhere. Famines, ethnic conflicts, social disintegration, terrorism, pollution and drug and human trafficking can no longer be confined within national borders. Some global challenges to human security arise because threats within countries rapidly spill beyond national frontiers, such as greenhouse gases and trade in drugs. Other threats take on a global character because of the disparities between countries-disparities that encourage millions of people to leave their homes in search of a better life, whether the receiving country wants them or not. And frustrations over inequalities in incomes and political power often build up into serious civil conflicts between groups, whether ethnic, religious or social.

Those suffering chronic poverty are caught in the midst of a set of basic conflicts which perpetuate their insecurity through 'capability poverty', resourcelessness and choicelessness. Some of these conflicts are silent and invisible e.g. the crisis due to ecological factors. Several others are visible as demonstrated by the sufferers of class, caste, ethnic gender, religious (communal) and racial discriminations. Together they contribute towards the continuity of chronic poverty in a cumulative manner by sustaining the logic of power relations and marginality of the chronic poor in the discourse of power. They envelop the institutions and processes of state, market and community. The most visible and loud conflicts in the context of chronic poverty are found to exist around a) class, b) caste, and c) tribes (ethno-regional issues).

About Class based Conflicts

The class based conflicts have industrial and rural spheres. Both kinds of conflicts are sinking into marginality in terms of their impact. In the industrial arena, economic liberalism has led to flexible labour market policies like subcontracting, outsourcing and the engagement of temporary and part-time workers in core activities of the labour process. India's integration into the global economy and far reaching structural adjustment for it in the 1990s has weakened the strategic position of the trade unions. According to the Labour Bureau figures of the Government of India, there has been a decline in the number of man-days lost due to strikes and lockouts in 2000 compared to the figures for 1992. Furthermore, more man-days are lost due to lockouts than strikes (J. John, 2001).

In the rural arena, 298 million persons constitute the labour force engaged in agricultural and allied activities which is 79 per cent of the total workforce. A majority of the workforce engaged in agriculture consists of small and marginal farmers and agricultural labourers. About 80 per cent of total rural labour households (over 30 per cent of total rural households) are agricultural labour households. Of them, the Scheduled Castes and the Scheduled Tribes constitute nearly 50 per cent. In general agricultural labourers suffer from seasonal unemployment, job insecurity, poverty, indebtedness, and lack of access to productive assets. They suffer from lack of social security and inability to form their own organizations. The economic reform measures have worsened their condition due to recent hike in the prices of food grains. There is also decline in their position in comparison to their counterparts in other activities in both rural and urban areas inspite of absolute rise in their wages. The hope of 'land to the tillers' generated before independence has receded beyond the realm of realization.

A significant section of owner-cultivators ('farmers') have become vulnerable to poverty due to the promotion of capital-intensive agriculture. In recent years farmers of Andhra Pradesh, Karnataka, Maharashtra and Punjab have committed suicides in significant numbers due to crop failures and indebtedness. According to newspapers there were 2409 suicides by farmers between 1995 and 1998, but it needs further study. According to one observer our country is a heaven for middlemen who earn their fabulous commissions and a hell for farmers who sweat and toil (Ramarao, 2003). Situations of direct and indirect conflict between the poor in rural and urban spheres of the economy and the propertied sections and the state are spreading in various parts of the country. A cycle of conflicts, control and suppression and re-emergence with added strength appears to occur in significant number of rural areas in most of the poor states. The issues causing conflict in rural areas are security of employment, minimum wages, share in the produce, securing of surplus lands, reduction and liquidations of debts and violence by the land owning classes.

There are also tensions and clashes in the context of sexual and cultural oppression and political denial. In fact the year 2000-01 has been a difficult one for rural economy. Income has declined. Agricultural production has been sluggish; food production has declined by almost 5 per cent. Suicides persist. The rural development programmes have recorded declining growth. A combined view of the situation of the rural labourers, marginal farmers, and the rural sector's contribution to the national economy gives a depressing picture. It is marked by limited growth of high and upper middle-income households (7.6 million households in rural and 10 million households in urban areas), increased regional disparity (Bihar and Gujarat at 1:7), and the general tenor of the National Agricultural Policy (July, 2000), which ignores the agricultural labour and marginal farmers and may accentuate the pre-existing inequities with possibilities of social strife and disenchantment (Prasad, 2001).

The situation in the urban settings is diffused. But there is growing discontent due to the increasing belief that the current development policies do not have the capability to create the framework within which the conditions of the poor might improve. In urban India slums are growing at the rate of 5 per cent. 24 per cent to 28 per cent of the urban population in Karnataka, Maharashtra and Delhi lives in slums as a fall out of poverty and deprivation. This provides a setting of recurring conflict between the urban poor and the Government Machinery as they are created out of 'illegal encroachment of government land'. There is high frequency of inter-community strife and conflicts. In fact violence is forced upon them as a way of living. The slum dwellers work mostly in the unorganized sector (in jobs requiring less skill and training). Their incomes are quite insufficient to enable them to lead a dignified life and enjoy basic rights.

Paradoxically, the condition of the working class in the organised sector is found to be drifting from resistance to hopelessness and less conflict in the context of the new economic policies. The new labour laws have diminished the space for class conflict in the organised sector of industrial India. There are three major events which have contributed towards the decline of the 'class power' of the organised workers in the last decade – i) disinvestment in the public sector, ii) retrenchment and contractualization of the private industrial establishments, and iii) global recession in the industrial sector. An overview of the changing labour relations scenario may be presented by comparing the figures of industrial disputes in India in 1992 and 2002. It is seen that the figure has declined from 1714 to 413. There was also phenomenal decline in the number of workers involved in disputes and man days lost in the last decade. It needs further enquiry to be able to understand the implications of declining number of trade union strikes in an era of economic transition in favour of entrepreneurs.

On Caste Oriented Conflicts

Caste based conflicts are increasing in the context of enlargement of the capacity of two blocks-the political power of the dominant castes and political mobilisation of the Dalit castes or the Scheduled castes. It is causing conflict in the electoral arena, labour market, and civil society.

The quest for political power among the Scheduled Castes around the provisions of 'Reserved seats' in legislature has been a major feature of Indian Democracy. They achieved a significant breakthrough with the growth of coalition politics in 1969-71. The making of OBC and Dalit Vote Banks was a singular contribution of socialist politics which contributed towards a 'Silent Revolution' in the era of "Green Revolution"

(Jeffrelot, 2002). At the same time there is marginal increase in the percentage of Dalits below the poverty line during the privatization-globalization regime from 44.7 per cent in 1987-88 to above 48 per cent in 1993-94, which is significantly higher than estimates for the general population (39 per cent). The literacy gap between the SCs and rest of the population has also remained more than 17 per cent between 1961 and 1991. According to the Census of 1991 more than 80 per cent rural Dalit women were found to be illiterate. They were also sufferers at the hands of the dominant castes in different parts of India. Between 1995 and 1997, a total of 90,925 cases were registered between with the police under different categories of crimes and atrocities against the Dalits. Nearly 70 per cent of all the offences were reported from the BIMARU states-Bihar, Madhya Pradesh, Rajasthan and Uttar Pradesh.

Mass murders of the Dalits by dominant castes in Andhra Pradesh and Bihar has underlined the depth of conflict between the castes in rural India over the last several years. According to an estimate, the period between 1990 and 1999 witnessed 35 instances of caste-based massacres, the total number of victims being about 400. More than 350 of those killed were from among the lower castes (Frontline, 1999). In short the issue of caste-class convergence in the context of chronic poverty in an era of dominant caste democracy and liberalizationglobalisation is promoting anti-Dalit caste violence in rural areas and decline in the opportunities for the Dalits in the urban-industrial economy.

According to the Sixth Report of the National Commission for Scheduled Castes and Scheduled Tribes (1999-2001), the extent of crimes and atrocities on persons belonging to Scheduled Castes is much higher than those on Scheduled Tribe. The cases of atrocities on Scheduled Castes are about 6-7 times more than STs, though the population of SCs is only twice that of STs. Uttar Pradesh (6122), Rajasthan (5623), and Madhya Pradesh (4667) have reported highest incidence of crime against Scheduled Castes. These three states account for 65.4 per cent of the total cases of atrocities on SCs in the country during 1999. The position of registered cases of atrocities in other states was Gujarat (1781), Andhra Pradesh (1749), Karnataka (1277), Tamil Nadu (883), Bihar (820), Orissa (772), Maharashtra

(605), Kerala (514), Haryana (121), Himachal Pradesh (54), Punjab (39) and Delhi (18). There had been a declining trend in crimes committed on members of SCs, STs, between 1997 and 2000. In the case of SCs, number of crimes came down from 32,997 in 1995 and 27,944 in 1997 to 23,742 in 2000; and for STs from 4644 in 1997 to 3958 in 2000. This decline deserves closer study to find out the relative roles of state, political mobilization, media and NGOs and increasing vigilance and resistance by SCs and STs.

One of the most obvious reasons for so many attacks on SC men and women is related to the refusal of the SCs to work without dignity and appropriate wages. The assertiveness of these castes for higher wages, freedom of choice of work and endeavor to achieve mobility as cultivators are among the most frequent reasons for atrocities against SCs.

Tribes and Conflicts

The Tribal dimension of chronic poverty is most pronounced in the context of conflicts and movements. They constitute 8 per cent of the population. 83 per cent of them live in the area between West-Bengal and Gujarat, 12 per cent in the North eastern region, 4 per cent in Nilgiri Hills and 1per cent in J&K and Himachal Pradesh. It is believed that confrontation has been the quintessence of the situation in the tribal areas after the rise of 'state' as a formal system of political and administrative authority. The ever-increasing exploitation of the tribals and elimination of their lands led to revolts and rebellion in many parts of India. 'Leave them alone' (or 'exclusion') as in the hills of North-East and 'light' administration (or 'partial exclusion') elsewhere was the response of the Imperial Regime in the face of determined resistance to their advancement and consolidation. The dawn of independence ushered in a new era of high hopes and soaring aspirations with an ebullient nation committed to the ideals of democracy, equity and social justice. The cause of weaker sections, particularly the tribal people, was accepted as a national task with clear premises and constitutional commitments. But the hopes were belied. The tribal people in fact faced regression as the personalized administration gave way to an amorphous faceless system. Influx of immigrants, alienation of their lands and underdevelopment are three major problems of the Tribal communities.

According to the Report of MPs and Experts (Bhuria Committee Report, 1995), "Notwithstanding the rhetoric of the past four decades, on account of absence of effective democratic decentralization at even district levels, demands and agitations for separate states in the country have taken root in Jharkhand, Bodoland, Uttarakhand, etc. Iniquitous policies and actions and economic imbalance have led to resentment among the deprived regions. Assertions on the basis of region, ethnicity, languages, etc. have been made. They have come to feel that without the political power of a state, they are not able to claim their rightful due"1.

In economic terms, the Scheduled Tribes (ST) have been found to receive a total household income of Rs. 19,556 and a per capita income of Rs. 3,504, which are 76 and 78 per cent respectively, of the national average. Both incidence and intensity of poverty are higher among the Scheduled Tribes in comparison with the national average. They have recorded a literacy level of about 40 per cent in comparison to an all India average of 54 per cent. Only about one-fourth of ST women are literate. Literacy levels are extremely low for STs in Bihar, Rajasthan, Uttar Pradesh, Madhya Pradesh and Orissa.

More than 87 per cent of the total population has been depending on agriculture for their livelihood, supplemented by collection and sale of minor forest products. However the percentage of cultivators has declined from 68 per cent to 54.5 per cent in 1991 and the proportion of agricultural labour is increasing correspondingly. Vast areas of tribal lands have been acquired under the Land Acquisition Act and still are being acquired for industrial and infrastructural development. Out of the total 213 lakh displaced persons (1951– 1990), 85.4 lakhs are Scheduled Tribes. They constitute about 40 per cent of the total number of displaced persons. From the total 83.8 lakh rehabilitated persons, 21.2 lakhs i.e. 39.4 per cent belong to STs. Dams (41 lakhs), mining (6.5 lakhs) and industries (3.8 lakhs) are the major causes of tribal displacements. A land mark judgement of Supreme Court in the case of Samatha vs. The State of Andhra Pradesh and others (11th July, 1997) has placed a check on this. The Supreme Court has ordered that government lands, forest lands and tribal lands in the Scheduled Areas cannot be leased out to non-tribals or to private companies for mining and industrial operations.

Social insecurity among the Scheduled Tribes, particularly the ST women, is also a cause of concern. Out of nearly 4000 cases of atrocities committed against Scheduled Tribes in 2000, there were 391 cases (9.8per cent) of rape. The incidents of atrocities on Scheduled Tribes were highest in Madhya Pradesh (1756), followed by Rajasthan (1221), Gujarat (367), Orissa (335), Andhra Pradesh (178), Maharashtra (171), Tamil Nadu (105) and Kerala (81). The direct and indirect relationships between the efforts of STs to move out of exploitative dependencies and the acts of atrocities is a relevant question for further systematic enquiry. At the same time, it may be concluded that the extreme forms of exploitation and violation of civil rights that exist in areas such as Chattishgarh and Jharkhand have turned them into places of long standing insurgency. Another reason for the rising violence in forest areas is encroachment by migrants who are taking over the land of the local people. This causes conflict over resource use.

Such a profile of tribal India makes it obvious that the tribals are the worst sufferers of resourcelessness and choicelessness as well as the most disenchanted section of the Indian population in post-colonial India. They are leading components in a variety of mobilizations in the last two decades including movements for environmental protection (Narmada Bachao), states reorganization (Jharkhand, Uttarakhand, and Chattisgarh), political separation (the separatist movements of the North-Eastern Tribals), and resistance to globalization (Kashipur). Such conflictual mobilizations have brought the issue of chronic poverty of tribal India to the attention of national media and policy analysts in recent years thereby prompting the governments to come forward with a variety of anti-poverty measures and development packages. Creation of three new provinces Jharkhand (out of Bihar), Chattisgarh (out of Madhya Pradesh) and Uttaranchal (out of Uttar Pradesh) is a major effort to address the challenge of tribal alienation and unrest. It also marks the beginning of assertiveness for tribal autonomy and dignity in the Hindi belt of India.

5

Evolution of a Sociological Concept

In social sciences it is often difficult to trace the origin of concepts. Concepts, theories and ideas are often products of collective endeavours. It would be extremely difficult to identify who used the term "globalization" for the first time. According to Malcolm Waters (1995) whose book titled *Globalization* is a fine primer, Roland Robertson was one of the early users of the term. More recently, Roland Robertson and Kathleen White edited *Globalization: Critical Concepts* in 6 volumes is a tour de force which present some of the most important essays on this subject.

No matter who coined it first, at the dawn of the 21st century globalization as a concept, as a slogan, as a term is used more frequently than any other terms. In Singapore, from the inflow of foreign capital, technology, workers or "foreign talents", music, movies, popular culture, almost everything has resonance with globalization. Globalization is a heroic process, globalization is a sinister process, depending on which side of the debate one stands. Some tend to see globalization as a brakeless train crushing everything in its path, others see benefit in getting on board the train towards economic growth and modernization.

SOCIOLOGY AND GLOBALIZATION

Globalization as a concept in social science has a short history. Even in the revised version of Raymond Williams' *Key Words* (1983) there is no entry on globalization. The Harper

Collins *Dictionary of Sociology* (1991) has an entry on "globalization of production" but no entry on globalization as such. The *Oxford Concise Dictionary of Sociology* (1994) has an entry on globalization together with globalization theory. It brought about by a variety of social and cultural developments...". The entry refers to the book edited by Martin Albrow and Elizabeth King (1990) *Globalization, Knowledge and Society*. The term globalization was probably first used as a book title in the Albrow and King edited book (1990) which was published drawing on the essays published in various issues of *International Sociology* the journal of International Sociological Association (1986-1990) Some of the journal articles contained globalization as a phrase in the titles in the 1980s and even earlier. One could even claim that the first social science text that dealt with the subject of globalization was *The nmunist Manifesto* (1848). One could even argue that Ibn Khaldun (1332-1406), the author of *Prolegomenon to the Universal History* was the real claimant of the credit. Globalization as a social process is old and has a much longer history. Many writers have traced the early globalizing processes in the dissemination of religion and culture, interactions of people, groups, communities through trade and commerce from the ancient times.

Sociology has been traditionally defined as the study of society. And as the boundaries of society have expanded from local community, through states to global society, sociology has become the study of the global society. This is a good illustration of how ideas, knowledge and (social) sciences expand with the changes and expansion of realities.

Sociology, it is often said, deals with the social life. In fact, all social sciences deal with social life or its various aspects. It is difficult to conceptualize *social* as a category. In sociology, there are two meanings of social. Social used in the sense of Wallerstein or for that matter Marx, encompasses technology, economy, politics and culture. Sociology is interested in the understanding of these broad processes, especially at their interrelatedness.

There is, however, a narrow meaning of social, which is often equated with social system, or what some people call societal. Here society is an abstract system of social relations, a web or network of social relations. Following Talcott Parsons, (and before him, Durkheim) some social scientists sought to view sociology as the *scientific* study of society. I put the stress on scientific because one of the goals of science is to define one's field narrowly so that specialized and predictable knowledge can be produced and accumulated. Sociologists with a positivistic bent of mind were quite happy with the narrow definition of sociology, hence the delimited conceptualization of society in the sense of social system. In this formulation, the field of study of economics is economic system; the field of political science is political system and so on. All social sciences could live happily in a world of segregated systems of knowledge! However, a large number of sociologists having dissatisfied with this narrow conceptualization of society, sought to view society and the scope of sociology broadly. They also found the earlier compartmentalization unnecessary, unproductive and overly abstract. All these so-called subsystems interact. Albert Hirschman called for the need of trespassing into each other's domains. The rise of macro-sociology is a clear response to the attempt to overcome a delimited view of sociology. Barrington Moore, Wallerstein, Tilly, Skocpol and others have looked at society in the broadest sense of the term, in that the inspiration came from Marx, Weber and later Braudel and other social historians.

Globalization, though it means many things to many people, is one of the master processes of our time. Globalization as a field in sociology is a legatee of the macro-sociological interests and development. Globalization study addresses itself to the connectivity of broad processes of technological, economic, political, cultural interrelationships. Whether one looks at the economic, cultural or media connectivity worldwide, one has to take a much broader understanding of society and social institutions. Sociology focuses its analytical lenses on the flows and processes in society whether at the local, national or global levels. In other words, sociology has a genuine claim over the field of globalization. Some contemporary writers accuse sociology, an archetypical social science, as a prisoner of nationstate.

Anthony Giddens and Immanuel Wallertsien have both lamented that sociology has been the study of modern nation states. The definitions as well as the boundaries of society, which sociology seeks to study, often overlap with those of nation-state. Since the interest taken by sociologists such as Roland Robertson of Pittsburgh and others since the late 1970s, sociology has redefined its scope and field as the social scientific study of the global processes. Ulrich Beck has explicitly called for the development of new concepts to capture the new realities of interconnectedness, plurality, multi-locality and multiplicity. Sociology has established its claim over globalization as a field of study historically. A return to national society centered focus would be a major regressive step towards objectivist, scientistic sociology and a return to what C Wright Mills called "abstracted empiricism". Or worse, sociology might become a residual discipline busy picking up areas left unattended by other social sciences. Sociology is not the only branch of social sciences that has a claim to study society because other branches of social sciences do study aspects of society. For example, institutional economists deal with social structure and cultural values to explain economic processes and market behaviors. Political scientists such as Robert Putnam have done important sociological studies of political processes. Such fields as political sociology illustrate the cross over of political science and sociology all the time. Social sciences are tasked to analyze society in all its various aspects and constellations.

The long-standing relationship between sociology and globalization, gives sociology as a discipline a unique position to study all aspects of the field of globalization, a master process in human society. This does not preclude the claims of other disciplines to the subject of globalization and it reminds us the importance of each field's autonomy to venture out and explore using its own traditions and conceptual frames.

While globalization as a framework is naturally biased in favour of macro-sociological issues, questions were raised to the viability of using this framework to study social realities on the ground. This led to a rethink of macro-macro relationship. Glocalization as a concept arose to help alleviate the conceptual difficulties of macro-micro relationship.

Although it would be difficult to trace the first user of the term "glocalization" in its original Japanese usage, the first time the term was used in English can be attributed to Professor

Roland Robertson, a British/American sociologist, who migrated from United Kingdom to the United States where he spent most of his academic career at the University of Pittsburgh, Pennsylvania, USA. Robertson's original interests in sociology were in the areas of sociology of religion, sociological theories and cultural sociology. He also ventured into areas of comparative sociology and modernization studies. His interest and knowledge of Japanese society led him to find out the use of the term "glocalization" in Japan in Japanese language, a term the marketing experts were using by which they meant that products of Japanese origin should be localized – that is, they should be suited to local taste and interests – yet, the products are global in application and reach, hence a new term "glocalization" was coined. Robertson and other sociologists interested in the subject of global processes could not help noticing that many of the social categories and practices assume a local flavour or character despite the fact that these products were invented elsewhere. Dutch sociologist Jan Nederveen Pieterse has for some time used terms such as mélange, hybridity, syncretism to capture similar processes with regard to culture. According to Nederveen Pieterse, (2004) there are three views on the issue of globalization of cultures. The first view is the clash of cultures view expressed in terms of clash of the civilizations by writers like Samuel Huntington. The second notion is best expressed in the phrase of "McDonaldization" of the world (Ritzer, 2000). This view obviously suggests a homogenized world, a world dominated by a single culture that erases differences of local cultures. The third view is that of hybridization or synthesis. Much of human evolution of culture can be seen as exchanges, diffusion, etc. where cross-breeding, borrowing and adjusting to the local needs and so on were very common.

EVOLUTION OF THE CONCEPT GLOBALIZATION

According to the dictionary meaning, the term "glocal" and the process noun "glocalization" are "formed by telescoping global and local to make a blend" (*The Oxford Dictionary of New Words*, 1991:134 quoted in Robertson, 1995:28). The term was modeled on Japanese word *dochakuka,* which originally meant adapting farming technique to one's own local condition. In the business world the idea was adopted to refer to global localization. The word as well as the idea came from Japan (Robertson, 1995:28). According to Wordspy, glocalization means "the creation of products or services intended for the global market, but customized to suit the local cultures." Although the term globalization has come to frequent use since the late 1980s, there were several related terms that social scientists used and continue to use. One such related word, which has been in use in social sciences and related fields for quite some time is, indigenization.

Some social scientists claimed that social sciences such as sociology and political science, even psychology were products of western social experiences therefore when these fields of inquiry were transported and transplanted to non-European or non-western contexts such as Latin America, Asia or Africa there was a need for indigenization of these subjects. The idea of indigenization has created quite a controversy among social scientists because it raises fundamental questions about the applicability of social scientific ideas and concepts. However, indigenization can be seen as similar to localization. In both these concepts, there is an assumption of an original or authentic "locality" or "indigenous system". One of the consequences of globalization is that it opens up doubts about the originality and authenticity of cultures. If one takes a long-term view of globalization, "locality" or "local" itself is a consequence of globalization. There are hardly any sites or cultures that can be seen as isolated or unconnected from the global processes.

Robertson, one of the pioneers in the study of globalization, did not view globalization as a recent phenomenon nor did he see it as a consequence of modernization. The theories of modernization came under serious attack in sociology because of such assumptions as unilinearity and convergence. As our knowledge of the world increased, many writers pointed out that the cultural differences are not all that superficial and nonlinearity and mutiliniearity are better descriptions of global modernity. Besides divergence rather than convergence seems to have been the consequence of modernization. Yet the divergent cultures and societies can be studied with the help of a globalized social science and there was no need for diverse, indigenized social sciences. Social sciences to claim scientific status could not afford to forfeit its claim to universality and universal knowledge. Social sciences must be context sensitive but not context dependent. It is in this context that Robertson conceptualized globalization in the twentieth century as *"the interpenetration of the universalization of particularization and the particularization of universalism"*. Khondker (1994) building on Robertson's framework argued that globalization or globalization should be seen as an interdependent process. "The problem of simultaneous globalization of the local and the localization of globality can be expressed as the twin processes of *macro-localization* and *micro-globalization*. Macro-localization involves expanding the boundaries locality as well as making some local ideas, practices, institutions global. The rise of world wide religious or ethnic revivalist movements can be seen as examples of macro-localization.

Microglobalization involves incorporating certain global processes into the local setting. Consider social movements such as the feminist movements or ecological movements or consider new production techniques or marketing strategies which emerge in a certain local context and over a period these practices spread far beyond that locality into a larger spatial and historical arena. Consider print industry or computer industry with a specific location of its emergence has now become a global phenomena. Overcoming space is globalization. In this view of globalization, globalization is globalization. This view is somewhat different from the way Giddens conceptualizes the relationship between the global and the local. Globalization, for Giddens, "is the reason for the revival of local cultural identities in different parts of the world" (Giddens, 2000:31). While in this view local is the provider of the response to the forces that are global, we argue that local itself is constituted globally. Ritzer in discussing globalization has added another – convoluted term "grobalization" to refer to what he calls "growth imperatives [pushing] organizations and nations to expand globally and to impose themselves on the local" (2004:xiii). For Ritzer, globalization is the sum total of globalization and "grobalization".

Wong argues, following Wind (1998), that a global company does not mean that it has gone global all the way. There are companies that are part global, part regional or part local involving different domains such as portfolio, supply chain, research and development and business processes. In terms of mode of business practices, there could be independent operations, joint venture or alliances (Wong, 1998:156).

KEY PROPOSITIONS

The main propositions of gloclaization are not too different from the main arguments of a sophisticated version of globalization. 1. Diversity is the essence of social life; 2. Globalization does not erase *all* differences; 3. Autonomy of history and culture give a sense of uniqueness to the experiences of groups of people whether we define them as cultures, societies or nations; 4. Globalization is the notion that removes the fear from many that globalization is like a tidal wave erasing all the differences. A number of books and articles on the subject of globalization give the impression that it is a force that creates a uniform world, a world where barriers disappear and cultures become amalgamated into a global whole. The tensions and conflicts between cultures are nothing but the problems of a transitory phase. Ironically, the phase of transition has been around for a long period of time. And as we have entered the third millennia many of the age-old problems of differences of cultures and religion remain. 5. Glocalizaton does not promise a world free from conflicts and tensions but a more historically grounded understanding of the complicated – yet, pragmatic view of the world.

GLOBALIZATION IS NOT WESTERNIZATION

Some writers view globalization as the worldwide spread of "westernization". This view is either erroneous or contains only partial truth. From a superficial point of view, various processes outwardly seem that the world is, indeed, becoming westernized. One could see the popularity of the western music, movies, and "McDonalds" as examples of westernization. More and more countries are seeing the opening of McDonalds. More and more countries playing the top chart of the pop list of USA and Hollywood movies and US-made television serials (such as, *Friends* and *The Simpsons* are becoming ubiquitous to the extent that some writers even use the term "Americanization" to describe these processes of cultural transmission. However, a closer look will reveal that these cultural goods have different meanings in different societal and cultural contexts with uneven impact on classes and agegroups. Some of the products are consumed without any modification, others are modified and indigenized to suit the local contexts and there are exceptional situations where the intentions are completely inverted.

In the past, many writers found it necessary to distinguish modernization from westernization. Modernization was believed to be a set of cultural practices and social institutional features that historically evolved in Europe and North America, commonly referred to as the West. The need to separate westernization from modernization (in the past) was motivated more by nationalism than pure intellectual reasons, because historically speaking, most of the modern cultural traits began in the West, a historical fact which was difficult to accommodate in a nationalistic political culture. The Western scholars in the nineteenth century were also guilty of making exaggerated claims of western superiority. Max Weber, a German sociologist was correct to claim that the western rationality and science had become universal but his denigration of non-western cultures did not sit well among the larger intellectual community. Many Indian sociologists took pains to delineate the differences between modernization and westernization. Similar discussions exist with regard to so-called westernization of the Ottoman Empire, modernization of Japan since the Meiji restoration of 1868 or modernization of China in the early part of the 20th century such as the May 4th Movement of 1919. In the modernization process, many of the late modernizing societies were borrowing ideas and knowledge and technology most of which were generated in the early modernized societies in Europe. The geography of the West kept shifting. In the nineteenth century, when Germany was modernizing, the idea of the West was limited to Western Europe only (mainly Britain and France). In some post-colonial situations the demarcation was based more on political expedience than logical or intellectual merits. Good westernization came to be regarded as modernization and bad modernization was designated as westernization. The distancing from westernization can also be understood as a reaction to centuries of domination and exploitation of the colonies by the western (mainly European) powers. However, over time a more objective consideration of history indicate that many of the traits that spread worldwide originated in certain geographical regions yet as these traits were transplanted elsewhere, they became mutated and assumed different forms in different contexts. For example, parliamentary democracy evolved in England, with roots that go back to *Magna Carta* of 1215. However, as Westminster-style parliamentary democracy was institutionalized in India, Malaysia, and other former British colonies, they mutated in light of the local milieu.

Westernization as a term is not equivalent to globalization. Nevertheless, westernization can be seen as an aspect of globalization. Certain institutional features and cultural traits that originated in the west were put in place in many other geographical regions lock stock and barrel under the framework of global interconnections and diffusion or forced implantation under colonial age. Yet, over time these institutions and practices mutated and assumed new meanings. Therefore, westernization can be seen as the beginning of the process. The cultural features borrowed or imitated themselves mutate in the source countries. Thus, westernization as a category has limited conceptual value. One can associate certain literary forms, genres, and traits as part of the cultural zone we vaguely call "the west", yet these are mere influences as one can see in artistic, literary, architectural styles. For example, the great Indian film maker late Satyajit Ray was influenced by Hollywood films and the art of film making, but he did not want to replicate Hollywood movies in Calcutta. His movies were modern capturing local themes which he projected with a modern art form and technology. Hence it was truly global, or more appropriately, glocal. Presently, Singapore is establishing linkages with both Bollywood and Indian film industries as well seeking to play the role of an outsourced location for hi-tech Hollywood productions. Globalization, like modernization, is often a fusion. Westernization as a concept has some value if used only as a descriptive rather than analytic category. As an analytic category it is rather limited.

Writers such as John Meyer have used the idea of isomorphism (a term borrowed from science, botany, in particular) which means replication of the same form yet separated from the main source. His research has shown that modern education – not western education though it was perhaps modified and institutionalized in the west – has spread worldwide and a similar set of values and practices have emerged in diverse settings. For example, college graduates command more social prestige and respect almost regardless of cultural contexts. Some cultures can give more rewards than others. Globalization shows tendencies towards isomorphism, yet some people may continue to mistake this process for westernization.

In the context of Singapore, the first generation leaders always emphasized the fact that although Singapore's economic development was dependent on western technology and capital, and it was reliant on multinational corporations to foster economic growth, the state maintained a certain degree of autonomy and formulated broad social development strategy.

GLOBALIZATION AND HYBRIDIZATION

In the discussion of globalization some writers tend to conflate it with hybridization. This may be somewhat misleading. Globalization involves blending, mixing adapting of two or more processes one of which must be local. But one can accept a hybrid version that does not involve local. In the context of higher education in Singapore a hybridized version comprising the original British model and the US model was accepted. One could find many such examples in matters of technology and business practices where two different systems or modes are combined for better results. Globalization to be meaningful must include at least one component that addresses the local culture, system of values and practices and so on. One of the areas in Singapore where the evidence of globalization is quite visible is the area of mass communication and especially in the area of television programming. From televised drama, sitcoms, and even "reality shows" one finds attempts of globalization. Although some attempts are not always successful and there are instances when one can see unabashed imitation, by and large the idea of globalization and fusion remain appealing to many Singaporeans.

Technology and Globalization

Singapore, located in Southeast Asia, has attained the developed country status or High Income Economy according to the World Bank classification. Having experienced rapid state-led economic development under a favorable global economic climate, Singapore has been pursuing the goal of creating a knowledge-based economy since 1990s. Singapore's economic growth since her emergence in 1965 as an independent state entailed heavy investment in education and development of human resource in science and technology. Singapore's advancement in areas of knowledge and high technology is dependent to a large extent on international collaboration. Two aspects of Singapore's growth are striking: linkage with global market and a highly rational approach to governance, which is often evidenced by a near-absence of corruption. These two aspects have direct bearing on the issues of technological developments in Singapore. An additional factor that one has to take into account is the cultural diversity of Singapore's population. Singapore is both a multiethnic and multi-religious society, which provides an added dimension to the context of formulation of ethical standards. Its 4 million people (in 2004) comprise 76% Chinese, 14% Malay, 7% Indian, and 3% others. As many as one quarter of Singapore's population is non-citizens which indicate Singapore's reliance on foreign human resources both at working class jobs as well as high end knowledge workers. Multicultural population-base and the varying sensitivity of various groups have influenced policies concerning biotechnology.

According to Stephen Haggard, "Singapore had already broken away from the typical policy pattern of a developing country as early as 1970. By the 1980s Singaporean policymakers were identifying the country with small European economies such as Switzerland" (Haggard, 1999:355). It has been noted by a number of writers (Rodan, 1989; Wade, 1990 and Haggard, 1999) that Singapore's economic development and social modernization did not take place following a pure free market model. Singapore state was very much involved in guiding the market forces. On the one hand Singapore has relied heavily for multinational corporations to launch economic growth but it also built a high rate of savings through central Provident Fund. Singapore's development model showed certain mixed or hybrid quality. Soon after Singapore's independence, policymakers began to focus attention on development in sciences and technology. The strive for such development was aided in the process by close relationship with the Multinational Corporations who brought investments and employed technically qualified Singaporeans. Right from the early days of national development, Singapore was well integrated with not only the international economic system bit also with global knowledge systems. Singapore's exportoriented economic development in the 1980s was dominated by IT and computer peripherals. In the 1990s emphasis on biotechnology followed an earlier emphasis on IT.

Singapore's development since her independence in 1965 can be described as a transformation from a Third World society to a First World economy. Much of that development can be attributed to Singapore's adoption of modern technology. Choices of technology were not always preceded by controversies and debates. Both the government and the general public showed a great deal of pragmatism in the choice of technology. Although in most instances, technology was adopted without much modification, the mode of use, and so on there were imprints of adaptation and globalization. One such area is in the area of electronic road pricing system. The technology of monitoring cars from a scanner fitted in a gantry was not a Singaporean invention, but they way that technology was used was very Singaporean. Because of the drive to catch up, Singapore has always been ahead in adopting new technology. It is in recent years having achieved the developed status; some Singaporeans are showing concern with issues of privacy and so on because some of the new technology is intrusive. Singapore's love affairs with technology is evident in the fact that Singapore ranks among the top three countries in the world in terms usage of personal computers as well as hand phones. The only country ahead of Singapore in the number of Short Messaging Service (SMS) is Hong Kong. Whenever a new technology is invented, Singapore would be one of the first places where that technology would show up.

Singaporeans have a favorable attitude towards technology. Singapore International Airlines as well as Port Authority of Singapore (PSA) remain equipped with the state of the art technology. ATM machines in Singapore were introduced in the early 1980s. Singapore's public transport system is another place where one would find a great many applications of new technology. However, all cases of adaptation technology may not be seen as examples of globalization. In many instances, for example, computer technology in Singapore was implemented without any modifications. However as Singapore entered a new phase of research in the 1990s, namely in the area of biotechnology we fins evidence of globalization. Biotechnological research calls for a careful consideration of and orientation towards local cultural and ethical contexts. A good deal of attention has been given to these areas in Singapore. Another area where examples of globalization can be found in both Malaysia and Singapore is the area of architectural designs. In the post-socialist world, Singapore remains a unique society where 90% of the population lives in the houses built and then sold to the citizens. When Singapore was embarked on massive public housing program, it borrowed the so-called international style of very basic and practical designs, yet a new concept of public space – though limited to the residents of the housing blocs – evolved. These spaces known as void-decks were places for wedding, funeral or any such communal gatherings. New designs blending the western and local motifs emerged in Singapore. Although the initial architectural thrust of Singapore can be viewed as "brutalism" driven by a sheer pragmatic consideration, over the years more attention has been given to the notions of fusion and hybridity, or in other words globalization.

6

Political Obligation

To have a political obligation is to have a moral duty to obey the laws of one's country or state. On that point there is almost complete agreement among political philosophers. But how does one acquire such an obligation, and how many people have really done what is necessary to acquire it? Or is political obligation more a matter of *being* than of *doing* — that is, of simply being a member of the country or state in question? To those questions many answers have been given, and none now commands widespread assent. Indeed, a number of contemporary political philosophers deny that a satisfactory theory of political obligation either has been or can be devised. Others, however, continue to believe that there is a solution to what is commonly called "the problem of political obligation," and they are presently engaged in lively debate not only with the skeptics but also with one another on the question of which theory, if any, provides the solution to the problem.

Whether political obligation is the central or fundamental problem of political philosophy, as some have maintained (e.g., McPherson), may well be doubted. There is no doubt, however, that the history of political thought is replete with attempts to provide a satisfactory account of political obligation, from the time of Socrates to the present. These attempts have become increasingly sophisticated in recent years, but they have brought us no closer to agreement on a solution to the problem of political obligation than the efforts of, say, Thomas Hobbes and John Locke in the seventeenth century. Nor have these sophisticated attempts made it unnecessary to look back to earlier efforts to resolve the problem. On the contrary, an appreciation of the troublesome nature of political obligation seems to require an examination of its place in the history of political thought.

This essay begins, therefore, with a brief history of the problem of political obligation. It then turns, in Part II, to the conceptual questions raised by political obligation, such as what it means for an *obligation* to be *political*. In Part III the focus is on the skeptics, with particular attention to the self-proclaimed philosophical anarchists, who deny that political obligations exist yet do not want to abolish the state. Part IV surveys the leading contenders among the various theories of political obligation now on offer, and Part V concludes the essay with a consideration of recent proposals for pluralistic or "multiple principle" approaches.

POLITICAL OBLIGATION IN HISTORICAL PERSPECTIVE

The phrase "political obligation" is apparently no older than T. H. Green's *Lectures on the Principles of Political Obligation*, delivered at Oxford University in 1879-80. The two words from which Green formed the phrase are much older, of course, and he apparently thought that combining them required no elaborate explanation or defence. In any case, there was nothing novel about the problem Green addressed in his lectures: "to discover the true ground or justification for obedience to law". Sophocles raised this problem in his play *Antigone*, first performed around 440 BCE, and Plato's *Crito* recounts Socrates' philosophical response to the problem, in the face of his own death, some forty years later.

Socrates on Obeying the Law

In 399 BCE an Athenian jury found Socrates guilty of impiety and corrupting the morals of the youth, for which crimes the jury condemned him to death. According to Plato's account, Socrates' friends arranged his escape, but he chose to stay and drink the fatal hemlock, arguing that to defy the judgment against him would be to break his "agreements and commitments" and to "mistreat" his friends, his country, and the laws of Athens. Socrates' arguments are sketchy, and Crito, his interlocutor, does little to challenge them, but they are nevertheless suggestive of the theories of political obligation that have emerged in the two and a half millennia since his death.

These arguments fall into four categories. First, Socrates maintains that his long residence in Athens shows that he has entered into an agreement with its laws and committed himself to obey them — an argument that anticipates the social contract or consent theory of political obligation. Second, he acknowledges that he owes his birth, nurture, and education, among other goods, to the laws of Athens, and he hints at the gratitude theory of obligation when he concludes that it would be wrong of him to disobey its laws now. Third, he appeals to what is now known as the argument from fairness or fair play when he suggests that disobedience would be a kind of mistreatment of his fellow citizens. As he asks Crito, "if we leave here without the city's permission, are we mistreating people whom we should least mistreat?" (50a) There is, finally, a trace of utilitarian reasoning, as when Socrates imagines "the laws and the state" confronting him with this challenge: "'do you think it possible for a city not to be destroyed if the verdicts of its courts have no force but are nullified and set at naught by private individuals?'" (50b). None of these arguments is fully developed, but their presence in the *Crito* is testimony to the staying power of intuitions and concepts — commitment and agreement, gratitude, fair play, and utility — that continue to figure in discussions of obligation and obedience.

Plato's *Crito* is noteworthy not only as the first philosophical exploration of political obligation but also as the last to appear for centuries. The Cynics and others did question the value of political life, and indirectly the existence of an obligation to obey the law, but they left no record of a discussion of the subject as sustained as even the five or six pages in the *Crito*. When the morality of obedience and disobedience next became a much discussed issue, it was a religious as much as a philosophical discussion.

Divine Command

Throughout history, the belief that political society and its rules are divinely ordained has been so strong as to keep many people, and probably most, from considering the possibility that disobeying those rules might ever be justified. With the advent of Christianity, however, that possibility had to be taken seriously. For the Christian, the distinction Jesus draws (Matthew 22:15-22) between the tribute owed to Caesar and that owed to God makes it clear that what the rulers command may be at odds with what God wants done. That point became even clearer when the rulers tried to suppress Christianity. Nevertheless, Christian doctrine held that there is an obligation to obey the law grounded in divine command, with the most important text being Paul's Epistle to the Romans (13:1-2): "For there is no authority except from God, and those that exist have been instituted by God. Therefore he who resists the authorities resists what God has appointed, and those who resist will incur judgment."

As a theory of political obligation, divine command faces two general problems. First, it presupposes the existence of divinity of some sort; and second, the commands of the divine being(s) are not always clear. It is one thing to know that we should give to Caesar what is Caesar's and to God what is God's, for example, and quite another to know what exactly is Caesar's due. For Christians, however, the main challenge was to reconcile Paul's text with the uncomfortable fact that rulers were often hostile to Christianity — or, with the rise of Protestantism in the sixteenth century, hostile to what one took to be true Christianity. To this challenge, one response was simply to hold that hostile or vicious rulers must be endured, for God must have given them power as a sign of His displeasure with a wicked people. Other responses, though, made room for disobedience.

One such response was to distinguish the divinely ordained office from the officer who occupied it. That is, God ordains that political authority must exist, because the condition of human life since the fall from grace requires such authority; but God does not ordain that this or that particular person hold a position of authority, and He certainly does not want rulers to abuse their authority by ruling tyrannically. This distinction, employed as early as the fourth century by St. John Chrysostom, was invoked throughout the middle ages. A second response to the problem Romans 13 posed was to distinguish disobedience from resistance. According to Martin Luther and others who drew this distinction, Christians may not actively resist their rulers, but they must disobey them when the rulers' commands are contrary to God's. Yet a third response was to note the possibility of conflict between two or more of one's rulers. In other words, if more than one person holds political authority over you, and if they issue conflicting commands, then you may satisfy Paul's injunction by obeying the authority whose commands are more congenial to your understanding of true Christianity, even when such obedience entails resisting the commands of others in authority.

These last two responses played an especially important part in the political disputes that accompanied the Protestant Reformation. Under the pressure of those disputes, however, another theory of political obligation became increasingly prominent, as Protestants came to rely on the belief that political authority derives from the consent of the governed.

The Social Contract

Although the idea of the social contract long antedates the modern era (Gough 1967), its full development occurred in the seventeenth century, when Thomas Hobbes and John Locke used the theory to rather different ends. Jean-Jacques Rousseau, Immanuel Kant, and other philosophers have also relied on social contract theory, but the classic expressions of the contract theory of political obligation remain Hobbes's *Leviathan* (1651) and Locke's *Second Treatise of Government* (1690).

For Hobbes, social contract theory established the authority of anyone who was able to wield and hold power. If we imagine ourselves in a state of nature, he argued, with no government and no law to guide us but the law of nature, we will recognize that everyone is naturally equal and independent. But we should also recognize that this state of nature will also be a state of war, for the "restlesse desire for Power after power" that drives all of us will lead to "a warre of every man against every man". To escape so dreadful a condition, people surrender their independence by entering into a covenant to obey a sovereign power that will have the authority to make, enforce, and interpret laws. This form of the social contract Hobbes called "sovereignty by institution." But he also insisted that conquerors acquire authority over those they subject to their rule — "sovereignty by acquisition" — when they allow those subjects to go about their business. In either case, Hobbes said, the subjects consent to obey those who have effective power over them, whether the subject has a choice in who holds power or not. Because they consent, they therefore have an obligation to obey the sovereign, whether sovereignty be instituted or acquired.

Exactly how much Locke differs from Hobbes in his conclusions is a matter of scholarly dispute, but there is no doubt that he puts the same concepts to work for what seem to be more limited ends. According to Locke, the free and equal individuals in the state of nature establish government as a way of overcoming the "inconveniencies" of that state. Moreover, Locke's social contract appears to have two stages. In the first stage the naturally free and equal individuals agree to form themselves into a political society, under law, and in the second they establish the government. This move allows Locke to argue, contrary to Hobbes, for a right of revolution on the ground that overthrowing the government will not immediately return the people to the state of nature. Nor does he hold, with Hobbes, that mere submission to a conqueror constitutes a form of consent to the conqueror's rule.

Locke does agree with Hobbes, of course, in deriving obligations to obey the law from the consent of the governed. In developing his argument, however, he reveals three problems that have bedevilled social contract theory. One problem has to do with the nature of the contract: is it historical or hypothetical? If the former, then the problem is to show that most people truly have entered into such a contract. If the contract is meant to be a device that illustrates how people *would have* given their consent, on the other hand, then the difficulty is that a hypothetical contract "is no contract at all". The second problem has to do with the way Hobbes and Locke rely on *tacit* consent. If only express or explicit statements of agreement or commitment count as genuine consent, then it appears that relatively few people have consented to obey the laws of their country; but if tacit or implied consent is allowed, the concept of consent may be stretched too far. Hobbes does this when he counts submission to a conqueror as consent, but

Locke also runs this risk when he states, in §119 of the *Second Treatise*, that the "very being of anyone within the territories" of a government amounts to tacit consent. Finally, it is not clear that consent is really the key to political obligation in these theories. The upshot of Hobbes's theory seems to be that we have an obligation to obey anyone who can maintain order, and in Locke's it seems that there are some things to which we cannot consent. In particular, we cannot consent to place ourselves under an absolute ruler, for doing so would defeat the very purposes for which we enter the social contract — to protect our lives, liberty, and property (Pitkin 1965).

One of the first to find fault with the argument from consent or contract was David Hume. In "Of the Original Contract," published in 1752, Hume takes particular exception to the appeal to tacit consent. To say, he protests, that most people have given their consent to obey the laws simply by remaining in their country of birth is tantamount to saying that someone tacitly consents to obey a ship's captain "though he was carried on board while asleep and must leap into the ocean and perish the moment he leaves her". For Hume, it seems, the obligation to obey the law derives not from consent or contract but from the straightforward utility of a system of laws that enables people to pursue their interests peacefully and conveniently.

Utility and Obligation

For all its influence in other areas of legal, moral, and political philosophy, utilitarianism has found few adherents among those who believe that there is a general obligation to obey the laws of one's country. Part of the reason for this situation may be the fact that Jeremy Bentham, John Stuart Mill, and others who followed Hume's path had little to say about political obligation. A more powerful reason, though, is that utilitarians have trouble accounting for obligations of any kind. If one's guiding principle is always to act to maximize expected utility, or promote the greatest happiness of the greatest number, then obligations seem to have little or no binding force.

Some utilitarian philosophers have struggled to overcome this problem, either by pointing to reasons to believe that respecting obligations serves to promote utility or by restricting calculations of utility to rules or norms rather than to individual acts. Whether their efforts have been successful remains a matter of debate. There seems to be a consensus, however, that the most sophisticated attempts to provide a utilitarian grounding for political obligation, such as those of Rolf Sartorius and R. M. Hare (1976), have proved unsuccessful. As a result, utilitarianism seldom figures in the debates of those contemporary political philosophers who continue to believe that there is, in some political societies, a general obligation to obey the law.

CONCEPTUAL MATTERS

In the twentieth century political philosophers devoted themselves at least as much to the analysis of the problem of political obligation, and to the concepts it involves, as to full-scale attempts to devise theories of the obligation to obey the law. As in the four historically significant theories surveyed in the previous section, however, the presumption has continued to be that the answer to the problem of political obligation must be stated in moral terms. When T. H. Green set out in 1879 "to discover the true ground or justification for obedience to law," for example, he was looking for more than prudence alone can provide. "You ought to obey the law because you will suffer if you do not" may be a powerful reason for obedience, but it is not a reason that speaks to Green's concern with "the moral function or object served by law ...". For Green, and for almost everyone else who has pondered it, the problem of political obligation is a moral problem, and the obligation in question is a kind of moral obligation. Anyone who has an obligation to obey the law thus has a moral duty to discharge, at least when there are no overriding moral considerations that justify disobedience.

Obligation and Duty

As the previous sentence suggests, obligations are also duties. That is true, at any rate, when the obligation in question is political obligation. To be sure, some philosophers have uncovered differences between obligations and duties, the most important of which is that obligations must be voluntarily undertaken or incurred, but duties need not be. The obligation to keep a promise or fulfil a contract, for example, arises only when one has done something that generates the obligation — made a promise or signed a contract — but the duties of charity and truth telling supposedly fall on us regardless of what, if anything, we voluntarily commit to do. John Rawls relies on this distinction when he argues that most citizens of a reasonably just political society have no general obligation to obey its laws, even though they do have a "natural duty" to support just institutions — a duty that has the general effect of requiring them to obey. For the most part, however, the distinction between obligation and duty has played no significant role in the debates over the supposed moral responsibility to obey the law. To invoke the distinction here would run counter to the tendency in both ordinary language and philosophical discussion to use the terms interchangeably, as when we speak of the "duty" to keep a promise or an "obligation" to tell the truth. It would also work against those who maintain that political obligations need not be acquired voluntarily, perhaps because they believe that the duty to obey the law is a "role obligation" akin to the "obligations" imposed by membership in a family (e.g., Hardimon 1994). Furthermore, those who follow the Rawlsian natural-duty approach typically argue that political obligation is grounded in a natural duty of some sort. In short, there seems to be nothing to gain from insisting on a sharp distinction between obligations and duties in this context. This essay will proceed, then, like almost everything written on either side of the question, on the understanding that a political obligation, if it exists, is a moral duty to obey the law.

To have an obligation is to be bound to do or not do something, as the etymological connection to the Latin *ligare* indicates; and to have a political obligation is to be bound to obey the law. But what is the force of this obligation? And why is it a *political* rather than a *legal* obligation? Both of these questions have proved troublesome.

Obligation and Morality

In the case of the first question, the problem is to determine whether the obligation to obey the law outweighs, overrides, or excludes competing moral consideration. If there is an obligation or duty to obey the law *as such*, simply because it is the law, then it is an obligation to obey no matter what the content of a particular law may be. Yet few people will say that someone who breaks the speed limit while driving a desperately ill person to the hospital is acting immorally; and many will say that some laws, such as those prohibiting consensual homosexual acts, are themselves immoral. We may grant that the law carries moral force, in other words, but we cannot grant that it holds a monopoly on that kind of force. Whether one ought to obey the law in a particular case is something that must be decided *all things considered* — that is, in light of other moral considerations that may arise. But what kind of an *obligation* is it that may be overridden or outweighed in this manner?

There are three responses to this question, broadly speaking. The first and most common is to hold that political obligations are morally binding, but not absolutely so. They are, instead, *prima facie* obligations. Like the obligation to keep a promise or meet the terms of a contract, the obligation to obey the law binds one to obedience, *ceteris paribus*, but it may be overridden in special circumstances, when other things are decidedly not equal. Nevertheless, the obligation is both presumptive and, at least on some accounts, quite strong. According to M. B. E. Smith's definition, for instance, "a person *S* has a prima facie obligation to do an act *X* if, and only if, there is a moral reason for *S* to do *X* which is such that, unless he has a moral reason not to do *X* at least as strong as his reason to do *X*, *S*'s failure to do *X* is wrong".

Others will allow that the overriding reason need not be strictly moral, as in the case of friends who break the law against gambling on their weekly poker night. On either account, though, there will be a presumption that one ought to obey the law. Someone who is under a political obligation thus should presume that she has a duty to obey the laws of her polity, and she should consider disobedience only when it seems that obeying a particular law may be, on balance, the wrong course of conduct. To have a political obligation, then, is not to have an obligation to obey laws *a*, *b*, and *c*, but perhaps not law *d*; it is to have a general obligation to obey the laws of one's polity as such. This general obligation, though, will not always require obedience to particular laws when all things are considered. A second response is to maintain that political obligations may be overridden because they are not (fully) moral obligations. In her recent book on the subject, Margaret Gilbert argues that political obligations fall between "the dictates of morality," on the one hand, and "one's inclinations and ... self-interest," on the other. A political obligation is thus a "genuine obligation," in Gilbert's terms, but it is not necessarily a moral requirement, all things considered. Like all genuine obligations, a political obligation has binding force — in this case, binding the obligated person to obey lawful commands. "Yet it may be," Gilbert says, "that one need not, all things considered, obey that command. One may, indeed, be morally required *not* to do so ...".

The third response is to hold that a prima facie obligation is not really an obligation at all. As one writer tempted by this view says, with particular reference to political obligation, it "makes little sense to insist there is such an obligation if those who stand under it are entitled to exercise their own moral discretion regarding the propriety of their obedience to law". Either we have an obligation to do (or not do) *X*, in which case we are simply and absolutely bound to do (or not do) it, or we do not. Those who take this view must conclude, therefore, either that anyone who has a political obligation should always obey the law, being guilty of immoral conduct if he does not, or that no one ever has been or will be under a political obligation. Given the reasons already noted for believing disobedience to be morally justified in some circumstances, few of those who take obligations to be absolutely binding will be inclined to draw the first conclusion. To conceive of obligations as necessarily absolute is thus to slide toward the conviction that there is no duty to obey the law as such, at least not if this duty is understood as a general obligation to obey the law of one's polity.

What, then, is the force of a political obligation? Is it "merely" a prima facie obligation, or is it, if it exists at all, absolutely binding? Or is it a genuine but non-moral obligation, as Gilbert seems to think? The advantage of Gilbert's position is that it avoids the problem of resolving the question of whether the obligation is prima facie or absolute. That is, one may acknowledge that political obligations are truly binding, so that anyone who has such an obligation is bound to obey the law, but also acknowledge that this obligation must give way when it conflicts with moral obligations. The disadvantage, however, is that Gilbert's position appears to deny what seems to be the common belief — namely, that all genuine obligations carry some moral force. To be sure, it may be easy to think of cases in which morality requires us to break promises or vows, but this does not mean that the promise or vow is completely lacking in moral content — not unless we take a moral obligation to be an all-things-considered requirement. But if we allow that all genuine obligations carry some moral force, if not enough to be always dispositive, we are in effect accepting the distinction between prima facie and absolute obligations. Either that or we need to introduce a related distinction between genuine obligations, which are moral but subject to being overridden, and some other kind of moral requirement, responsibility, or "ought" that is capable of overriding moral obligations.

Or we could take the third route and insist that genuine obligations, including political obligations, must be absolutely binding. But this is to require more of political obligation than almost any obligation can bear. In fact, the usual candidates for absolutely binding moral requirements are highly abstract and truly fundamental — to do God's will in all of one's actions, to do good and avoid evil, to promote the greatest happiness of the greatest number, to submit only to laws that one makes for oneself, and the like. Unless one holds the implausible view that the obligation to obey the law is a fundamental requirement of this kind — that is, the moral duty from which all other moral duties derive — there is no good reason to deny that political obligations are as liable to be overridden as almost all of our other obligations, such as those that follow from promises, contracts, oaths, and vows.

We should not be troubled, then, by the charge that "it makes little sense to insist there is such an obligation [i.e., a political obligation] if those who stand under it are entitled to exercise their own moral discretion regarding the propriety of their obedience to law." It is true that the law does not invite us to examine its content before deciding whether to obey, nor does it typically present us with a set of options from which to choose. As Joseph Raz and others have observed, the law claims exclusive or ultimate authority within its domain. From the standpoint of moral or political philosophy, however, there is no reason to cede such authority to "the law." We may not want people to stop in their tracks so that they can ponder the moral implications of obedience every time the law directs them to do something, but neither should we want them to obey unquestioningly whatever is presented to them as a law. Political obligation resembles military duty in this respect. Anyone who believes that a military force is necessary will almost certainly accept the need for a chain of command, which entails a duty on the part of subordinates to obey the orders of those who outrank them.

Obligation, Political and Legal

What does this prima facie or defeasible nature of political obligation imply by way of an answer to the second question, which concerns the distinction between political and legal obligation? If those who have a political obligation have a duty to obey the law, *ceteris paribus*, then why not call it a *legal* obligation? Or why not conclude, with Bhiku Parekh, that the question of whether we have a duty to obey the law is really a matter of *civil obligation* — that is, "the obligation to respect and uphold the legitimately constituted civil authority" — that entails *legal obligations* "to obey the laws enacted by the civil authority" rather than political obligation? "Political" is the broader term, according to Parekh, and someone who has a truly political obligation will owe her polity more than mere obedience to its laws. Such a person will have a positive duty to take steps to secure the safety and advance the interests of her country. Following Parekh's distinction, then, we may say that someone who pays taxes discharges a legal obligation, no matter how grudgingly she pays them, but someone who pays taxes *and* contributes voluntarily to public projects fulfills a truly political obligation.

Other philosophers also distinguish political from legal obligations, but not in the far-reaching way that Parekh does. Indeed, it seems that we already have a term, "civic duty," that does the work he wants to assign to "political obligation." Exhortations to do our civic duty typically urge us to do more than merely obey the law. These exhortations would have us vote in elections and be well-informed voters; buy government bonds; limit our use of water and other scarce resources; donate blood, service, or money (beyond what we owe in taxes) in times of crisis; and generally contribute in an active way to the common good. Whether we really have a civic duty to do any or all of these things may be a matter of dispute, but appeals to civic duty are certainly quite common, and it is hardly clear that there is something to be gained by reclassifying them as appeals to political obligation.

How, then, do others draw the distinction? In general, the idea seems to be that political obligations are *systemic* and legal obligations *specific*. Among political philosophers, as previously noted, the problem of political obligation is the problem of determining whether there is a ground or justification for obedience to the law — not this or that law in particular but the law as such. This is the sense in which it is a systemic obligation, and that is why political philosophers have worried less about whether this or that law is binding than about the conditions under which one has an obligation to obey the laws in general. They look upon the system of laws as an aspect of the polity, albeit a vital one, and their question is what kind of polity can rightly claim that its members have a moral duty to obey its laws. Their answers have varied, of course, from Hobbes at one extreme, insisting that there is an obligation to obey the dictates of anyone who can maintain order, to anarchists at the other. Yet their concern has been the general or systemic one of establishing the grounds for obeying the laws as such.

For legal philosophers, however, the binding nature of laws in general is something to be assumed. The law claims ultimate or exclusive authority within its domain, and anyone who acknowledges that a legal system is in place must also acknowledge that its laws are binding. The obligation, though, is a legal obligation, or an obligation from the law's point of view. It need not be a moral obligation. According to legal positivists, in fact, a law will be morally binding only when it requires those subject to it to do what morality independently requires. Thus the laws that prohibit robbery, murder, and other acts that are *mala in se* — that is, inherently evil — are laws that people have both a moral and a legal obligation to obey; while laws that prohibit acts that are otherwise morally indifferent, such as driving on the left-hand side of the road, are merely legal obligations. Legal obligations are specific rather than systemic, then, because legal philosophers are concerned with the question of what counts as a law (or a valid law) with binding force, not with the moral justification of political systems that claim a right to be obeyed.

For political philosophers, the value of this distinction is that it allows one to hold that a person may be subject to a legal obligation even though she has no political obligation to obey the laws of the regime in power. There are at least two kinds of cases in which doing so can prove helpful. In the first, the regime is tyrannical, inept, or simply so unjust that only a Hobbesian would maintain that those subject to its commands have a moral obligation to obey. Nevertheless, people in this unhappy country manage to drive cars on roads that the regime maintains and marry according to its rules. In this situation we can acknowledge that people have legal obligations to obey certain laws — those that govern traffic and marriage — despite the absence of a political obligation to obey the laws as such. In the second, happier kind of case, we can acknowledge that the citizen of one country, to which she owes a political obligation, has a legal obligation to obey the laws of another country that she is visiting. This legal obligation lapses, however, when she returns to her own country, whereas the political obligation to her country is something she carries with her. If she is truly under a political obligation, she may be morally bound to pay taxes to her polity while abroad, and perhaps even to be recalled to perform military or some other kind of duty.

Political and legal obligations are related, in short, but they are not the same thing. A political obligation is a moral duty that only a citizen or perhaps a permanent resident can have, for it is an obligation that attaches only to members of a polity. Legal obligations, by contrast, attach themselves to anyone who is subject to the pertinent law or laws, including tourists who owe no allegiance to the country they happen to be visiting.

To appreciate the value of this distinction, and of this way of drawing it, it may help to reconsider §119 of Locke's *Second Treatise of Government*. There Locke insists that the obligation to obey the laws of a political society extends not only to those who have expressly consented to obey but also to anyone who owns property in that society, lodges within it for a week, or travels freely on its highways — indeed, "it reaches as far as the very being of any one within the territories of that government." If the obligation in question is a political obligation, then Locke would find himself in the embarrassing position of holding that the person who sneaks into a country with the aim of subverting it nevertheless has a moral duty to obey its laws. Such a position may not be absurd, but it is difficult to see how the "very being" of someone within the boundaries of a country can place him under a *political* obligation to obey the laws of a regime that he abhors. If Locke were to distinguish political from legal obligation, however, he could say that the subversive is under a legal but not a political obligation while within the territory of the regime he seeks to destroy. While he is there, in other words, he will be subject to its laws, at least in the eyes of those who enforce them, and thus under a legal obligation to obey the laws that apply to him. But he will not be under a political obligation, for he will have no moral duty to obey the laws of the political system he seeks to subvert. Indeed, Locke may have had something of this sort in mind when he distinguished "perfect members" of a political society, who expressly consent to place themselves under an obligation, from those whose tacit consent made them merely temporary subjects.

ANARCHIST CHALLENGES TO POLITICAL OBLIGATION

According to the foregoing analysis, a political obligation, if it exists at all, is a systemic, prima-facie moral duty to obey the laws of one's polity. But does such an obligation exist or obtain in any general or widespread sense? Most political philosophers have assumed that the answer is yes, and they have devoted their efforts to discovering what Green called "the true ground or justification for obedience to law." Some philosophers in the middle years of the twentieth century even asserted, on conceptual grounds, that political obligation needs no justification.

There have been dissenters, however, and in recent years they have come to occupy a prominent place among political philosophers. As they see it, there is no general obligation to obey the law, not even on the part of the citizens of a reasonably just polity. The most thorough-going of these dissenters have been anarchists proper — that is, those persons who insist that states and governments are wickedly coercive institutions that ought to be abolished. Yet other skeptics or dissenters have concluded that the anarchist proper is wrong about the need for the state but right about the obligation to obey the law. Like the anarchist proper, these "philosophical anarchists" hold that the state is illegitimate, but they deny that its illegitimacy entails "a strong moral imperative to oppose or eliminate states; rather they typically take state illegitimacy simply to remove any strong moral presumption in favour of obedience to, compliance with, or support for our own or other existing states".

Philosophical Anarchism

The arguments of these philosophical anarchists take either an "a priori" or an "a posteriori" form. Arguments of the first kind maintain that it is impossible to provide a satisfactory account of a general obligation to obey the law. According to Robert Paul Wolff, the principal advocate of this view, there can be no general obligation to obey the law because any such obligation would violate the "primary obligation" of autonomy, which is "the refusal to be ruled". As Wolff defines it, autonomy combines freedom with responsibility. To be autonomous, someone must have the capacity for choice, and therefore for freedom; but the person who has this capacity also has the responsibility to exercise it — to act autonomously. Failing to do so is to fail to fulfil this "primary obligation" of autonomy.

This primary obligation dooms any attempt to develop a theory of political obligation, Wolff argues, except in the highly unlikely case of a direct democracy in which every law has the unanimous approval of the citizenry.

Under any other form of government, autonomy and authority are simply incompatible. Authority is "the right to command, and correlatively, the right to be obeyed", which entails that anyone subject to authority has an obligation to obey those who have the right to be obeyed. But if we acknowledge such an authority, we allow someone else to rule us, thereby violating our fundamental obligation to act autonomously. We must therefore reject the claim that we have an obligation to obey the orders of those who purport to hold authority over us and conclude that there can be no general obligation to obey the laws of any polity that falls short of a unanimous direct democracy.

Arguments of the second, a posteriori form are more modest in their aims but no less devastating in their conclusions. In this case the aim is not to show that a satisfactory defence of political obligation is impossible but that no defence has proven satisfactory, despite the efforts of some of the best minds in the history of philosophy. All such attempts have failed, according to those who take this line, so we must conclude that only those relatively few people who have explicitly committed themselves to obey the law, perhaps by swearing allegiance as part of an oath of citizenship, have anything like a general obligation to obey the laws under which they live.

Against Philosophical Anarchism

Whether a priori or a posteriori, the arguments of the philosophical anarchists pose a serious challenge to those who continue to believe in a general obligation to obey the law. This challenge is made especially difficult by the powerful objections that Simmons and other a posteriori anarchists have brought against the existing theories of political obligation. The most effective response, of course, would be to demonstrate that one's favoured theory does not succumb to these objections, and we shall briefly consider attempts to respond in this fashion in the following section. Some general attempts to refute philosophical anarchism ought to be noted first, however.

Some of these attempts apply specifically to Wolff's a priori attack on political authority and obligation, while others apply to philosophical anarchism in general.

The arguments against Wolff usually concentrate on his conception of autonomy and its relation to authority. In brief, Wolff's critics argue that he is wrong to insist that moral autonomy is our "primary" or "fundamental obligation," for this would require us "to think that autonomy will always over-ride values such as not harming other people, supporting loved ones, doing a favour for a friend or even more mundane desires, such as that for a quiet life, with which this ideal of moral autonomy will from time to time conflict". Moreover, there is no reason to accept Wolff's claim that autonomy and authority are necessarily incompatible. Insofar as autonomy is a capacity, as Wolff says, it will need to be developed before it can be exercised, and various kinds of authority — including political authority — will foster its development and make its continued exercise possible. Nor is it clear how Wolff can reject political authority without also rejecting promises and contracts as illegitimate constraints on one's autonomy — a problem that leads even Simmons to judge Wolff's a priori philosophical anarchism a "failed attempt".

Critics have responded to philosophical anarchism in general in various ways, including the disparate complaints that it is a kind of false or hypocritical radicalism (Gans) and that it is all too genuine a threat to political order (Senor; Horton 2006/07, "Part Two"). The latter complaint has both an ontological and a conceptual aspect.

That is, the critics argue that philosophical anarchists fail to appreciate the social or embedded nature of human beings, which leads the anarchists to conceive of obligation in excessively individualistic or voluntaristic terms — which leads, in turn, to their denial of a general obligation to obey the law. The problem, however, is that it is a mistake to think "that political life is left more or less unchanged by dispensing with some conception of political obligation and adopting the perspective of philosophical anarchism. Unless it can be shown that we can continue to talk intelligibly and credibly of our government or our state, then a radical rethinking of our political relations is an unavoidable consequence". Whether the philosophical anarchists are willing to accept that consequence — and perhaps to become anarchists proper — or whether they can find a way to stop short of it thus becomes a major point of contention.

In the end, of course, the best response to philosophical anarchists, especially those of the a posteriori kind, will be to produce or defend a theory of political obligation that proves to be immune to their objections. At present, though, no single theory has the support of all of those who continue to believe in political obligation, let alone the assent of philosophical anarchists. Several theories remain in contention, however, as the next section will attest.

CONTEMPORARY THEORIES OF POLITICAL OBLIGATION

Although the lines that separate one theory from another are not always distinct, philosophical justifications of political obligation nowadays usually take the form of arguments from consent, gratitude, fair play, membership, or natural duty. Some philosophers advance a hybrid of two or more of these approaches, and others hold, as the concluding section shows, that a pluralistic theory is necessary. For the most part, though, those who believe that it is possible to justify a general obligation to obey the law will rely on one of these five lines of argument.

Consent

Most people who believe they have an obligation to obey the law probably think that this putative obligation is grounded in their consent. Political philosophers are less inclined to think this way, however, in light of the withering criticism to which Hume and more recent writers — notably A. John Simmons — have subjected consent theory. The critics' claim is not that consent cannot be a source of obligations, for they typically believe it can. The claim, instead, is that too few people have given the kind of express or actual consent that can ground a general obligation to obey the law, and neither hypothetical nor tacit consent will supply the defect, for reasons already canvassed.

Nevertheless, consent theory still has its adherents among political philosophers. Their versions of consent theory vary considerably, however, with two main approaches emerging in response to the criticisms. One, advanced by Harry Beran (1987), accepts the claim that only express consent can generate a political obligation, but calls for political societies to establish formal procedures for evoking such consent. That is, states should require their members openly to undertake an obligation to obey the law or to refuse to do so. Those who decline the obligation will then have the options of leaving the state, seceding to form a new state with like-minded people, or taking residence in a territory within the state reserved for dissenters. In the absence of such procedures, it seems that Beran's position is roughly the same as that of the a posteriori philosophical anarchist. Were these procedures in place, though, it is far from clear that the options available to the members will make their "consent" truly voluntary.

Other philosophers who adhere to consent theory argue in one way or another that the critics construe "consent" too narrowly. Thus John Plamenatz (1968, Postscript) and Peter Steinberger have maintained that voting or otherwise participating in elections should count as consent; and Steinberger produces a lengthy list of fairly ordinary activities — calling the police or fire department for help, sending children to a public school, using a public library, and more — that constitute "active participation in the institutions of the state". Mark Murphy and Margaret Gilbert have sounded variations on this theme by arguing, in Murphy's case, that "surrender of judgment is a kind of consent", or, in Gilbert's, that "joint commitment" is an important source of obligations, including political obligations (1993, 2006). For Murphy, surrender of judgment is consent in the usual sense of voluntary agreement or acceptance. As he says, "One consents to another in a certain sphere of conduct in the acceptance sense of consent when one allows the other's practical judgments to take the place of his or her own with regard to that sphere of conduct. (This consent may be either to a person or to a set of rules: both of these can be authoritative)". Gilbert differs from Murphy and others in taking a joint commitment to be something that need not arise voluntarily. According to her theory, "an understanding of joint commitment and a readiness to be jointly committed are necessary if one is to accrue political obligations, as is common knowledge of these in the population in question. One can, however, fulfil these conditions without prior deliberation or decision, and if one has deliberated, one may have had little choice but to incur them". Indeed, membership in a "plural subject" formed through non-voluntary joint commitments plays such a large part in Gilbert's theory that it may be better to place her with those who advocate an "associative" theory of political obligation than with the adherents of consent theory.

At this time there is little reason to believe that the critics of consent theory will be won over by these attempts to revive the theory by broadening our understanding of what counts as consent. There is even less reason, however, to believe that appeals to consent will simply wither away, at least among those who continue to believe in the existence of a general obligation to obey the law.

Gratitude

To move from consent to gratitude is to move from the most to the least popular foundation for a theory of political obligation. That is not to say that those who believe in political obligations seldom appeal to gratitude. To the contrary, the appeal is both long-standing — appearing some 2500 years ago in Plato's *Crito*, as we have seen — and widespread. The point is that it is rarely the sole or even primary basis for an attempt to justify the obligation to obey the law. Plato's account of Socrates' reasoning is typical in this regard, with gratitude but one of at least four considerations that Socrates relies on in explaining why he will not disobey the ruling of the jury that sentenced him to death. When Simmons included a chapter on the weakness of gratitude as a foundation for political obligation in his influential *Moral Principles and Political Obligations* (1979), in fact, there was no gratitude *theory* on which to concentrate his criticism.

That situation changed within a decade when A. D. M. Walker sketched such a theory in "Political Obligation and the Argument from Gratitude." Walker's argument takes the following form (1988):

1. The person who benefits from *X* has an obligation of gratitude not to act contrary to *X*'s interests.
2. Every citizen has received benefits from the state.
3. Every citizen has an obligation of gratitude not to act in ways that are contrary to the state's interests.
4. Noncompliance with the law is contrary to the state's interests.
5. Every citizen has an obligation of gratitude to comply with the law.

Whether this argument does indeed provide the basis for a satisfactory theory of political obligation seems to turn on two points. First, are obligations of gratitude at all pertinent where political *institutions* are concerned? Walker holds that one may have an obligation of gratitude not only to other persons but also to institutions, including the state or polity; but critics such as Simmons disagree. Gratitude is owed only to those who intentionally and at significant cost to themselves provide us with benefits, according to Simmons, and institutions cannot satisfy these conditions. The second point concerns the strength of obligations of gratitude. That is, one may grant that we can have obligations to institutions, including the state, yet hold that these obligations are "too weak to function as prima facie political obligations in the usual sense," for they "would be overridden frequently, not just in unusual circumstances". Walker, in response, points to Socrates as someone who obviously thought his obligation of gratitude was very strong indeed, and concludes that we "can afford to acknowledge that the extent of our indebtedness to the state is less than his, while still insisting that it grounds a strong, though not absolute, obligation of gratitude to comply with the law".

Fair Play

Although earlier philosophers, including Socrates, appealed to something resembling the principle of fairness (or fair play), the classic formulation of the principle is the one H. L. A. Hart gave it in "Are There Any Natural Rights?" As Hart there says, "when a number of persons conduct any joint enterprise according to rules and thus restrict their liberty, those who have submitted to these restrictions when required have a right to a similar submission from those who have benefited by their submission". John Rawls subsequently adopted this principle in an influential essay of his own, referring to the duty derived from the principle as the "duty of fair play" (1964). What the principle of fair play holds, then, is that everyone who participates in a reasonably just, mutually beneficial cooperative practice — Hart's "joint enterprise according to rules" — has an obligation to bear a fair share of the burdens of the practice. This obligation is owed to the others who cooperate in the enterprise, for cooperation is what makes it possible for any individual to enjoy the benefits of the practice. Anyone who acts as a free rider is acting wrongly, then, even if his or her shirking does not directly threaten the existence or success of the endeavor. Those who participate in the practice thus have rights against as well as obligations to one another: a right to require others to bear their share of the burdens and an obligation to bear one's share in turn.

The principle of fair play applies to a political society only if that society can reasonably be regarded as a cooperative enterprise. If it can, the members of the polity have an obligation of fair play to do their part in maintaining the enterprise. Because the rule of law is necessary to the maintenance of such a polity — and perhaps even constitutive of it — the principal form of cooperation is abiding by the law. In the absence of overriding considerations, then, the members of the polity *qua* cooperative practice must honour their obligation to one another to obey the laws. In this way the principle of fair play provides the grounding for a general obligation to obey the law, at least on the part of those whose polity is reasonably regarded as a cooperative enterprise.

The argument from fair play has met with serious criticism, however, including that of Rawls, who abandoned fair play as an account of political obligation for citizens generally in *A Theory of Justice*. The critics have brought forward three particular criticisms. The most sweeping is that of Robert Nozick, who objects that the principle of fair play would allow others to place us under an obligation to them simply by conferring benefits on us. To make his point, Nozick imagines a group of neighbours creating a public entertainment system and assigning every adult in the neighbourhood a day on which he or she is responsible for planning and broadcasting the program. As a resident of the neighbourhood, you occasionally hear and enjoy the programs, but you never consent to take part in this scheme. When your assigned day arrives, are you obligated to take a turn? The principle of fair play says yes, according to Nozick, but the correct answer is "surely not."

The second objection, raised by M. B. E. Smith, is that "the obligation of fair play governs a man's actions only when some benefit or harm turns on whether he obeys". This implies that the principle of fair play will generate an obligation to cooperate only when the cooperative enterprise is small enough that any participant's failure to obey the rules could reasonably be expected to damage the enterprise. Political societies are not small, cooperative enterprises, however, and we can readily think of cases in which someone's disobedience neither deprives anyone of any benefits nor harms the polity in any noticeable way. It follows, then, that the principle of fair play cannot ground a general obligation to obey the law, however useful it may be in other circumstances.

Those who raise the third objection agree that considerations of fairness sometimes do generate obligations, but they insist, like Smith, that these considerations do not obtain in the political context. In this case, however, the complaint is that fair play considerations apply only to cooperative schemes that produce benefits one may refuse. If it produces *nonexcludable* goods, which everyone receives regardless of whether she contributed to their production or even wants them, then there can be no fair-play obligation to bear a share of the burdens of the enterprise. But this is typically the case in political societies, which produce goods such as public order and national defence that one cannot meaningfully refuse to accept. As Simmons puts it, there is a difference between *receiving* and *accepting* benefits, and receiving them is not enough to place someone under an obligation. If there is a political obligation, then, it cannot follow from the kind of nonexcludable goods that states provide.

As one might expect, advocates of the fair-play account have not remained silent in the face of these criticisms. The leading advocate, George Klosko, has written two books elaborating and defending the principle of fairness as the foundation of political obligation (1992, 2005), and it sometimes seems that every fresh attack on fair play provokes a swift response. And the attacks have certainly continued. Perhaps the best that can be done to convey the present state of the debate is to indicate how fair-play advocates have responded to the three criticisms sketched above.

With regard to Nozick's objection, the response is usually to hold that his example of the neighbourhood entertainment system is beside the point (Bell 1978). That is, Nozick is probably right to say that one would have no obligation to operate the system on his or her assigned day, but he is wrong to think fair play would require one to do so. There is no fair play obligation in cases such as this, either because the passive receipt of benefits is not enough to show that one is a *participant* in a cooperative practice or because the benefits are "of relatively little value". To Smith's objection, the response is that fairness is not a consideration only when harm or benefit to some person or practice is involved. To fail to do one's part in a cooperative enterprise is to *wrong* those who cooperate even when it does not clearly harm either them or the enterprise as such. Finally, responses to Simmons' objection have taken two directions. One is to say that Simmons has drawn too sharp a distinction between the acceptance and receipt of benefits. Between the person who passively receives the benefits of a cooperative practice and the one who knowingly and willingly accepts them is the person — very many people, in fact — who actively participates in the practice without being fully aware, in the ordinary course of life, that he or she is undertaking an obligation to do his or her part by participating in a cooperative practice. Others respond to Simmons' criticism by denying that obligations must be incurred voluntarily. What matters is not that one accepts the benefits of the practice, according to Klosko's influential account, but that three conditions are met: "Goods supplied must be (i) worth the recipients' effort in providing them; (ii) 'presumptively beneficial'; and (iii) have benefits and burdens that are fairly distributed". If, in sum, a state may be reasonably regarded as a cooperative enterprise, and if it provides its members with goods that are presumptively beneficial — or "indispensable for satisfactory lives" — then its members have an obligation grounded in fairness to obey its laws.

Membership or Association

A fourth attempt to ground a general obligation to obey the law has emerged in the last twenty years or so in the form of the "membership" or "associative" theory. According to the proponents of this theory, political obligation is best understood as an *associative* obligation grounded in membership. If we are members of a group, then we are under an obligation, *ceteris paribus*, to comply with the norms that govern it. Nor does this obligation follow from our consenting to become members, for it holds even in the case of groups or associations, such as families and polities, that people typically do not consent to join. Voluntary or not, membership entails obligation. Anyone who acknowledges membership in a particular polity must therefore acknowledge that he or she has a general obligation to obey its laws.

At the core of the associative approach is the idea is that political obligation is a form of non-voluntary obligation on a par with familial obligations. In Ronald Dworkin's words, "Political association, like family and friendship and other forms of association more local and intimate, is in itself pregnant of obligation". The same idea, with an explicit analogy between family and polity, is at work in John Horton's account of political obligation:

My claim is that a polity is, like the family, a relationship into which we are mostly born: and that the obligations which are constitutive of the relationship do not stand in need of moral justification in terms of a set of basic moral principles or some comprehensive moral theory. Furthermore, both the family and the political community figure prominently in our sense of who we are: our self-identity and our understanding of our place in the world.

As members of families and political communities, on this view, we are subject to what Michael Hardimon calls "noncontractual role obligations" — that is, obligations that simply flow from "roles into which we are born".

The associative account of political obligation has at least three attractive features. The first is the refusal of its proponents to treat 'voluntary' and 'involuntary' as two parts of a dichotomy. It is true, they say, that most people do not voluntarily undertake to become members of a polity, but that hardly means that membership has been forced or imposed on them. There is a middle ground, and it is fertile soil for a theory of political obligation, just as it is for those who believe that being a member of a family entails obligations that we have neither chosen, on the one hand, nor incurred against our will, on the other. A second attraction of the associative account is that it squares with a common intuition, as a great many people apparently do think of themselves as members of political societies who have an obligation to obey their polities' laws. This intuition, moreover, points to the third attractive feature, which is the way in which the obligation to obey the laws grows out of the sense of *identity* that members of a polity commonly share.

Like the other theories of political obligation, however, the membership account has met with considerable criticism, with three main objections being raised. First, the critics maintain that the analogy between the polity and the family is neither persuasive nor attractive. It is unpersuasive because the members of the modern polity lack the close and intimate relationships with one another that family members typically share; and it is unattractive because it raises the possibility that the paternalism appropriate within the family may be extended to the polity. Second, the critics object that the associative account conflates the *sense* of obligation with obligation itself. As Wolff and other philosophical anarchists have argued, the fact that many people feel a sense of identity with and obligation to their countries does not mean that they really have such an obligation; nor need one be a philosophical anarchist to share this conclusion. Finally, there is the problem of what may be called group character. All groups have members, including groups that are not decent, fair, or morally praiseworthy; but if membership is sufficient to generate an obligation to obey, then the members of unjust and exploitative groups will have an obligation to obey the rules. In the case of the polity, this leads to the unpalatable and counter-intuitive conclusion that the routinely exploited and oppressed "members" of an unjust polity are under an obligation to obey its laws.

Can the proponents of the associative theory meet or overcome these objections? That, of course, remains a matter of debate, with the latest round being Horton's vigorous response to the critics in his two-part "In Defence of Associative Political Obligations" (Horton 2006/07).

Natural Duty

The final contender in the political obligation debates is an approach that follows John Rawls in distinguishing obligations from natural duties. As noted earlier, Rawls believes that a person must do something to acquire an obligation, such as make a promise or sign a contract, whereas natural duties "apply to us without regard to our voluntary acts". One implication of this distinction is that most people have no general obligation to obey the laws of their polity, for they have not done what is necessary to incur such an obligation. Everyone, however, is subject to the natural duty of justice, which "requires us to support and to comply with just institutions that exist and apply to us", and this duty takes the place, for Rawls, of political obligation. As he says, "there are several ways in which one may be bound to political institutions. For the most part the natural duty of justice is the more fundamental, since it binds citizens generally and requires no voluntary acts in order to apply".

To find the Rawlsian natural-duty approach to political obedience (if not obligation) persuasive, one will have to agree that there is a natural duty of justice that entails a duty to support and comply with just institutions that apply to us. Agreeing to that does not require acceptance of the contractual reasoning through which Rawls defines the natural duties, but such acceptance will certainly help. A difficult problem remains, however, even if we grant the existence of a natural duty to support and comply with just institutions. This problem is that the natural-duty approach runs afoul of what Simmons calls "the particularity requirement" that any attempt to solve the problem of political obligation must satisfy: "that we are only interested in those moral requirements [including obligations and duties] which bind an individual to one *particular* political community, set of political institutions, etc." We may have a natural duty to support and comply with just institutions, in other words, but that duty does not confine us to supporting and complying with any particular just institution. If I, a citizen of the United States, find that my country and Canada are both just polities, a natural duty to support Canadian institutions that is apparently as strong as my duty to support those of the U.S. But in that case there seems to be no special bond between me and the institutions of my country. Yet it is that kind of special bond, as Simmons points out, that theories of political obligation are supposed to provide.

Defenders of the natural-duty approach have tried to show, in response, that there is something about the relationship between a person and her country that establishes a special political bond — some sense in which its institutions "apply" to her in a way that the institutions of other political societies, no matter how just, do not. Thus Jeremy Waldron draws a distinction between "insiders" and "outsiders" that "explains much of the specialness of an individual's relation to the institutions of his own country, at least so far as moral requirement is concerned". A New Zealander, to use his example, has the special insider relation to the laws of New Zealand because those laws "have been set up precisely to address the question of the rights and duties of someone in his position vis-a-vis his fellow New Zealanders". Because they "apply" to him in a way they cannot apply to a citizen of another country, the example shows how the appeal to natural duty can handle the problem of particularity or special allegiance.

Christopher Heath Wellman makes a similar move in his attempt to derive political obligation from "samaritanism." The duty to be a good samaritan is a natural duty, on his account, because it "does not depend upon a previous transaction or preexisting association between the rescuer and the rescuee; if a person is sufficiently imperiled and one can save her at no unreasonable cost, one cannot justify one's failure to rescue by pointing out that one never agreed to do so or that one had no morally significant relationship with her ..." Wellman then goes on to argue that "legal obedience is required as one's fair share of helping to rescue others from peril", including the "political peril ... [that] is fundamentally a *coordination* problem". Wellman admits that samaritanism by itself cannot explain how a person may have special ties to his compatriots or country, but he does claim that it leads to an obligation to obey the laws of the particular state in which one resides. In that respect, at least, his theory aims to overcome the particularity problem.

Once again, however, the critics are proving stubborn, as Simmons' recent lengthy critique of natural-duty arguments attests. Even a sympathetic critic may wonder whether the natural-duty approach relies implicitly, and especially where the particularity requirement is concerned, on arguments borrowed from other theories. Both Waldron and Wellman draw on the fair-play approach, for example, as when Wellman suggests "that we understand our political obligations as our fair share of the communal samaritan chore of rescuing others from the perils of the state of nature". Which, in the end, is doing the argumentative work here, natural duty or fair play?

Conclusion: A Plurality of Principles?

One response to this question might be to say that both

concepts are at work, and a good thing that they are, for no one concept or principle by itself can ground a satisfactory theory of political obligation. In fact, that is a response that a number of philosophers have made, either implicitly or explicitly, in recent years. Gilbert (2006) and Steinberger (2004), for example, seem to have developed hybrid theories without ever advertising them as such. Gilbert's theory fuses the consent and associative approaches through her reliance on joint *commitments* to a *plural subject*, or group. For his part, Steinberger combines the consent and natural-duty approaches, arguing that any "generalized attempt to divorce obligations from natural duties, to find justifications for the former that are entirely independent of the latter, is ... doomed to fail".

Others, notably Klosko (2006) and Jonathan Wolff (1995, 2000), have explicitly called for a pluralistic or multiple-principle approach to political obligation. There is no single answer to the problem of political obligation, as they see it, because the problem has more than one aspect. Not every "member" of a polity will stand in the same relation to its laws, for instance, which means that it is a mistake to think that everyone must have the same general obligation to obey. Nor is every obligation of equal force. Some are weak, such as the notorious obligation to stop at a traffic signal when no one else is around, and others are quite strong. Klosko thus thinks it necessary to rely on the principle of fairness to supply the core of a justification, but to supplement it with appeals to natural duty and the common good.

As yet there has been little reaction to these attempts to fuse approaches and draw on multiple principles in the attempt to provide a satisfactory theory of political obligation. Those who doubt that such a theory can be constructed, however, are likely to say that combining principles, whether in hybrid or pluralist fashion, will not help, for putting together a set of principles that are weak and unsatisfactory individually will hardly produce a strong and satisfying theory. On the other hand, those who believe that political obligation is fundamentally a problem of showing that those who live in a polity governed by the rule of law do indeed have a *general* obligation to obey its laws (Mapel, 2005), are likely to see no need for a plurality of principles to make their case. Whether a plurality of principles is necessary, in sum, remains one of many open questions about political obligation.

The idea of "political obligation" is that there is (at least under certain circumstances) a moral obligation to obey the government and its law even if, apart from this obligation, there would be no moral obligation to do so. It is supposed to be a moral obligation, not simply a legal obligation or a matter of expediency. If we disobey we should feel guilty, we should feel that we have done something ethically wrong.

Political obligation makes certain action (or inaction) obligatory even when apart from this obligation it would not be. Murder is against the law, but even if it were not illegal or we recognised no obligation to obey the law, we would still (presumably) recognise a moral obligation not to commit murder. But we do not regard it as morally wrong to stand our car in a 'no standing' zone unless we acknowledge a moral obligation to obey the law precisely because it is the law. The claim is that there is a moral obligation to obey the law just because it is the law, apart from its content.

The idea that there is such an obligation goes back a long way. In Plato's *Crito* Socrates is presented as acknowledging an obligation not to run away from Athens even though he is to be put to death unjustly; he explains that one's country is "either to be persuaded, or if not persuaded, to be obeyed". "Let every soul be subject unto the higher powers. For there is no power but of God: the powers that be are ordained of God. Whosoever therefore resisteth the power, resisteth the ordinance of God: and they that resist shall receive to themselves damnation... Wherefore ye must needs be subject, not only for wrath, but also for conscience sake". Theologians (some theologians) interpreted this to mean that "for conscience sake" we must obey the powers that be, even if they are unjust, as long as what they command is not contrary to what God commands.

Some modern political thinkers have secularised and democratised this doctrine. They say that we ought (not just legally but morally ought) to obey a decision that has been arrived at by majority vote even if we were not persuaded by the arguments for it and voted against it. The usual argument is that by living is a country and taking part in its political process we have "tacitly" undertaken to obey whatever is decided, at least if the process is democratic. The most influential source of this idea of tacit consent is probably John Locke: "Every man, that hath any possessions, or enjoyment, of any part of the dominions of any government, doth thereby give his tacit consent, and is as far forth obliged to obedience to the laws of that government, during such enjoyment, as any one under it; whether this his possession be of land, to him and his heirs for ever, or a lodging only for a week; or whether it be barely travelling freely on the highway; and in effect, it reaches as far as the very being of any one within the territories of that government".

Some writers argue that anyone who votes in an election thereby tacitly commits him/herself to obeying the government elected, however much they may have opposed its policy—by voting against Hitler in the 1933 election, a voter would have acquired a political obligation to obey Hitler's government. (Hitler did not get a majority in that election, but the coalition government he formed was the legal outcome of the election process). Some who adopt this position say that the obligation to obey if you have voted is a "prima facie" obligation, which may be overriden by some other obligation.

Against all this, we ought to reject the doctrine of "political obligation" altogether. In an organisation, such as a democratic state, in which the constitution gives the majority the power to determine the organisation's policy and actions, then the minority has to admit that when the officials implement the policy decided by the majority they are acting in a properly authorised way and are not misusing the organisation's name, power and resources; i.e. they are obliged to admit that the majority and its agents are acting legally. But this is as far as their "obligation" extends. The minority are not obliged to admit that the policy is right, and they are not morally obliged to conform to it or help carry it out themselves. They are fully entitled to act on their own belief. They may choose to obey if there are penalties for disobedience, but if they choose to risk the penalties there is no reason why their conscience should reproach them.

The obligation of officials goes further than the obligation of private citizens or members, but not much further. Officials who disagree so seriously with the majority policy that they are not willing to carry it out should resign, or at least make it clear that they will not carry it out (the majority may then remove them from office, or they may think that their services are worth more than the implementation of the policy). For example, a military officer or soldier should refuse an order that goes against his or her conscience, even if it has been produced through the proper lawful process. ("Conscience" is the term we use for a serious ethical judgment; it means a judgment arrived at through ordinary thinking processes— it does not imply any special faculty of moral judgment or any religious doctrine.) Refusal of orders by conscientious officials is an important safeguard against abuse of government power.

In my view, then, commitment to democracy does not mean accepting a moral obligation personally to carry out the will of the majority. It means supporting the legal (or quasi-legal) rule that the organisation's official policies should be decided by majority vote.

That policies should be decided this way is not, in my view, a self-evident axiom. Everyone seems to think that in some organisations some decisions should be made in some other way. Even when the majority rule is accepted, there are different ways of implementing it, and weight is sometimes given to other considerations besides mere numbers (e.g. to geographical dispersion). "Democracy" is a generic term. Exactly what constitutional arrangements you should commit ourselves to supporting is a question that each of us should decide in view of the circumstances by considering which arrangement is, in our individual judgments, most likely normally to produce the right decisions (i.e. decisions that conform to the value system we individually subscribe to, which is of course modifiable through discussion with others). A commitment to supporting that arrangement in general is not a commitment to accepting each decision it produces.

7

Political Parties, Pressure Groups and Lobbies

A political party is a political organization that typically seeks to attain and maintain political power within government, usually by participating in electoral campaigns, educational outreach or protest actions. Parties often espouse an expressed ideology or vision bolstered by a written platform with specific goals, forming a coalition among disparate interests.

Voting Systems

The type of electoral system is a major factor in determining the type of party political system. In countries where first past the post voting systems there is an increased likely hood for the establishment of a two party system. Countries that have a proportional representation voting system, as exists throughout Europe, or to a greater extent preferential voting systems, such as in Australia or Ireland, three or more parties are often elected to public office.

Nonpartisan

In a nonpartisan system, no official political parties exist, sometimes reflecting legal restrictions on political parties. In nonpartisan elections, each candidate is eligible for office on his or her own merits. In nonpartisan legislatures, there are no typically formal party alignments within the legislature. The administration of George Washington and the first few sessions of the US Congress were nonpartisan. Washington also warned against political parties during his Farewell

Address. The unicameral legislature of Nebraska is the only state government body that is nonpartisan in the United States today. Many city and county governments are nonpartisan. In Canada, the territorial legislatures of the Northwest Territories and Nunavut are nonpartisan. Nonpartisan elections and modes of governance are common outside of state institutions. Unless there are legal prohibitions against political parties, factions within nonpartisan systems often evolve into political parties. Tokelau also has a nonpartisan parliament.

SINGLE DOMINANT PARTY

In single-party systems, one political party is legally allowed to hold effective power. Although minor parties may sometimes be allowed, they are legally required to accept the leadership of the dominant party. This party may not always be identical to the government, although sometimes positions within the party may in fact be more important than positions within the government. Communist states such as China are some of the examples; others can be found in Fascist states such as Nazi Germany was between 1933 and 1945. The single-party system is thus usually equated with dictatorships and tyranny.

In dominant-party systems, opposition parties are allowed, and there may be even a deeply established democratic tradition, but other parties are widely considered to have no real chance of gaining power. Sometimes, political, social and economic circumstances, and public opinion are the reason for others parties' failure. Sometimes, typically in countries with less of an established democratic tradition, it is possible the dominant party will remain in power by using patronage and sometimes by voting fraud.

In the latter case, the definition between Dominant and single-party system becomes rather blurred. Examples of dominant party systems include the People's Action Party in Singapore, the African National Congress in South Africa, the Democratic Party of Socialists of Montenegro in Montenegro and the Social Democratic Party in Sweden. One party dominant systems also existed in Mexico with the Institutional Revolutionary Party until the 1990s, in the southern United States with the Democratic Party from the late 19th century until the 1970s, and in Indonesia with the *Golongan Karya*

(Party of the Functional Groups) from the early 1970s until 1998.

Two Political Parties

Two-party systems are states such as the United States, United Kingdom, Jamaica, and Ghana in which there are two political parties dominant to such an extent that electoral success under the banner of any other party is almost impossible. One right wing coalition party and one left wing coalition party is the most common ideological breakdown in such a system but in two-party states political parties are traditionally catch all parties which are ideologically broad and inclusive. For the system to work, one of the parties must obtain a sufficient working majority after an election and it must be in a position to be able to govern without the support from the other party.

The United Kingdom is widely considered a two-party state, as historically power alternates between two dominant parties (currently the Labour Party and the Conservative Party). However, the Liberal Democrats, as well as numerous other parties and independents, hold a substantial number of seats in Parliament. A plurality voting system (such as that in the United States) usually leads to a two-party system, a relationship described by Maurice Duverger and known as Duverger's Law.

Multiple Parties

Multi-party systems are systems in which more than two parties are represented and elected to public office. Australia, Canada, Pakistan, India, the Republic of Ireland and Norway are examples of countries with two strong parties and additional smaller parties that have also obtained representation. The smaller or "third" parties may form a part of a coalition government together with one of the larger parties or act independently from the other dominant parties.

More commonly, in cases where there are three or more parties, no one party is likely to gain power alone, and parties work with each other to form coalition governments. This has been an emerging trend in the politics of the Republic of Ireland and is almost always the case in Germany on national and state level, and in most constituencies at the communal level.

Furthermore since the forming of the Republic of Iceland there has never been a government not led by a coalition (usually of the Independence Party & one other oftentimes the Social Democratic Alliance. The major drawback of any coalition government is that it is potentially vulnerable to rapid changes and tends to lack stability.

Balanced Multiple-party Systems

Extensive studies including simulations and polls by Donald Arthur Kronos, have shown that an effectively two-party system such as that currently used in the United States could be modified into a balanced plurality voting system through the addition of a negative vote option to better represent the intentions of the voters. This differs from a standard Plurality voting system or an anti-plurality voting system in that rather than either allowing a choice of whom to vote for or allowing a choice of whom to vote against, a balanced system would allow each vote to be either for or against any candidate. In the case of balanced range voting an individual could in fact cast a combination of for and against votes.

The problem with the traditional plurality voting system is that any attempt to prevent a candidate from getting elected tends to result in a false positive vote, generally for a candidate thought to have an advantaged position over other candidates, thereby causing or increasing such advantage. A balanced plurality election would allow the voter to represent a true negative vote, thus eliminating or at least reducing the occurrence of false positive votes.

A balanced multiple-party system significantly reduces the odds of a well known but largely unpopular candidate winning an election, by allowing those who oppose the election of that candidate to cast a more accurate vote than would have been possible in an unbalanced system of only negative votes or only positive votes. Of course the option of a positive vote is also necessary in order to have balance. Simply changing to an all negative vote system would just reverse the polarity of the imbalance rather than remove it.

The number of votes per voter is not a factor in the system being balanced. It should be consistent within an election across all voters to be fair. This also has the mathematical effect of eliminating the feedback loop that would otherwise give an unfair advantage over time to exactly two parties. This feedback loop happens in a traditional plurality voting system when a voter attempts to represent a negative vote where only positive votes are available. The voter is forced to evaluate the choices available and determine what is most likely to reduce the odds of a win by the opposed candidate. For example, since the history of a party may give some indication of the electability of a candidate endorsed by the party, the closest thing to a vote against a candidate in a general election would be a vote for the candidate of the party that the voter believes has won the most elections historically. If the opposed candidate is in fact running under that same party, then the obvious choice is the next most historically successful party's candidate. This causes only two parties to have any reasonable viability once a history has been established. A balanced voting system would eliminate this feedback loop for voters who take advantage of it.

The addition of a negative vote option to balance a party system can theoretically be applied to a popular vote, an electoral college vote, or both. In cases where an electoral college is expected to in some way represent the popular vote, it would of course make sense to allow balanced voting options for both the electoral college and the populace. The concept of a balanced election system is applicable to many types of voting systems including instant runoff voting and other such multiple vote systems and can be applied equally well to plurality voting or proportional representation systems.

Party Funding

Political parties are funded by contributions from party members, individuals and organizations which share their political ideas or who stand to benefit from their activities or governmental public funding. Political parties and factions, especially those in government, are lobbied vigorously by organizations, businesses and special interest groups such as trades unions. Money and gifts to a party, or its members, may be offered as incentives.

In the United Kingdom, it has been alleged that peerages have been awarded to contributors to party funds, the benefactors becoming members of the Upper House of

Parliament and thus being in a position to participate in the legislative process. Famously, Lloyd George was found to have been selling peerages and to prevent such corruption in future, Parliament passed the Honours (Prevention of Abuses) Act 1925 into law. Thus the outright sale of peerages and similar honours became a criminal act, however some benefactors are alleged to have attempted to circumvent this by cloaking their contributions as loans, giving rise to the 'Cash for Peerages' scandal. Such activities have given rise to demands that the scale of donations should be capped. As the costs of electioneering escalate, so the demands made on party funds increases. In the UK some politicians are advocating that parties should be funded by the State; a proposition that promises to give rise to interesting debate. Along with the increased scrutiny of donations there has been a long term contraction in party memberships in a number of western democracies which itself places more strains on funding. For example in the United Kingdom and Australia membership of the two main parties in 2006 is less than an 1/8 of what it was in 1950, despite significant increases in population over that period. In I· land, elected representatives of the Sinn Fein party take only the average industrial wage from their salary as a representative, while the rest goes into the party budget. Other incomes they may have are not taken into account. Elected representatives of the Socialist Party (Ireland) take only the average industrial wage out of their entire earnings.

Public financing for parties and candidates during elections has several permutations and is increasingly common. There are two broad categories of funding, direct, which entails a montetary transfer to a party, and indirect, which includes broadcast time on state media, use of the mail service or supplies. According to the Comparative Data from the ACE Electoral Knowledge Network, out of a sample of over 180 nations, 25% of nations provide no direct or indirect public funding, 58% provide direct public funding and 60% of nations provide indirect public funding. Some countries provide both direct and indirect public funding to political parties. Funding may be equal for all parties or depend on the results of previous campaigns or the number of candidates participating in an election. Frequently parties rely on a mix of private and public funding and are required to disclose their finances to the Electoral Management Body.

Colours and Emblems for Parties

Generally speaking, over the world, political parties associate themselves with colours, primarily for identification, especially for voter recognition during elections. Red usually signifies leftist, communist or socialist parties. Conservative parties generally use blue or black. Pink sometimes signifies moderate socialist. Yellow is often used for libertarianism or classical liberalism. Green is the colour for green parties, Islamist parties and Irish nationalist and republican parties in Northern Ireland. Orange is sometimes a colour of nationalism, such as in the Netherlands, in Israel with the Orange Camp or with Ulster Loyalists in Northern Ireland; it is also a colour of reform such as in Ukraine. In the past, Purple was considered the colour of royalty (like white), but today it is sometimes used for feminist parties. White also is associated with nationalism. "Purple Party" is also used as an academic hypothetical of an undefined party, as a centralist party in the United States (because purple is created from mixing the main parties' colours of red and blue) and as a highly idealistic "peace and love" party— in a similar vein to a Green Party, perhaps. Black is generally associated with fascist parties, going back to Benito Mussolini's blackshirts, but also with Anarchism. Similarly, brown is often associated with Nazism, going back to the Nazi Party's brown-uniformed storm troopers.

Colour associations are useful for mnemonics when voter illiteracy is significant. Another case where they are used is when it is not desirable to make rigorous links to parties, particularly when coalitions and alliances are formed between political parties and other organizations, for example: Red Tory, "Purple" (Red-Blue) alliances, Red-green alliances, Blue-green alliances, Traffic light coalitions, Pan-green coalitions, and Pan-blue coalitions.

Political colour schemes in the United States diverge from international norms. Since 2000, red has become associated with the right-wing Republican Party and blue with the left-wing Democratic Party. However, unlike political colour schemes of other countries, the parties did not choose those colours; they were used in news coverage of 2000 election results and ensuing legal battle and caught on in popular usage. Prior to the 2000 election the media typically alternated which colour represented which party each presidential election cycle. The colour scheme happened to get inordinate attention that year, so the cycle was stopped lest it cause confusion the following election.

The emblem of socialist parties is often a red rose held in a fist. Communist parties often use a hammer to represent the worker, a sickle to represent the farmer, or both a hammer and a sickle to refer to both at the same time. The emblem of Nazism, the swastika or *"hakenkreuz,"* has been adopted as a near-universal symbol for almost any organized hate group, even though it dates from more ancient times.

Symbols can be very important when the overall electorate is illiterate. In the Kenyan constitutional referendum, 2005, supporters of the constitution used the banana as their symbol, while the "no" used an orange.

INTERNATIONAL ORGANIZATIONS OF POLITICAL PARTIES

During the 19th and 20th century, many national political parties organized themselves into international organizations along similar policy lines. Notable examples are the International Workingmen's Association (also called the First International), the Socialist International (also called the Second International), the Communist International (also called the Third International), and the Fourth International, as organizations of working class parties, or the Liberal International (yellow), Christian Democratic International and the International Democrat Union (blue). Worldwide green parties have recently established the Global Greens. The Socialist International, the Liberal International, and the International Democrat Union are all based in London. Some countries (e.g. Hong Kong) outlaw formal linkages between local and foreign political organizations, effectively outlawing international political parties.

Party Line (Politics)

In politics, the line or the party line is an idiom for a political party or social movement's canon agenda, as well as specific ideological elements specific to the organization's partisanship. The common phrase toeing the party line describes a person who speaks in a manner that conforms to his political party's agenda. Likewise, a party-line vote is one in which most or all of the legislators from each political party voted in accordance with that party's policies. In several countries, a whip attempts to ensure this.

The Marxist-Leninist concept of democratic centralism involves strict adherence to, and defence of, a communist party's positions in public, while in inner-party debate sessions, the line can be questioned, criticized, and changed if necessary. Used loosely, the phrase "the party line" may also refer to the non-party organizations such as religious groups, business offices, or social network a that may have a semi-official organizational policy or position that is unrelated to any political party.

POLITICAL PARTIES IN INDIA

The Constitution of India stipulates that India be a federal polity with a central government in New Delhi, and state governments for the various states and Union territories. Consequently, political parties in India are classified as national and state (regional) parties based on their realms of influence.

The Indian political parties are categorized into two main types. National level parties and state level parties. National parties are political parties which, participate in different elections all over India. For example, Indian National Congress, Bhartiya Janata Party, Bahujan Samaj Party, Samajwadi Party, Communist Party of India, Communist Party of India (Marxist) and some other parties. State parties or regional parties are political parties which, participate in different elections but only within one state. For example Shiv Sena participates only in Maharashtra, Telegu Desam in Andra Pradesh, Akali Dal in Punjab, Dravida Munnetra Kazagham (DMK) in Tamil Nadu and there are other such state parties. There are some small communist parties who participate only within one state. Some states have more than one state party. For example in Tamil Nadu another important state party is All India Anna Dravida Munnetra Kazagham (AIADMK). Because of these long party names many party names are abbreviated to their initials.

Some the political parties have their origin from before India's independence, for example, Indian National Congress, Forward Bloc, Akali Dal, National Conference and some other parties. Some of these parties were either social or political organization before India's independence and they became political parties after India's independence. But many of the present parties were established after India's independence. Members, who split from larger parties, established some of these parties. For example in the 1960s, Lok Dal was established by people who split from the Indian National Congress. Communist Party of India (Marxist) was established after the split in Communist Party of India and there are other such examples.

In Indian politics, there are political parties in which one person pulls all the strings. This feature existed even before India's independence, when Mahatma Gandhi was the father figure of the Indian National Congress until his death in 1948 even though he resigned from the Congress in 1933. Indira Gandhi for some period was in complete control of her party. Her party was also named, Congress (Indira). Shiv Sena is dominated by Bal Thakarey. Even when the Shiv Sena won the state elections in Maharashtra, Bal Thakarey handled the establishment of the state government but did not appoint himself as the Chief Minister but appointed someone else for this post.

Some of these parties, like the Shiv Sena in which one person pulls all the strings, have their stronghold in the public not because of their leader but because of party ideology. While other parties are completely dependable on the respect the leader of the party has in the public. One such party is Samata Party and its leader is George Fernandes. Another such party was Lok Shakti and its leader was Ramakrishna Hegde.

Many of the large national parties have a pre-election agreement with smaller parties on joint candidates in some constituencies. This candidate belongs to one of the parties and the other party supports this candidate. This is done to prevent a possibility of parties, with common national agenda or common state agenda, nominate their own different candidates causing the splitting of the votes of their wing and so losing the constituency to the rival wing. In Indian politics there are also many independent candidates. These candidates participate in election constituencies independently without the support of any party. In very few cases the larger parties also support independent candidates.

Another feature unique to Indian politics is the high number of film actors who join the Indian politics. The Indian cinema produces films in different languages. The largest and the most popular film industry is the Hindi language film industry. Many national parties recruit Hindi movie actors in their parties. While many state parties with state chauvinism attract local film industry actors in their parties. These actors do not only appear along side with the party politicians to attract the mob towards the politicians gatherings, but they even participate as candidates in elections. Some of the state parties in south India were established by former movie actors.

ADVOCACY GROUP

Advocacy groups (also pressure groups, lobby groups and some interest groups and special interest groups) use various forms of advocacy to influence public opinion and/or policy; they have played and continue to play an important part in the development of political and social systems. Groups vary considerably in size, influence and motive; some have wide ranging long term social purposes, others are focused and are a response to an immediate issue or concern.

Motives for action may be based on a shared political, faith, moral or commercial position. Groups use varied methods to try to achieve their aims including lobbying, media campaigns, publicity stunts, polls, research and policy briefings. Some groups are supported by powerful business or political interests and exert considerable influence on the political process, others have few such resources.

Some have developed into important social, political institutions or social movements. Some powerful Lobby groups have been accused of manipulating the democratic system for narrow commercial gain and in some instances have been found guilty of corruption, fraud, bribery and other serious crimes; lobbying has become increasingly regulated as a result. Some groups, generally ones with less financial resources may use direct action and civil disobedience and in some cases are accused of being a threat to the social order or 'domestic extremists'.

A single-issue groups may form in response to a particular issue area sometimes in response to a single event or threat. In some cases initiatives initially championed by advocacy groups later become institutionalized as important elements of civic life. Groups representing broad interests of a group may be formed with the purpose of benefiting the group over an expended period of time and in many ways, for example as Consumer organizations, Professional associations, Trade associations and Trade unions.

Lobby groups lobby for a change to the law or the maintenance of a particular law and big business funds very considerable lobbying influence on legislators, for example in the in the USA and in the UK where lobbying first developed. Some Lobby groups have considerable financial resources at their disposal. Lobbying is regulated to stop the worst abuses which can develop into corruption. In the United States the Internal Revenue Service makes a clear distinction between lobbying and advocacy.

Influential Advocacy Groups

There are many significant advocacy groups through history, some of which could be considered to operate with different dynamics and could better be described as social movements. Here are some notable groups operating in different parts of the world:-

- British Medical Association formed at a meeting of 50 doctors in 1832 for the sharing of knowledge; lobbying led to the Medical Act 1858 and the formation of the General Medical Council which has registered and regulated doctors in the UK to this date.
- Campaign for Nuclear Disarmament non-proliferation of nuclear weapons and unilateral nuclear disarmament in the UK since 1957 who's logo is now an international peace symbol.
- Center for Auto Safety Formed in 1970 to give consumers a voice for auto safety and quality in the United States
- Drug Policy Alliance (Drug law: USA)

- Energy Lobby Representatives of large oil, gas, coal, and electric utilities corporations attempting to influence governmental policy in the United States
- Greenpeace Formed in 1970 as the Don't Make a Wave Committee to resist Nuclear weapons testing in the United States.
- National Rifle Association Formed in New York is 1871 to protect the rights of gun-owners
- Oxfam Formed in 1942 as the 'Oxford Committee for Famine Relief'.
- Pennsylvania Abolition Society Formed in Philadelphia in 1775 with a view to abolish slavery in the United States
- People for the Ethical Treatment of Animals Animal rights
- Royal Society for the Protection of Birds Founded in Manchester in 1889 to campaign against the 'barbarous trade in plumes for women's hats'.
- Sierra Club Formed in 1892 to help protect the Sierra Nevada.
- Stop the War Coalition against the War on Terrorism which included a march of between 750,000 and 2,000,000 people in London in 2003.
- Suffragettes Voting rights for women after direct action and hunger strikes from 1865-1928 in the United Kingdom
- Sunday School movement Formed in about 1751 to pomoting universal schooling in the UK
- Tories Formed in 1678 to resist the British Exclusion Bill; it developed into one of the first political parties, now known as the Conservative Party.

Corruption and Illegal Activity

In some instances Advocacy groups are convicted of illegal activity. Major examples include:

- Jack Abramoff Indian lobbying scandal Corrupt and fraudulent lobbying in relation to Native American gambling enterprises

- Tobacco Master Settlement Agreement between the Attorneys General of 46 states and the four largest US tobacco companies who agreed to pay $206 billion over the first twenty-five years of the agreement.

Adversarial Groupings

On some controversial issues there are a number of competing advocacy groups, sometimes with very different resources available to them:

- Pro-choice movement vs Pro-life movement (abortion policy in the United States)
- SPEAK campaign vs Pro-Test (animal testing in United Kingdom)
- The Automobile Association vs Pedestrians' Association (now 'Living Streets') (road safety in the United Kingdom since 1929)
- Tobacco Institute vs Action on Smoking and Health (tobacco legislation)
- Flying Matters vs Plane Stupid (aviation policy in the United Kingdom since 2007)

Benefits and Incentives

The general theory is that individuals must be enticed with some type of benefit to join an interest group. Known as the Free Rider Problem, it refers to the difficulty of obtaining members of a particular interest group when the benefits are already reaped without membership. For instance, an interest group dedicated to improving farming standards will fight for the general goal of improving farming for every farmer, even those who are not members of that particular interest group. So there is no real incentive to join an interest group and pay dues if they will receive that benefit anyway. Interest groups must receive dues and contributions from its members in order to accomplish its agenda. While every individual in the world would benefit from a cleaner environment, that Environmental protection interest group does not, in turn, receive monetary help from every individual in the world.

Selective material benefits are benefits that are usually given in monetary benefits. For instance, if an interest group gives a material benefit to their member, they could give them travel discounts, free meals at certain restaurants, or free subscriptions to magazines, newspapers, or journals. Many trade and professional interest groups tend to give these types of benefits to their members. A selective solidary benefit is another type of benefit offered to members or prospective members of an interest group. These incentives involve benefits like "socializing congeniality, the sense of group membership and identification, the status resulting from membership, fun and conviviality, the maintenance of social distinctions, and so on. A solidary incentive is when the rewards for participation are socially derived and created out of the act of association.

An expressive incentive is another basic type of incentive or benefit offered to being a member of an interest group. People who join an interest group because of expressive benefits likely joined to express an ideological or moral value that they believe in. Some include free speech, civil rights, economic justice, or political equality. To obtain these types of benefits, members would simply pay dues, donate their time or money to get a feeling of satisfaction from expressing a political value. Also, it would not matter if the interest group achieved their goal, but these members would be able to say they helped out in the process of trying to obtain these goals, which is the expressive incentive that they got in the first place. The types of interest groups that rely on expressive benefits or incentives would be environmental groups and groups who claim to be lobbying for the public interest.

Some public policy interests are not recognized or addressed by a group at all, and these interests are labelled latent interests.

LOBBYING

Lobbying (also Lobby) is a form of advocacy with the intention of influencing decisions made by legislators and officials in the government by individuals, other legislators, constituents, or advocacy groups. A lobbyist is a person who tries to influence legislation on behalf of a special interest or a member of a lobby. Governments often define and regulate organized group lobbying which has become very influential on policy.

In the United States the Internal Revenue Service makes a clear distinction for nonprofit organizations between lobbying and advocacy limiting the former to "asking policymakers to take a specific position on a specific piece of legislation, or that ask others to ask the same"; in common language, the definition of lobbying is normally broader. Other activities seek to influence policies, possibly including public demonstrations and the filing of "friend of the court briefs" are termed as "advocacy".

The House of Commons Public Administration Select Committee argued that while there are shortcomings in the regulation of the lobbying industry in the United Kingdom, "The practice of lobbying in order to influence political decisions is a legitimate and necessary part of the democratic process. Individuals and organisations reasonably want to influence decisions that may affect them, those around them, and their environment.

Government in turn needs access to the knowledge and views that lobbying can bring." Governments often define and regulate organized group lobbying. Economist Thomas Sowell defends corporate lobbying as simply an example of a group having better knowledge of its interests than the people at large do of theirs.

Lobby groups may concentrate their efforts on the legislatures, where laws are created but make also use the judicial branch to advance their causes. The National Association for the Advancement of Coloured People, for example, filed suits in state and federal courts in the 1950s to challenge segregation laws. Their efforts resulted in the Supreme Court declaring such laws unconstitutional. At any given time, there are hundreds of cases in state and federal courts in which Advocacy groups are suing in hopes of winning lawsuits to help their members. Court victories, in addition to their legal benefits, can make the headlines and give interest groups a lot of publicity.

They may use a legal device known as amicus curiae, literally "friend of the court," briefs to try and influence court cases. Briefs are written documents filed with a court, typically by parties to a lawsuit. Amicus curiae briefs are briefs filed by people or groups who are not parties to a suit. These briefs are entered into the court records, and give additional background on the matter being decided upon. Advocacy groups use these briefs to both share their expertise and promote their positions.

LOBBYING BY COUNTRY

United Kingdom

The terms 'lobby' and 'lobbying referred to discussions which attempted to influence an MP's vote by either their fellow parliamentary colleagues, by one of their constituents or by any outside organisation and which took place in the lobby of parliament. A professional lobbying industry (also known as 'public affairs') has been steadily growing in recent years and was estimated to be worth £1.9 billion and employ 14,000 people in 2007 with some MPs being contacted 100 times a week. It is recognised that funding political parties can also be an indirect form of effective political influence. Following legislation of disclosure of contributions to campaigning, donations to parties some were described as loans. Some contributions to party funds were being used to 'Buy peerages' allowing the person to participate directly in the legislative process.

Recently many recent MPs and in particular Ministers are recruited by lobby firms and lobbyists have been recruited by ministers as 'special advisors' using what is termed the Revolving door of influence. In 2009 the House of Commons Public Administration Select Committee recommended that a statutory register of lobbying activity and lobbyists would improve transparency to the dealings between Whitehall decision makers and outside interests. Parliament controversially responded to this recommendation by saying that self-regulation was more practice. The Conservative leader, David Cameron, predicted that it was "the next big scandal waiting to happen" and was one that had "tainted our politics for too long, an issue that exposes the far-too-cosy relationship between politics, government, business and money".

United States

The ability of individuals, groups, and corporations to lobby the government is protected by the right to petition in the First Amendment of the United States Constitution. Lobbyists use time spent with legislators to explain the goals of the organizations which they represent and the obstacles elected officials face when dealing with issues, to clients. Lobbying activities are also performed at the state level, and lobbyists try to influence legislation in the state legislatures in each of the 50 states. At the local municipal level, some lobbying activities occur with city council members and county commissioners, especially in the larger cities and more populous counties. Since 1998, 43 percent of the 198 members of Congress who left government to join private life have registered to lobby using the 'revolving door of influence'. The Lobbying Disclosure Act of 1995 and Honest Leadership and Open Government Act of 2007 increased regulation and transparency. In 2009 U.S. President Barack Obama signed two related executive orders and three presidential memoranda on his first day in office to help ensure his administration would be a more open, transparent, and accountable government.

European Union

The more political influence the European Union gains on a global level, and the more policy areas it covers, the more interesting it becomes for lobbyists. With its enlargement in 2004 this development has taken a further step, bringing in not only a lot more players and stakeholders but also a wide range of different political cultures and traditions. Currently around 15,000 Brussels-based lobbyists (consultants, lawyers, associations, corporations, NGOs etc.) seek to influence the EU's legislative process. Some 2,600 special interest groups have a permanent office in Brussels. Their distribution is roughly as follows: European trade federations (32%), consultants (20%), companies (13%), NGOs (11%), national associations (10%), regional representations (6%), international organizations (5%) and think tanks (1%),.

The fragmented nature of EU institutional structure provides multiple channels through which organized interests may seek to influence policy-making. Lobbying takes place at the European level itself and within the existing national states. The most important institutional targets are the Commission, the Council, and the European Parliament. The Commission has a monopoly on the initiative in Community decision-making. Since it has the power to draft initiatives, it makes it ideally suited as an arena for interest representation. There are three main channels of indirect lobbying of the Council. First, lobbying groups routinely lobby the national delegations in Brussels. The second indirect means of lobbying the Council is for interest groups to lobby members of the many Council-working groups. The third means of influencing the Council is directly via national governments. As a consequence of the co-decision procedures, the European Parliament attracts attention from lobbyists who target the rapporteur and the chairman of the committee. The reporters are MEPs appointed by Committees to prepare the parliament's response to the Commission's proposal and to those measures taken by the Parliament itself.

Lobbying in Brussels was born only in the late 1970s. Up to that time, "diplomatic lobbying" at the highest levels remained the rule. There were few lobbyists involved in the system and except for some business associations, representative offices were rarely used. The event that sparked the explosion of lobbying was the first direct election of the European Parliament in 1979. Up until then the Parliament consisted of a complex, and companies increasingly felt the need of an expert local presence to find out what was going on in Brussels. The foundation of lobbying was therefore the need to provide information. From that developed the need to influence the process actively and effectively. The next important step in lobbying development was the Single European Act of 1986 which both created the qualified majority vote for taking decisions in the Council and enhanced the role of the Parliament, again making EU legislation more complex and lobbying further more important and attractive for stakeholders.

In the wake of the Abramoff scandal in Washington and the massive impact that this had on the lobbying scene in the United States, the rules for lobbying in the EU—which until now consist of only a non-binding code of conduct—may also be tightened.

France

In France, the political system does not integrate the lobbying practice. Much French republican thought has been suspicious of the claims of "particular interests," which are often contrasted with the "general interest" of the nation. This is one interpretation of Rousseau's *Social Contract*, for example. So while lobbying has always been practiced in France, organized lobbying made a significant appearance in France only in the early 1980s. Since then, it has steadily grown; many interest groups routinely seek to influence the French institutions as the Government and the French Parliament ("National Assembly" and "Senate"). In order to make up the lost time, more and more French enterprises try to organize their own lobbies by creating their own public affairs department. In recent years, growing numbers of grassroots and grasstop lobbies have been organized by citizen groups, representing interests such as genetically modified organisms and software piracy.

But there is currently no regulation at all for lobbying activities in France and, as a consequence, this practice suffers from a lack of transparency. There is no regulated access to the French institutions and no register. For example, the internal rule of the National Assembly (art. 23 and 79) forbid to members of Parliament to be linked with a particular interest. However, MPs don't have to declare their interest and the list of MPs' assistants is not public. At last, there is no rule at all for consultation of interest groups by the Parliament and the Government. Nevertheless, a recent parliamentary initiative (motion for a resolution) has been launched by several MPs so as to establish a register for representatives of interest groups and lobbyists who intend to lobby the MPs. The purpose of this initiative is to introduce standards of conduct and access to the National Assembly. Through the use of a register, these standards of conduct and access will enable the Assembly to identify and maintain a list of the representatives of interest groups who follow legislative activity and to supervise fully the access of those representatives to the National Assembly. This motion has not been adopted yet.

Other Countries

Only countries where lobbying is regulated in parliament bills include:

- Georgia (1998)
- Hungary (2006).
- Lithuania (2001)
- Poland (2005)
- Israel (1994).

Etymology

The BBC holds that "lobbying" comes from the gathering of Members of Parliament and peers in the hallways (or lobbies) of Houses of Parliament before and after parliamentary debates. One story states that the term originated at the Willard Hotel in Washington, DC, where it was used by Ulysses S. Grant to describe the political wheelers and dealers frequenting the hotel's lobby in order to access Grant, who was often found there, enjoying a cigar and brandy.

The term "lobbying" appeared in print as early as 1820:

> *"Other letters from Washington affirm, that members of the Senate, when the compromise question was to be taken in the House, were not only "lobbying about the Representatives' Chamber" but also active in endeavoring to intimidate certain weak representatives by insulting threats to dissolve the Union."*

— April 1, 1820, New Hampshire Sentinel

Dictionary Definitions

- 'Lobbying' (also 'Lobby') is a form of advocacy with the intention of influencing decisions made by the government by individuals or more usually by Lobby groups; it includes all attempts to influence legislators and officials, whether by other legislators, constituents, or organized groups.
- A 'lobbyist' is a person who tries to influence legislation on behalf of a special interest or a member of a lobby.

ELECTORAL POLITICS

In ancient Greek democracies (e.g., Athens) public officials were occasionally elected but more often were chosen by lot. In Rome the popular assemblies elected the tribunes. In the Middle Ages elections were abandoned, except for such processes as elections to the papacy and, in a more limited sense, of the Holy Roman emperor by a small and partly hereditary body of electors. In the modern period, elections have been inseparable from the growth of democratic forms of government. Elections were associated with the parliamentary process in England from the 13th cent. and were gradually regularized by acts prescribing the frequency of elections (the Triennial Act of 1694, and the Septennial Act of 1716), by successive reform bills widening the franchise in the 19th cent., and by the adoption of the secret ballot in 1872.

Elections in the United States

In colonial America the election of church and public officials dates almost from the founding of the Plymouth Colony, and the paper ballot was instituted in elections to the Massachusetts governorship in 1634. Under the U.S. Constitution the right to hold elections is specified, but the method and place are left to the states, with Congress having the power to alter their regulations. The Constitution specified that elections to the House of Representatives be direct, or popular, and that the election of the Senate and of the president and vice president be indirect, Senators being chosen by the state legislatures and the president and vice president by electors selected by the people. The Seventeenth Amendment (1913) provided for popular election of senators. Political candidates are usually chosen by delegate convention, direct primary, nonpartisan primaries, or petition. The candidate who receives the most votes is usually elected, but an absolute majority may be required; a majority has not been required in the U.S. federal elections since 1850 except in the electoral vote cast for the president and vice president. (In presidential nominating conventions an absolute majority is required; the Democrats required a two-thirds vote of the delegates from 1832 to 1936.)

Voting frauds and disorder at the polls were common after the rise of political machines, and the enactment of registration laws after 1865 did little to ameliorate conditions. Corrupt practices acts, poll watching, the institution of primary elections, and the introduction of voting machines after 1892 have been more effective in ensuring honest elections. Nonetheless, the disputes over the counting of the votes in Florida in the 2000 presidential election clearly revealed that some machine voting systems are more reliable than others and that less reliable systems can potentially distort the results. All states have some residency requirements as a condition for suffrage. Originally the vote was typically restricted to white men who met certain property qualifications; such restrictions were later liberalized and removed. The Fourteenth Amendment (1868) and Fifteenth Amendment (1870) were designed to forbid the disenfranchisement of African-American men after the Civil War, and the Nineteenth (1920) conferred the vote on women. The Twenty-third Amendment (1961) permitted residents of the District of Columbia to vote in the presidential elections, while the Twenty-fourth Amendment (1964) outlawed payment of poll or other taxes as a condition for voting. The Twenty-sixth Amendment (1971) lowered the voting age from 21 to 18. The so-called motor voter law (National Voter Registration Act, 1993) was designed to reverse declining voter registrations by permitting registration at motor vehicle departments and other agencies. Certain classes of felons and some others are deprived of the vote.

Types of Representation

In the United States, Canada, Mexico, Great Britain, and many other nations, usually the one candidate who receives the most votes is elected from a district. If an absolute majority is needed to win, a run-off election maybe required. In Denmark, Norway, Sweden, Russia, Ukraine, Brazil, and other nations (including some local elections in the United States), proportional representation is used to more adequately represent political or other minorities within the electorate. Two methods are used—the voter ranking system in a multiseat district, and the party list system in which parties gaining a threshold vote win one seat and those well above the threshold dividing the remaining seats proportionally. While a proportional system provides representation for minorities and eliminates gerrymandering, primaries, and run-off elections, it can weaken the representative-constituent relationship, encourage multiple parties, and necessitate coalition rather than majority governments. Some nations, for example, Italy, Germany, and Spain, use a combination of direct election and proportional representation.

ELECTION

An election is a formal decision-making process by which a population chooses an individual to hold public office. Elections have been the usual mechanism by which modern representative democracy operates since the 17th century. Elections may fill offices in the legislature, sometimes in the executive and judiciary, and for regional and local government. This process is also used in many other private and business organizations, from clubs to voluntary associations and corporations. The universal use of elections as a tool for selecting representatives in modern democracies is in contrast with the practice in the democratic archetype, ancient Athens. Elections were considered an oligarchic institution and most political offices were filled using sortition, also known as allotment, by which officeholders were chosen by lot.

Electoral reform describes the process of introducing fair electoral systems where they are not in place, or improving the fairness or effectiveness of existing systems. Psephology is the study of results and other statistics relating to elections (especially with a view to predicting future results). To *elect* means "to choose or make a decision", and so sometimes other forms of ballot such as the referendum are referred to as elections, especially in the United States.

History

Elections were used as early in history as ancient Greece and ancient Rome, and throughout the Medieval period to select rulers such as the Holy Roman Emperor and the Pope. Elections were also used to select rajas by the *gana* in several [[History of India | ancient Indian] caliphs, Uthman and Ali, in the early medieval Rashidun Caliphate; and to select the Pala king Gopala in early medieval Bengal. The modern "election", which consists of public elections of government officials, didn't emerge until the beginning of the 17th century when the idea of representative government took hold in North America and Europe.

Questions of suffrage, especially suffrage for minority groups, have dominated the history of elections. Males, the dominate cultural group in North America and Europe, often dominated the electorate and continue to do so in many countries. Early elections in countries such as Great Britain and the United States were dominated by landed or ruling class males. However, by 1920 all Western European and North American democracies had universal male suffrage (except Switzerland) and many countries began to consider women's suffrage. Despite legally mandated universal suffrage for males, political barriers were sometimes erected to prevent fair access to elections.

Functions

Who is Elected

The government positions for which elections are held vary depending on the locale. In a representative democracy, such as the United States, some positions are not filled through elections, especially those that require certain skills. For example, judges are usually appointed rather than elected to help protect their impartiality. There are exceptions to this practice, however; some judges in the United States are elected, and in ancient Athens military generals were elected. In some cases, as for example, in soviet democracy—there may exist an intermediate tier of electors between constituents and the elected figure. However, in most representative democracies, this level of indirection usually is nothing more than a formality. For example, the President of the United States is elected by the Electoral College, and in the Westminster System, the Prime Minister is formally chosen by the head of state (and in reality by the legislature or by their party).

Types of Elections

In most democratic political systems, there are a range of different types of election, corresponding to different layers of public governance or geographical jurisdiction. Some common types of election are:

- Presidential election
- General election
- Primary election
- By-election
- Local election
- Co-option.

A referendum (plural *referenda* or *referendums*) is a democratic tool related to elections in which the electorate votes for or against a specific proposal, law or policy, rather than for a general policy or a particular candidate or party. Referenda may be added to an election ballot or held separately and may be either binding or consultative, usually depending on the constitution. Referenda are usually called by governments via the legislature, however many democracies allow citizens to petition for referenda directly, called *initiatives*.

Referenda are particularly prevalent and important in direct democracies, such as Switzerland. The basic Swiss system, however, still works with representatives. In the most direct form of democracy, anyone can vote about anything. This is closely related to referenda and may take the form of consensus decision-making. Reminiscent of the ancient Greek system, anyone may discuss a particular subject until a consensus is reached. The consensus requirement means that discussions can go on for a very long time. The result will be that only those who are genuinely interested will participate in the discussion and therefore the vote. In this system there need not be an age limit because children will usually become bored. This system is however only feasible when implemented on a very small scale.

CHARACTERISTICS

Suffrage

The question of who may vote is a central issue in elections. The electorate does not generally include the entire population; for example, many countries prohibit those judged mentally incompetent from voting, and all jurisdictions require a minimum age for voting.

Historically, other groups of people have also been excluded from voting. For instance, the democracy of ancient Athens did not allow women, foreigners, or slaves to vote, and the original United States Constitution left the topic of suffrage to the states; usually only white male property owners were able to vote. Much of the history of elections involves the effort to promote suffrage for excluded groups. The women's suffrage movement gave women in many countries the right to vote, and securing the right to vote freely was a major goal of the American civil rights movement. Extending voting rights to excluded groups (such as convicted felons, members of certain minorities, and the economically disadvantaged) continues to be a goal of voting rights advocates. Suffrage is typically only for citizens of the country. Further limits may be imposed: for example, in Kuwait, only people who have been citizens since 1920 or their descendants are allowed to vote, a condition that the majority of residents do not fulfil. However, in the European Union, one can vote in municipal elections if one lives in the municipality and is an EU citizen; the nationality of the country of residence is not required.

In some countries, voting is required by law; if an eligible voter does not cast a vote, he or she may be subject to punitive measures such as a small fine.

Nomination

A representative democracy requires a procedure to govern nomination for political office. In many cases, nomination for office is mediated through preselection processes in organised political parties.

Non-partisan systems tend to differ from partisan systems as concerns nominations. In a direct democracy, one type of non-partisan democracy, any eligible person can be nominated. In some non-partisan representative systems no nominations (or campaigning, electioneering, etc.) take place at all, with voters free to choose any person at the time of voting—with some possible exceptions such as through a minimum age requirement—in the jurisdiction. In such cases, it is not required (or even possible) that the members of the electorate be familiar with all of the eligible persons, though such systems may involve indirect elections at larger geographic levels to ensure that some first-hand familiarity among potential electees can exist at these levels (i.e., among the elected delegates).

As far as partisan systems, in some countries, only members of a particular political party can be nominated. Or, an eligible person can be nominated through a petition; thus allowing him or her to be listed on a ballot.

Electoral Systems

Electoral systems are the detailed constitutional arrangements and voting systems that convert the vote into political decision. The first step is to tally the votes, for which various different vote counting systems and ballot types are used. Voting systems then determine the result on the basis of the tally. Most systems can be categorized as either proportional or majoritarian. Among the former are party-list proportional representation and additional member system. Among the latter are First Past the Post (FPP) (relative majority) and absolute majority. Many countries have growing electoral reform movements, which advocate systems such as approval voting, single transferable vote, instant runoff voting or a Condorcet method; these methods are also gaining popularity for lesser elections in some countries where more important elections still use more traditional counting methods.

While openness and accountability are usually considered cornerstones of a democratic system, the act of casting a vote and the content of a voter's ballot are usually an important exception. The secret ballot is a relatively modern development, but it is now considered crucial in most free and fair elections, as it limits the effectiveness of intimidation.

Scheduling

The nature of democracy is that elected officials are accountable to the people, and they must return to the voters at prescribed intervals to seek their mandate to continue in office. For that reason most democratic constitutions provide that elections are held at fixed regular intervals. In the United States, elections are held between every three and six years in most states, with exceptions such as the U.S. House of Representatives, which stands for election every two years. There is a variety of schedules, for example presidents: the President of Ireland is elected every seven years, the President of Finland every six years, the President of France every five years, the President of Russia and President of United States every four years.

Pre-determined or fixed election dates have the advantage of fairness and predictability. However, they tend to greatly lengthen campaigns, and make dissolving the legislature (parliamentary system) more problematic if the date should happen to fall at time when dissolution is inconvenient (e.g. when war breaks out). Other states (e.g., the United Kingdom) only set maximum time in office, and the executive decides exactly when within that limit it will actually go to the polls. In practice, this means the government remains in power for close to its full term, and choose an election date it calculates to be in its best interests (unless something special happens, such as a motion of no-confidence). This calculation depends on a number of variables, such as its performance in opinion polls and the size of its majority. Elections are usually held on one day. There are also advance polls and absentee voting, which have a more flexible schedule. In Europe, a substantial proportion of votes are cast in advance voting.

Election Campaigns

When elections are called, politicians and their supporters attempt to influence policy by competing directly for the votes of constituents in what are called campaigns. Supporters for a campaign can be either formally organized or loosely affiliated, and frequently utilize campaign advertising. It is common for political scientists to attempt to predict elections via Political Forecasting methods. A political campaign is an organized effort which seeks to influence the decision making process within a specific group. In democracies, political campaigns often refer to electoral campaigns, wherein representatives are chosen or referendums are decided. Political campaigns also include organized efforts to alter policy within any institution or organization.

Politics is as old as humankind and is not limited to democratic or governmental institutions. Some examples of political campaigns are: the effort to execute or banish Socrates from Athens in the 5th century BC, the uprising of petty nobility against John of England in the 13th century, or the 2005 push to remove Michael Eisner from the helm of The Walt Disney Company.

Campaign Message

The message of the campaign is what ideas that the candidate wants to share with the voters. The message often consists of several talking points about policy issues. The points summarize the main ideas of the campaign and are repeated frequently in order to create a lasting impression with the voters. In many elections, the opposition party will try to get the candidate "off message" by bringing up policy or personal questions that are not related to the talking points. Most campaigns prefer to keep the message broad in order to attract the most potential voters. A message that is too narrow can alienate voters or slow the candidate down with explaining details. For example, in the election of 2008 John McCain originally used a message that focused on his patriotism and political experience: "Country First"; later the message was changed to shift attention to his role as "The Original Maverick" within the political establishment. Barack Obama ran on a consistent, simple message of "change" throughout his campaign. If the message is crafted carefully, it will assure the candidate a victory at the polls. For a winning candidate, the message is refined and then becomes his or her political agenda in office.

Soundbites

The habit of modern Western media outlets (especially radio and television) of taking short excerpts from speeches has resulted in the creation of the term "soundbite". Examples might include:

- "John Doe is a businessman, not a politician. His background in finance means he can bring fiscal discipline to state government."
- "As our society faces a rapid upswing in violent crime and an ever worsening education system, we need leaders who will keep our streets safe and restore accountability to our schools. John Doe is that leader."
- "Over the past four years, John Doe has missed over fifty City Council meetings. How can you lead if you don't show up? Jane Doe won't turn a blind eye to the government."

Campaign Finance

Fundraising techniques include having the candidate call or meet with large donors, sending direct mail pleas to small donors, and courting interest groups who could end up spending millions on the race if it is significant to their interests.

ORGANIZATION

In a modern political campaign, the campaign organization (or 'machine') will have a coherent structure of personnel in the same manner as any business of similar size.

Campaign Manager

Successful campaigns usually require a campaign manager

to coordinate the campaign's operations. Apart from a candidate, they are often a campaign's most visible leader. Modern campaign managers may be concerned with executing strategy rather than setting it-particularly if the senior strategists are typically outside political consultants such as primarily pollsters and media consultants.

Political Consultants

Political consultants advise campaigns on virtually all of their activities, from research to field strategy. Consultants conduct candidate research, voter research, and opposition research for their clients.

Activists

Activists are the 'foot soldiers' loyal to the cause, the true believers who will carry the run by volunteer activists. Such volunteers and interns may take part in activities such as canvassing door-to-door and making phone calls on behalf of the campaign.

Campaign Ethics and Campaign Time

Modern political campaigns have set new standards for how successful campaigns are conducted day-to-day. The campaign is conducted in what would seem to the public like pseudo-military style, with a strict chain of command, zero tolerance for certain prohibited actions, and an extended daily schedule that starts early and ends much later than most "day jobs."

Prohibited actions may include, but are not limited to: lying about numbers generated (e.g. phone calls made, doors knocked, volunteers recruited, etc.-this is increasingly an issue in offices that are wirelessly connected, without direct oversight; going outside the chain of command (e.g. talking to a superior's superior who happens to be a friend in order to get special favours or report information); non-press-shop members talking to the press; blogging (considered another form of "talking to the press," which can interfere with message discipline); and being arrested (or otherwise becoming a potential easy target for opponent smear campaigns).

The daily schedule of a political campaign is hyperextended, and often has no definite beginning or end, only a series of tasks to be completed by certain benchmark times (or, most often, "COB" ("close of business"). COB for political campaigns is generally defined as "the time at night at which your supervisor is required to report his/her numbers" (or shortly beforehand), so that your numbers reporting (generally the last action a political campaigner takes before COB) can be factored into theirs. For example, a Field Organizer may have collected 9 new committed volunteers for an event during the day; he will be required to report this at 8:45pm to his Regional Field Director, so that the Regional can report that all Field Organizers in the region recruited 52 total volunteers for said event; which needs to be reported to the Deputy State Field Director by 9:00, so that THEY can speak to the State Field Director at 9:15 and report that 827 volunteers have been recruited for events around the state; and so on, up the chain of command.

Once each of these reporting sequences is finished, organizers at all levels may do paperwork, send emails, call friends, and do other things which are not effective to do during business hours or "voter contact time." Political campaigns are generally about contacting voters and volunteers at the nuts-and-bolts level; and so dependent on state law, local peculiarities and the preferences of campaign organizers and volunteers, a certain block of time (usually ending at 8pm or 9pm) is set aside each night for "voter/volunteer contact." (Violation of this block of time to conduct other activities often cannot happen or needs a strong justification, such as attending an important meeting.) Only a very small fraction of campaign workers (such as people who deal with vendors) do the bulk of their work during traditional business hours.

Techniques

A campaign team (which may be as small as one inspired individual, or a heavily-resourced group of professionals) must consider how to communicate the message of the campaign, recruit volunteers, and raise money. Campaign advertising draws on techniques from commercial advertising and propaganda. The avenues available to political campaigns when distributing their messages is limited by the law, available resources, and the imagination of the campaigns' participants. These techniques are often combined into a formal strategy known as the campaign plan. The plan takes account of a campaign's goal, message, target audience, and resources available. The campaign will typically seek to identify supporters at the same time as getting its message across.

Campaign Advertising

Campaign advertising is the use of paid media (newspapers, radio, television, etc.) to influence the decisions made for and by groups. These ads are designed by political consultants and the campaign's staff.

Media Management

The public media (in US parlance 'free media' or 'earned media') may run the story that someone is trying to get elected or to do something about such and such.

Mass Meetings, Rallies and Protests

Holding protests, rallies and other similar public events (if enough people can be persuaded to come) may be a very effective campaign tool. Holding mass meetings with speakers is powerful as it shows visually, through the number of people in attendance, the support that the campaign has.

Modern Technology and the Internet

The internet is now a core element of modern political campaigns. Communication technologies such as e-mail, web sites, and podcasts for various forms of activism to enable faster communications by citizen movements and deliver a message to a large audience. These Internet technologies are used for cause-related fundraising, lobbying, volunteering, community building, and organizing. Individual political candidates are also using the internet to promote their election campaign. In 2008, the Barack Obama for President campaign relied heavily on social media, and new media channels to engage voters, recruit campaign volunteers, and raise campaign funds.

Husting

A husting, or the hustings, was originally a physical platform from which representatives presented their views or cast votes before a parliamentary or other election body. By metonymy, the term may now refer to any event, such as debates or speeches, during an election campaign where one or more of the representative candidates are present.

Other Techniques

- Writing directly to members of the public (either via a professional marketing firm or, particularly on a small scale, by volunteers)
- By distributing leaflets or selling newspapers
- Through websites, online communities, and solicited or unsolicited bulk email
- Through a new technique known as Microtargeting that helps identify and target small demographic slices of voters
- Through a whistlestop tour-a series of brief appearances in several small towns
- Hampering the ability of political competitors to campaign, by such techniques as counter-rallies, picketing of rival parties' meetings, or overwhelming rival candidates' offices with mischievous phone calls (most political parties in representative democracies publicly distance themselves from such disruptive and morale-affecting tactics, with the exception of those parties self-identifying as activist
- Organizing political house parties
- Using endorsements of other celebrated party members to boost support
- Remaining close to or at home to make speeches to supporters who come to visit as part of a front porch campaign
- Vote-by-mail, previously known as 'absentee ballots' have grown significantly in importance as an election tool. Today, campaigns in most states must have a strategy in place to impact early voting
- Sale of official campaign merchandise (colloquially known as chum, in reference to the baiting technique) as a way of commuting a competitor's popularity into campaign donations, volunteer recruitment, and free advertising

CAMPAIGN TYPES

Informational Campaign

An informational campaign is a political campaign designed to raise public awareness and support for the positions of a candidate (or his party). It is more intense than a paper campaign, which consists of little more than filing the necessary papers to get on the ballot, but is less intense than a competitive campaign, which aims to actually win election to the office. An informational campaign typically focuses on low-cost outreach such as news releases, getting interviewed in the paper, making a brochure for door to door distribution, organizing poll workers, etc.

MODERN ELECTION CAMPAIGNS IN THE US

Types of Elections

The United States is unusual in that there are dozens of different types of elections and political offices available, from the sewer commission to the President of the United States. Elections happen every year on many different dates in many different areas of the country.

At the local level, some offices (e.g., school board, town council, etc.) may be officially non-partisan, with candidates of the same political party challenging each other and in many cases without any campaign references to political parties. Other offices (e.g., county treasurer, county district attorney, county sheriff) may be filled in partisan manners with parties endorsing like-minded candidates and then working on their behalf.

All state and national elections are partisan (except judicial elections in some states).

Process of Campaigning

Campaigns start anywhere from several months to several years before election day. The first part of any campaign for a candidate is deciding to run. Prospective candidates will often speak with family, friends, professional associates, elected officials, community leaders, and the leaders of political parties before deciding to run. Candidates are often recruited by political parties and lobby groups interested in electing like-minded politicians. During this period, people considering running for office will consider their ability to put together the money, organization, and public image needed to get elected. Many campaigns for major office do not progress past this point as people often do not feel confident in their ability to win. However, some candidates lacking the resources needed for a competitive campaign proceed with an inexpensive paper campaign or informational campaign designed to raise public awareness and support for their positions.

Once a person decides to run, they will make a public announcement. This announcement could consist of anything from a simple press release to concerned media outlets to a major media event followed by a speaking tour. It is often well-known to many people that a candidate will run prior to an announcement being made. Campaigns will often be announced and then only officially "kicked off" months after active campaigning has begun. Being coy about whether a candidacy is planned is often a deliberate strategy by a prospective candidate, either to "test the waters" or to keep the media's attention.

One of the most important aspects of the major American political campaign is the ability to raise large sums of money, especially early on in the race. Political insiders and donors often judge candidates based on their ability to raise money. Not raising enough money early on can lead to problems later as donors are not willing to give funds to candidates they perceive to be losing, a perception based on their poor fundraising performance.

Also during this period, candidates travel around the area they are running in and meet with voters; speaking to them in large crowds, small groups, or even one-on-one. This allows voters to get a better picture of who a candidate is than that which they read about in the paper or see on television. Campaigns sometimes launch expensive media campaigns during this time to introduce the candidate to voters, although most wait until closer to election day.

Campaigns often dispatch volunteers into local communities to meet with voters and persuade people to support the candidate. The volunteers are also responsible for identifying supporters, recruiting them as volunteers or registering them to vote if they are not already registered. The identification of supporters will be useful later as campaigns remind voters to cast their votes.

Late in the campaign, campaigns will launch expensive television, radio, and direct mail campaigns aimed at persuading voters to support the candidate. Campaigns will also intensify their grassroots campaigns, coordinating their volunteers in a full court effort to win votes. Voting in the United States often starts weeks before election day as mail-in ballots are a commonly used voting method. Campaigns will often run two persuasion programs, one aimed at mail-in voters and one aimed at the more traditional poll voters.

Campaigns for minor office may be relatively simple and inexpensive-talking to local newspapers, giving out campaign signs, and greeting people in the local square.

Political Consultants

Political campaigns in the United States are not merely a civic ritual and occasion for political debate, but a multi-billion dollar industry, dominated by professional political consultants using sophisticated campaign management tools, to an extent far greater than elsewhere in the world. Though the quadrennial presidential election attracts the most attention, the United States has a huge number of elected offices and there is wide variation between different states, counties, and municipalities on which offices are elected and under what procedures. Moreover, unlike democratic politics in much of the rest of the world, the US has relatively weak parties. While parties play a significant role in fundraising and occasionally in drafting people to run, campaigns are ultimately controlled by the individual candidates themselves.

Other Issues and Criticisms

Cost of campaign advertising: American political campaigns have become heavily reliant on broadcast media and direct mail advertising (typically designed and purchased through specialized consultants). Though virtually all campaign media are sometimes used at all levels (even candidates for local office have been known to purchase cable TV ads), smaller, lower-budget campaigns are typically more focused on direct mail, low-cost advertising (such as lawn signs), and direct voter contact. This reliance on expensive advertising is a leading factor behind the rise in the cost of running for office in the United States. This rising cost is considered by some to discourage those without well-monied connections, or money themselves, from running for office.

Independent expenditures: Money is raised and spent not only by candidate's campaign, but also by party committees, political action committees, and other groups (in the 2004 election cycle, much controversy has focused on a new category of organization, 527 groups). This is sometimes done through independent expenditures made in support or opposition of specific candidates but without any candidate's cooperation or approval. The lack of an overt connection between a candidate and third party groups allows one side of a campaign to attack the other side while avoiding criticism for going negative. A memorable example are the Swift Boat Veterans who criticized John Kerry in the 2004 Presidential campaign.

Future developments: Many political players and commentators agree that American political campaigns are currently undergoing a period of change, due to changing campaign-finance laws, increased use of the internet (which has become a valuable fundraising tool), and the apparently declining effectiveness of television advertising.

History

Political campaigns have existed as long as there have been informed citizens to campaign amongst. Often mass campaigns are started by the less privileged or anti-establishment viewpoints (as against more powerful interests whose first resort is lobbying). The phenomenon of political campaigns are tightly tied to lobby groups and political parties. The first 'modern' campaign is thought to be William Ewart Gladstone's Midlothian campaign in the 1880s, although there may be earlier recognizably modern examples from the 19th century.

Democratic societies have regular election campaigns, but political campaigning can occur on particular issues even in non-democracies so long as freedom of expression is allowed. American election campaigns in the 19th century created the first mass-base political parties and invented many of the techniques of mass campaigning. In the 1790-1820s, the Federalist Party and the Democratic-Republican Party battled it out in the so-called "First Party System".

Alternatives to Campaigning

Not all democratic elections involve political campaigning. Indeed, some democratic elections specifically rule out campaigning on the grounds that campaigning may compromise the democratic character of the elections (Abizadeh 2005), perhaps because of campaigns' susceptibility to the influence of money, or to the influence of special interest groups.

Difficulties with Elections

In many countries with weak rule of law, the most common reason why elections do not meet international standards of being "free and fair" is interference from the incumbent government. Dictators may use the powers of the executive (police, martial law, censorship, physical implementation of the election mechanism, etc.) to remain in power despite popular opinion in favour of removal. Members of a particular faction in a legislature may use the power of the majority or supermajority (passing criminal laws, defining the electoral mechanisms including eligibility and district boundaries) to prevent the balance of power in the body from shifting to a rival faction due to an election.

Non-governmental entities can also interfere with elections, through physical force, verbal intimidation, or fraud, which can result in improper casting or counting of votes. Monitoring for and minimizing electoral fraud is also an ongoing task in countries with strong traditions of free and fair elections. Problems that prevent an election from being "free and fair" take various form:

Lack of Open Political Debate or an Informed Electorate

The electorate may be poorly informed about issues or candidates due to lack of freedom of the press, lack of objectivity in the press due to state or corporate control, or lack of access to news and political media. Freedom of speech may be curtailed by the state, favouring certain viewpoints or state propaganda.

Unfair Rules

This can include Gerrymandering, exclusion of opposition candidates from eligibility for office, and manipulating thresholds for electoral success are some of the ways the structure of an election can be changed to favour a specific faction or candidate.

Interference with Campaigns

Those in power may arrest or assassinate candidates, suppress or even criminalize campaigning, close campaign headquarters, harass or beat campaign workers, or intimidate voters with violence.

Tampering with the Election Mechanism

This can include confusing or misleading voters about how to vote, violation of the secret ballot, ballot stuffing, tampering with voting machines, destruction of legitimately cast ballots, voter suppression, fraudulent tabulation of results, and use of physical force or verbal intimation at polling places.

8

Political Behaviour and Citizen Politics

The fact of scarcity, which exists everywhere, guarantees that people will compete for resources. Markets are one way to organize and channel this COMPETITION. Politics is another. People use both markets and politics to get resources allocated to the ends they favour. Even in a democracy, however, political activity is startlingly different from voluntary exchange in markets. People can accomplish many things in politics that they could not accomplish in the private sector. Some of these are vital to the broader community's welfare, such as control of health-threatening air pollution from myriad sources affecting millions of individuals or the provision of national DEFENCE. Other public-sector actions, such as subsidies to farmers and restrictions on the number of taxicabs in a city, provide narrow benefits that fall far short of their costs.

In democratic politics, rules typically give a majority coalition power over the entire society. These rules replace the rule of willing consent and voluntary exchange that exists in the marketplace. In politics, people's goals are similar to the goals they have as consumers, producers, and resource suppliers in the private sector, but people participate instead as voters, politicians, bureaucrats, and lobbyists. In the political system, as in the marketplace, people are sometimes (but not always) selfish. In all cases, they are narrow: how much they know and how much they care about other people's goals is necessarily limited. An advocate of the homeless working in the political arena typically lobbies for a shift of funding (reflecting a move of real resources) from other missions to help poor people who lack HOUSING.

The views of such a person, while admirable, are narrow. He or she prefers that the government (and other givers) allocate more resources to meet his or her goals, even though it means fewer resources for the goals of others. Similarly, a dedicated professional, such as the director of the National Park Service, however unselfish, pushes strongly for shifting government funds away from other uses and toward expanding and improving the national park system. His or her priority is to get more resources allocated to parks, even if goals espoused by others, such as helping the poor, necessarily suffer. Passionate demands for funding and for legislative favours (inevitably at the expense of other people's goals) come from every direction.

Political rules determine how these competing demands, which far exceed the government's ability to provide them, will be arbitrated. The rules of the political game are critical. Is the government purely democratic or a representative democracy? Who can vote? Over what domain of issues can the government make decisions? How much of the society's output is available for diversion to political allocation? The rules provide answers to these questions, influencing not only who gets what from society's product, but also how big the product itself will be and how much of it is diverted from the production of goods and services and devoted instead to influencing the political game.

Why do individuals and groups often seek their aims in the political sector rather than in markets? The motives range from public spirited to narrowly selfish:

- Political solutions can compel people, on threat of prison or worse, to financially support politically chosen goals. This solves the financial "free rider" problem caused by the fact that with solely voluntary provision, even citizens who do not pay for national defence or for, say, a sculpture in the town square can potentially benefit from the expenditures of those who do.
- Imperfections in the legal protection of one's rights, such as one's right to be safe from harmful air pollutants, or even one's civil rights, can be addressed politically.

- Even in a democracy, political action can allow one group to benefit at the expense mainly of the rest of society. Except for gifts and unintended spillovers, this does not happen in a FREE MARKET with protected PROPERTY RIGHTS, where those who pay *are* the ones who benefit, and transfers such as gifts are strictly voluntary. (Political victories, however, are often costly to those who win them; lobbying is not free.)

Some aspects of the political process, however, work against those who pursue their goals via the political route:

- One Congress or legislature cannot bind the next, and so a political solution, other than the grant or sale of private rights, lasts only as long as the political muscle of those who push it. Any political program, land allocation, or treaty can be reversed as political pressures change. In other words, a political solution cannot be purchased: it can only be rented. A political act is inherently less secure than a private purchase or trust arrangement, if property rights are secure.
- Truly innovative activity is often difficult to sell to the majority of the political group, such as the Congress or a specific committee, which must agree to the proposed action. In the free market, on the other hand, innovations typically are funded when only a few entrepreneurs and capitalists believe in them because only their capital, not that of all taxpayers, is at risk.

For ordinary citizens who are not politically active, political activity has very different consequences from market activity. Although such citizens may benefit from political action that others take, they are bound by all and must pay for some political outcomes, whether in their own interest or not. Ordinary citizens are outside the political process except when they vote and when they have concentrated, or special, interests and are politically well organized. Dairy farmers, for example, typically know little or nothing about how much they pay to operate the national park system or whether the parks are well managed. However, they are keenly informed about the federal milk program, which restricts milk production and keeps milk prices high. Thus, they do not have an incentive to act politically to control the costs of the national park system, but they do have an incentive to act to expand the milk program. Their counterparts, such as conservation advocates eager to expand the national park system, know little about the costs they are bearing to support the milk program and concentrate instead on expanding the park system and its budget.

Although political activity has benefits as well as costs, political behaviour causes some predictable problems for citizens in general:

- One-to-a-citizen ballot votes, the currency of the formal democratic marketplace, do not allow voters to show the intensity of their preferences, as dollar votes do when citizens focus their budgets—some spending more on housing, others on entertainment, EDUCATION, or their favourite CHARITY.
- The voter purchases a large bundle of policies and cannot pick and choose. In a representative government, the voters select a single candidate (the "bundle") to represent them on many different issues. Voters cannot vote for the position of one candidate on issue A, the position of another on issue B, and so on, as they do routinely when shopping for thousands of items in the marketplace. In a representative democracy, fine-tuning one's expression at the ballot box is impossible.
- An individual voter has virtually no chance of casting the decisive vote in an election. Even among the more than four thousand elections held each decade to fill the U.S. House of Representatives, a race decided by less than one hundred votes is newsworthy at the national level, and a recount is normally conducted. Moreover, the cost of an uninformed or mistaken vote that did make a difference would be spread among other citizens. This differs from the cost of a mistaken personal purchase, the full burden of which the buyer pays. People thus have little incentive to spend valuable time and effort learning about election issues beyond their narrow personal interest, monitoring politicians' overall performance, or even voting. Instead, voters are "rationally ignorant" on most issues. Thus, it makes sense for a politician to pay attention primarily to special interests on most issues, and to use the financial support

of special interests to campaign on "image" issues at election time.

- Because politicians do not sell their interests to their successors (the way the owners of companies, farms, and houses do), they have an incentive to provide current benefits while delaying costs into the future whenever possible. They have less incentive to invest today for the benefit of the future. Future voters cannot affect elections now, but will simply inherit what current voters leave to them—both debts and assets. In contrast, private assets can either be sold to benefit the owner directly or given by bequest. Only charitable instincts among voter-taxpayers (and perhaps the lobbying of special interest groups such as weapons system suppliers or owners of real estate that may go up in value if a project is built) will push for a costly project with benefits mainly in the future. Charitable instincts toward the future are present in the private sector, too (especially in private charities), and are reinforced by the fact that future PRODUCTIVITY and PROFITS are reflected in today's asset prices, including the stock price of a corporation.

One special interest that has gained at the expense of consumers and taxpayers is wool and mohair producers. During World War II, military planners discovered that U.S. wool producers could SUPPLY only half the wool the military wanted. Partly for this reason, and partly to give added income to wool growers, Congress passed the National Wool Act in 1954. Mohair, produced by Angora goats, had no military use but was included as an offshoot of the wool industry. Although wool was removed from the military's list of strategic materials in 1960, the program survived and continued to grow.

Under the Wool Act, growers were given subsidy checks to supplement what they received in the market for their wool. In 1990, the wool subsidy rate was 127 percent, so a farmer who got $1,000 for selling wool in the market also got a $1,270 check from the government. The subsidy rate for mohair was a much larger 387 percent. The subsidies were paid for by tariffs on imported wool. Thus, consumers were paying more for imported wool, which also drove up the market price paid for domestic wool, a close substitute. The economy operated less efficiently because less wool was imported, even though the imported wool would have cost less to produce and to buy. The subsidy program, together with the higher price caused by the wool tariff, meant that domestic land, labour, and capital resources were applied to the production of wool and mohair instead of to more valuable goods.

Nevertheless, political support for the program was strong, and Congress continued it. Thousands of very small checks were sent to small growers in every state. Almost half of the 1990 payments were less than $100. Many of those receiving them were willing to write letters and to vote for those who support the program. Nearly half of the money, though, went to the 1 percent of the growers who were the largest producers. The largest checks, nearly three hundred of them, averaged $98,000 and accounted for 27 percent of the program's 1990 cost. Recipients of these large checks could be counted on to contribute to organizing costs and to give campaign donations to members of congressional committees critical to the subsidy program. By contrast, because American taxpayers paid only a few dollars per family (Wool Act subsidies were $104 million in 1990), most taxpayers were unaware of the program and of how their elected representatives voted on it. Even though taxpayers were numerous and the Wool Act cost them a lot as a group, each taxpayer lost so little that none had an incentive to become organized or knowledgeable on the topic. Thus, the Wool Act, which harmed the interests of the great majority of voters, survived until 1996, the last year of a three-year phaseout of the program mandated by Congress in 1994. But organized interests are resilient. A subsidy program that effectively set minimum prices for both wool and mohair was part of the 2002 Farm Act and seems likely to persist for years to come.

Although such special interest groups are sometimes in line with more general interests of the citizens, there is little to confine their actions when they are not. For example, the general public wants national defence, and weapons contractors have an interest in providing the means to obtain defence. But the contractors and the government's military itself will push for far more elaborate, extensive, and costly means of defence than would a knowledgeable citizen with broader interests. Political activity is often seen as a way to solve problems not handled well by the private sector—sometimes including everything from pollution problems and national defence to the REDISTRIBUTION of income to the poor. Clearly, private-sector results in each of these areas are unsatisfactory to many, and there are massive, growing political programs aimed at each of these goals. But the problems just described reduce the ability of the political system to reach the sought-after goals—or to reach any goal in a least-cost manner.

Pollution control programs, from the Clean Air and Clean Water acts to the Superfund program, have received great political support. The cost to the economy of environmental programs is generally agreed to be more than $100 billion per year. Yet political manipulation of each program is widely recognized to have led to large imperfections in handling these problems. A classic case has been the political uses of the 1977 amendments to the Clean Air Act. Bruce Ackerman and William Hassler showed that by requiring the use of expensive scrubbers on coal-fired power plants, the amendments effectively protected eastern coal interests while harming both the health and the pocketbooks of millions of Americans. Robert Crandall of the Brookings Institution showed that eastern and midwestern manufacturing interests used the same amendments to stifle competition from new Sunbelt factories. Jonathan Adler has since documented a number of similar cases in which environmental policy initiatives have produced private benefits at public cost.

Bureaucratic performance in achieving the voters' goals is also a serious concern. Leaders of government agencies make strong, consistent attempts to gain larger budgets and more regulatory authority to further their programs. They often can achieve their ends with a "can't do" stance in place of the "can do" attitude needed for market success.

A perennial case in point is the "Washington Monument strategy" of the National Park Service. At budget time, the service frequently threatens to curtail visiting hours at its most popular attractions, such as the Washington Monument, if its budget request is not met, and it threatens to blame Congress and the budget process when tourists complain. Other agencies use this and similar tactics to seek more support for their narrow programs. In doing so, too often they impose enormous costs on society. It is hard to imagine a private firm—even a large, bureaucratic one—responding to hard budget times by curtailing its most popular product or service. The private firm would lose too much business to the competition.

Summary

Political behaviour in a democracy has both prospects and problems that differ from those of private, voluntary activity. Political action can force all citizens to comply with decisions made by their elected representatives. Because these political decisions are supposed to be for the benefit of all, the support of all is commanded. But because no single citizen's ballot is decisive, voters are not very effective at monitoring the intent and the EFFICIENCY of political action. Voter turnout is often low, and even very intelligent voters are notoriously uninformed on policy issues. Americans of voting age cannot, on average, even name their congressional representative. Such results are not as strange as they may sound when the impact of political rules on individual incentives is examined.

POLITICAL PSYCHOLOGY AND CHOICE

Political psychology is an interdisciplinary academic field dedicated to the relationship between psychology and political science, with a focus on the role of human thought, emotion, and behaviour in politics. It analyzes political science as related to entities such as voters, lawmakers, local and national governments and administrations, international organizations, political parties, and associations. While the grammar of "political psychology" tends to stress psychology as the central field, the discipline could also be accurately labelled "the psychology of politics," so as to more evenly recognize the interdisciplinary nature of the field.

Also not fully conveyed by the label is the wide scope of the disciplines from which political psychology draws, including anthropology, cognitive and personality psychology, sociology, psychiatry, international relations, and other more distant fields such as economics, philosophy, and the arts.

History of Political Psychology

The cross-fertilization between political science and psychology has risen to a modestly active level since its beginnings in the 1940s, though both fields have traditionally had a wider magnitude of collaboration with other disciplines, such as history with political science, and sociology with psychology.

PUBLIC CHOICE THEORY

In economics, public choice theory is the use of modern economic tools to study problems that are traditionally in the province of political science. From the perspective of political science, it may be seen as the subset of positive political theory which deals with subjects in which *material* interests are assumed to predominate. In particular, it studies the behaviour of politicians and government officials as mostly self-interested agents and their interactions in the social system either as such or under alternative constitutional rules. These can be represented a number of ways, including standard constrained utility maximization, game theory, or decision theory. Public choice analysis has roots in positive analysis ("what is") but is often used for normative purposes ("what ought to be"), to identify a problem or suggest how a system could be improved by changes in constitutional rules. Another related field is social choice theory.

Origins and Formation

The modern literature in Public Choice began with Duncan Black, who in 1948 identified the underlying concepts of what would become median voter theory. He also wrote *The Theory of Committees and Elections* in 1958. Gordon Tullock refers to him as the "father of public choice theory". James M. Buchanan and Gordon Tullock coauthored *The Calculus of Consent: Logical Foundations of Constitutional Democracy* (1962), considered one of the landmark works that founded the discipline of public choice theory. In particular (1962), the book is about the *political organization* of a free society. But its method, conceptual apparatus, and analytics "are derived, essentially, from the discipline that has as its subject the *economic* organization of such a society." The book focuses on positive-economic analysis as to the development of constitutional democracy but in an ethical context of consent. The consent takes the form of a compensation principle like Pareto efficiency for making a policy change and unanimity at least no opposition as a point of departure for social choice. Kenneth Arrow's *Social Choice and Individual Values* (1951) influenced formulation of the theory. Among other important works are Anthony Downs's *An Economic Theory of Democracy* (1957) and Mancur Olson's *The Logic of Collective Action* (1965).

Public choice theory is commonly associated with George Mason University, where Tullock and Buchanan are currently faculty members. Their early work took place at the University of Virginia and Virginia Polytechnic Institute and State University, hence identification of a Virginia school of political economy. Development of public choice theory accelerated with the formation of the Public Choice Society in the United States in 1965. The loci of the Society became its journal *Public Choice* and its annual meetings. The journal and meetings mainly attracted economists and political scientists. The economists brought their choice-based, model-building skill. The political scientists brought their broad knowledge of different political systems and detailed knowledge of institutions and political interaction. Scholars in related fields, such as philosophy, public administration, and sociology, also contributed.

In 1970 the median voter theory was accepted without question in public choice, but by 1980 it had been assaulted on so many fronts that it was almost abandoned. Works by Romer and Rosenthal (1979) and McKelvey (1976) showed that, when political issues are considered multidimensional rather than single dimensional, an agenda setter could start at any point in the issue space and, by strategically selecting issues, end up at any other point in the issue space, so that there is no unique and stable majority rule outcome.

During the same decade, the probabilistic voting theory started to replace the median voter theory, since it clearly showed how it was able to find Nash Equilibria also in multidimensional space. The theory was later completely formalized by Peter Coughlin..

Special Interests

Public choice theory is often used to explain how political decision-making results in outcomes that conflict with the preferences of the general public. For example, many advocacy group and pork barrel projects are not the desire of the overall democracy. However, it makes sense for politicians to support these projects. It may make them feel powerful and important. It can also benefit them financially by opening the door to future wealth as lobbyists. The project may be of interest to the politician's local constituency, increasing district votes or campaign contributions. The politician pays little or no cost to gain these benefits, as he is spending public money. Special-interest lobbyists are also behaving rationally. They can gain government favours worth millions or billions for relatively small investments. They face a risk of losing out to their competitors if they don't seek these favours. The taxpayer is also behaving rationally. The cost of defeating any one government give-away is very high, while the benefits to the individual taxpayer are very small. Each citizen pays only a few pennies or a few dollars for any given government favour, while the costs of ending that favour would be many times higher. Everyone involved has rational incentives to do exactly what they're doing, even though the desire of the general constituency is opposite. (It is notable that the political system considered here is very much that of the United States, with "pork" a main aim of individual legislators; in countries such as Britain with strong party systems the issues would differ somewhat.) Costs are diffused, while benefits are concentrated. The voices of vocal minorities with much to gain are heard over those of indifferent majorities with little to lose.

Decision Making Processes and the State

One way to organize the subject matter studied by Public Choice theorists is to begin with the foundations of the state itself. According to this procedure, the most fundamental subject is the origin of government. Although some work has been done on anarchy, autocracy, revolution, and even war, the bulk of the study in this area has concerned the fundamental problem of collectively choosing constitutional rules. This work assumes a group of individuals who aim to form a government. Then it focuses on the problem of hiring the agents required to carry out government functions agreed upon by the members.

The main questions are: (1) how to hire competent and trustworthy individuals to whom day-to-day decision-making can be delegated and (2) how to set up an effective system of oversight and sanctions for such individuals. To answer these questions it is necessary to assess the effects of creating different loci of power and decision-making within a government; to examine voting and the various means of selecting candidates and choosing winners in elections; to assess various behavioural rules that might be established to influence the behaviour of elected and appointed government officials; and to evaluate alternative constitutional and legal rights that could be reserved for citizens, especially rights relating to citizen oversight and the avoidance of harm due to the coercive power of government agents.

These are difficult assessments to make. In practice, most work in the field of Public Choice has dealt with more limited issues. Extensive work has been done on different voting systems and, more generally, on how to transform what voters are assumed to want into a coherent "collective preference". Of some interest has been the discovery that a general collective preference function cannot be derived from even seemingly mild conditions. This is often called Arrow's impossibility theorem. The theorem, an economic generalization of the voting paradox, suggests that voters have no reason to expect that, short of dictatorship, even the best rules for making collective decisions will lead to the kind of consistency attributed to individual choice.

Much work has been done on the loose connection between decisions that we can imagine being made by a full contingent of citizens with zero collective decision-making costs and those made by legislators representing different voting constituencies. Of special concern has been logrolling and other negotiations carried out by legislators in exercising their law-making powers. Important factors in such legislative decisions are political parties and pressure groups. Accordingly, Public Choicers have studied these institutions extensively. The study of how legislatures make decisions and how various constitutional rules can constrain legislative decisions is a major sub-field in Public Choice.

Bureaucracy

Another major sub-field is the study of bureaucracy. The usual model depicts the top bureaucrats as being chosen by the chief executive and legislature, depending on whether the democratic system is presidential and parliamentary. The typical image of a bureau chief is a person on a fixed salary who is concerned with pleasing those who appointed him. The latter have the power to hire and fire him more or less at will. The bulk of the bureaucrats, however, are civil servants whose jobs and pay are protected by a civil service system against major changes by their appointed bureau chiefs. This image is often compared with that of a business owner whose profit varies with the success of production and sales, who aims to maximize profit, and who can hire and fire employees at will.

Rent Seeking

A field that is closely related to public choice is "rent seeking." This field combines the study of a market economy with that of government. Thus, one might regard it as a "new political economy." Its basic thesis is that when both a market economy and government are present, government agents are a source of numerous special market privileges. Both the government agents and self-interested market participants seek these privileges in order to partake in the monopoly rent that they provide. When such privileges are granted, they reduce the efficiency of the economic system. In addition, the rent-seekers use resources that could otherwise be used to produce goods that are valued by consumers.

Rent seeking is broader than Public Choice in that it applies to autocracies as well as democracies and, therefore, is not directly concerned with collective decision-making. However, the obvious pressures it exerts on legislators, executives, bureaucrats, and even judges are factors that public choice theory must account for in its analysis collective decision-making rules and institutions. Moreover, the members of a collective who are planning a government would be wise to take prospective rent seeking into account.

Political Market Failure: Undemocratic Governments

Public Choice Theory has been developed largely in the context of democratic political systems of the variety that exist in Europe and North America. A pioneering work—and, perhaps, the only work to-date of its kind—seeking to analyze collective decision-making based on rules and institutions that characterize the Less Developed Countries was undertaken by Muzaffar Ali Isani at Georgetown University. It focuses largely on the assumptions of a generation of development economists who have articulated the role of the state or political action as an efficient alternative to 'economic' market failures. Isani has suggested that once we introduce 'political' market imperfections as generally found in these countries, we may be confronted with the possibility that far from correcting market failures, political action may actually prove to be a source of further distortions in the economy. He then goes on to develop an essentially economic paradigm of politics appropriate to many developing countries and which is consistent with the axioms of economic theory.

Perspective

Prior to the emergence of public choice theory, many economists tended to consider the state as an agent outside the scope of economic theory, whose actions depend on different considerations than those driving economic agents. (The many *other* economists who *did* place the state and its agents within such theory include Vilfredo Pareto.)

Public choice theory attempts to look at governments from the perspective of the bureaucrats and politicians who compose them, and makes the assumption that they act based on Budget-maximizing model in a self-interested way for the purpose of maximizing their own economic benefits (e.g. their personal wealth). The theory aims to apply economic analysis (usually decision theory and game theory) to the political decision-making process in order to reveal certain systematic trends towards inefficient government policies. There are also Austrian variants of public choice theory (suggested by Mises, Hayek, Kirzner, Lopez, and Boettke) in which it is assumed that bureaucrats and politicians may be benevolent but have access to limited information. The assumption that such benevolent political agents possess limited information for making decisions often results in conclusions similar to those generated separately by means of the rational self-interest assumptions. Randall Holcombe and Richard Wagner have also developed the notion of "Political Entrepreneurship".

Claims

One of the basic claims that results from public choice theory is that good government policies in a democracy are an underprovided public good, because of the rational ignorance of the voters. Each voter is faced with a tiny probability that his vote will change the result of the elections, while gathering the relevant information necessary for a well-informed voting decision requires substantial time and effort. Therefore, the rational decision for each voter is to be generally ignorant of politics and perhaps even abstain from voting. Rational choice theorists claim that this explains the gross ignorance of most citizens in modern democracies as well as low voter turnout. Rational abstention does, however, create the "Paradox of voting" whereby strict costs benefit analysis implies that nobody should vote.

Special Interests

While good government tends to be a pure public good for the mass of voters, there may be many advocacy groups that have strong incentives for lobbying the government to implement specific inefficient policies that would benefit them at the expense of the general public. For example, lobbying by the sugar manufacturers might result in an inefficient subsidy for the production of sugar, either direct or by protectionist measures. The costs of such inefficient policy are dispersed over all citizens, and therefore unnoticeable to each individual. On the other hand, the benefits are shared by a small special-interest group with a strong incentive to perpetuate the policy by further lobbying. The vast majority of voters will be unaware of the effort due to rational ignorance. Therefore, theorists expect that numerous special interests will be able to successfully lobby for various inefficient policies. In public choice theory, such scenarios of inefficient government policies are referred to as *government failure* — a term akin to *market failure* from earlier theoretical welfare economics.

"Expressive Interests" and Democratic Irrationality

Geoffrey Brennan and Loren Lomasky claim that democratic policy is biased to favour "expressive interests" and neglect practical and utilitarian considerations. Brennan and Lomasky differentiate between instrumental interests (any kind of practical benefit, both monetary and non-monetary) and expressive interests (forms of expression like applause). According to Brennan and Lomasky, the voting paradox can be resolved by differentiating between expressive and instrumental interests. While voters have virtually no instrumental incentive to vote, they do have an expressive interest in voting. Since voters vote for expressive reasons, politicians win by targeting the median expressive preferences. Bias in favour of expressive interests means that public policy often ignores important practical considerations. For example, there are instrumental costs to restricting international trade. Yet many people favour protectionism as an expression of nationalism, despite its economic costs.

This argument has led some public choice scholars to claim that politics is plagued by irrationality. In articles published in the Econ Journal Watch, economist Bryan Caplan contended that voter choices and government economic decisions are inherently irrational. Caplan's ideas are more fully developed in his book *The Myth of the Rational Voter* (Princeton University Press 2007). In opposition to the arguments put forward by economist Donald Wittman in his The Myth of Democratic Failure, Caplan claims that politics is biased in favour of irrational beliefs.

According to Caplan, democracy effectively subsidizes irrational beliefs. Anyone who derives utility from potentially irrational policies (such as protectionism) can receive private benefits while imposing the costs of such beliefs on the general public. Were people to bear the full costs of their "irrational beliefs", they would lobby for them optimally, taking into account both their instrumental consequences and their expressive appeal. Instead, democracy oversupplies policies based on irrational beliefs. Caplan defines rationality mainly in terms of mainstream price theory, pointing out that mainstream economists tend to oppose protectionism and government regulation more than the general population, and that more educated people are closer to economists on this score, even after controlling for confounding factors such as income, wealth or political affiliation. One criticism is that many economists do not share Caplan's views on the nature of public choice.

However, Caplan does have some data to support his position. Economists have, in fact, often been frustrated by public opposition to economic reasoning. As Sam Peltzman puts it "Economists know what steps would improve the efficiency of HSE [health, safety, and environmental] regulation, and they have not been bashful advocates of them. These steps include substituting markets in property rights, such as emission rights, for command and control.... The real problem lies deeper than any lack of reform proposals or failure to press them. It is our inability to understand their lack of political appeal "George Stigler's Contribution to the Economic Analysis of Regulation" 101 J. Pol. Econ. 818, 830 (October 1993).

Rent Seeking

Another major claim is that much of political activity is a form of rent seeking which wastes resources. Gordon Tullock, Jagdish Bhagwati, and Anne Osborn Krueger have argued that rent seeking has caused considerable waste. In a parallel line of research Fred McChesney claims that rent extraction causes considerable waste, especially in the developing world. As the term implies, rent extraction happens when officials use threats to extort payments from private parties.

Political Stance

From such results it is sometimes asserted that public choice theory has an anti-state tilt. But there is ideological diversity among public choice theorists. Mancur Olson for example was an advocate of a strong state and instead opposed political interest group lobbying. More generally, James Buchanan has suggested that public choice theory be interpreted as "politics without romance," a critical approach to a pervasive earlier notion of idealized politics set against market failure. As such it is more a correction of the earlier scientific record, almost requiring a certain pragmatism in comparing alternative politicized institutional structures.

Remedies for the Public Choice Problem

Many proposals have been advanced for reducing what is often seen as excessive or improper influence on public choices by those who invest most to influence them. From game theory we have the insight that a winning strategy in competitive games should have a random component so that the opponent can't anticipate one's moves. This is confirmed by the historical resort to having decisions made by officials selected at random, perhaps with a complex process of intermediate qualifying steps, called sortition. That is what is done in countries using a trial jury selected at random.

Applications and Wider Recognition

Public choice's application to government regulation was developed by George Stigler (1971) and Sam Peltzman (1976). William Niskanen is generally considered the founder of Public Choice literature on the bureaucracy. Several notable Public Choice scholars have been awarded the Nobel Prize in Economics, including James M. Buchanan (1986), George Stigler (1982), and Gary Becker (1992). In addition, Vernon Smith (2002) was President of Public Choice Society from 1988 to 1990.

Criticism

In their 1994 book *Pathologies of Rational Choice Theory*, political scientists Donald P. Green and Ian Shapiro argue that rational choice theory (of which public choice theory is a branch) has contributed less to the field than its popularity suggests. They write:

The discrepancy between the faith that practitioners place in rational choice theory and its failure to deliver empirically warrants closer inspection of rational choice theorizing as a scientific enterprise.

Linda McQuaig writes in *All You Can Eat*: The absurdity of public-choice theory is captured by Nobel Prize-winning economist Amartya Sen in the following little scenario: "Can you direct me to the railway station?" asks the stranger. "Certainly," says the local, pointing in the opposite direction, towards the post office, "and would you post this letter for me on your way?" "Certainly," says the stranger, resolving to open it to see if it contains anything worth stealing.

It should be noted that scenarios of this type contain an implicit assumption of zero probability of the two strangers ever interacting again. With a positive probability of future interactions and the propensity of humans to use tit-for-tat type strategies (someone harms or helps you, you return the favour in kind), the optimal totally self-interested decision may be to point to the train station. Furthermore, as David D. Friedman observes, the benefit of cheating the stranger *on one occasion* may not be worth the mental effort of conceiving a way to do so and weighing the odds of suffering the consequences.

Public Choice theorists have been criticized for failure to explain human actions motivated by non-rational or non-economic considerations. They respond, however, that the theory explains a broad variety of actions since humanitarian or even a madman's actions are also rational. This way, the argument goes, public choice allows to account for a much broader variety of actions than any other approach, and in the example above, Sen's rational actors may or may not act in a way he identified, since public choice approach does not mean the actors necessarily take advantage of one another; it only implies that the actions are 'rational'. Action to direct someone to a train station would thus be just as rational as the action to direct the stranger away for one's own reasons. Furthermore, only 'rationalism' helps to explain human motivation, whereas any other approaches such as humanitarian considerations or the willingness to get extra profit (which is in no way the same as 'rational action') would only explain a part of the developments and fails to present a comprehensive picture. Also, Bryan Caplan argues against rationality in politics, and Brennan and Lomasky account for expressive (non-economic) motives in politics.

Schram and Caterino (2006) contains a fundamental methodological criticism of public choice theory for promoting the view that the natural science model is the only appropriate methodology in social science and that political science should follow this model, with its emphasis on quantification and mathematization. Schram and Caterino argue instead for methodological pluralism.

ELECTIONS IN INDIA

Since independence, elections in India have evolved a long way, but all along elections have been a significant cultural aspect of independent India. In 2004, Indian elections covered an electorate larger than 670 million people—over twice that of the next largest, the European Parliament elections—and declared expenditure has trebled since 1989 to almost $300 million, using more than 1 million electronic voting machines. In 2009, the elections covered an even larger electorate of 714 million (larger than both EU and US elections combined).

The size of the huge electorate mandates that elections be conducted in a number of phases (there were four phases in 2004 General Elections and five phases in 2009). It involves a number of step-by-step processes from announcement of election dates by the Election Commission of India, which brings into force the 'model code of conduct' for the political parties, to the announcement of results and submission of the list of successful candidates to the executive head of the state or the centre. The submission of results marks the end of the election process, thereby paving way for the formation of the new government.

LIST OF NATIONAL ELECTIONS

Lok Sabha

Lok Sabha Elections, elect the Prime Minister of India, and are democratic elections that take place every 5 years, but the election could occur earlier, if the President of India, dissolves the parliament and calls for new elections.

Rajya Sabha

Rajya Sabha members are indirectly elected, and are almost entirely elected by Members of Assembly of individual states, while 12 member are nominated by the President of India, usually with the advice and consent from the Prime Minister of India. More info on Rajya Sabha can be found at

Presidential Election

The President of India, is indirectly elected, to a 5 year term, and the electoral college, is used, where the Member of Parliament of both the Lok Sabha and the Rajya Sabha, and the Members of Legislative Assemblies from all states and territories of India cast their vote.

INDIAN ELECTORAL SYSTEM

The Parliament of India comprises the head of country — the president — and the two Houses which are the legislature.

The President of India is elected for a five-year term by an electoral college consisting of members of federal and state legislatures. Parliament of India has two chambers. The House of the People (*Lok Sabha*) has 545 members, 543 members elected for a five-year term in single-seat constituencies and two members appointed to represent the Anglo-Indian community. (as envisaged by the Constitution of India, as of now the members of Lok Sabha are 545, out of which 543 are elected for 5-year term and 2 members represent the Anglo-Indian community). The two unelected members are a relic from the past. The 550 members are elected under the plurality ('first past the post') electoral system.

Council of States (*Rajya Sabha*) has 245 members, 233 members elected for a six-year term, with one-third retiring every two years. The members are elected by legislators of the state and union (federal) territories. The elected members are chosen under the system of proportional representation by means of the Single Transferable Vote. The twelve nominated members are usually an eclectic mix of eminent artists (including actors), scientists, jurists, sportspersons, businessmen and journalists and common people.

History of Elections in India

India got its first Lok Sabha in April 1952, after the first General Elections were successfully concluded and the Indian National Congress (INC) came into power with 245 seats in its kitty. Here is a brief history of Lok Sabha tenures...

Lok Sabha is composed of representatives of the people chosen by direct election on the basis of the adult suffrage. The maximum strength of the House envisaged by the Constitution is 552, which is made up by election of up to 530 members to represent the States, up to 20 members to represent the Union Territories and not more than two members of the Anglo-Indian Community to be nominated by the President, if, in his/her opinion, that community is not adequately represented in the House.

HISTORY OF POLITICAL PARTIES

The dominance of the Indian National Congress was broken for the first time in 1977, with the defeat of the party led by

Indira Gandhi, by an unlikely coalition of all the major other parties, which protested against the imposition of a controversial Emergency from 1975–1977. A similar coalition, led by VP Singh was swept to power in 1989 in the wake of major allegations of corruption by the incumbent Prime Minister, Rajiv Gandhi. It, too, lost its steam in 1990.

In 1992, the heretofore one-party-dominant politics in India gave way to a coalition system wherein no single party can expect to achieve a majority in the Parliament to form a government, but rather has to depend on a process of coalition building with other parties to form a block and claim a majority to be invited to form the government. This has been a consequence of strong regional parties which ride on the back of regional aspirations. While parties like the TDP and the AIADMK had traditionally been strong regional contenders, the 1990s saw the emergence of other regional players such as the Lok Dal, Samajwadi Party, Bahujan Samaj Party and Janata Dal. These parties are traditionally based on regional aspirations, e.g. Telengana Rastra Samiti or strongly influenced by caste considerations, e.g. Bahujan Samaj Party which claims to represent the Dalits.

Presently, the United Progressive Alliance led by the Congress Party is in power, while the National Democratic Alliance forms the opposition. Manmohan Singh was re-elected.

The Election Commission

Elections in India are conducted by the Election Commission of India, the authority created under the Constitution. It is a well established convention that once the election process commences; no courts intervene until the results are declared by the election commission. During the elections, vast powers are assigned to the election commission to the extent that it can function as a civil court, if needed

Electoral Process

Electoral Process in India takes at least a month for state assembly elections with the duration increasing further for the General Elections. Publishing of electoral rolls is a key process that happens before the elections and is vital for the conduct of elections in India. The Indian Constitution sets the eligibility of an individual for voting. Any person who is a citizen of India and above 18 years of age is eligible to enroll as a voter in the electoral rolls. It is the responsibility of the eligible voters to enroll their names. Normally, voter registrations are allowed latest one week prior to the last date for nomination of candidates.

Pre Elections

At first before the elections the dates of nomination, polling and counting takes place. The model code of conduct comes in force from the day the dates are announced.. No party is allowed to use the government resources for campaigning. The code of conduct stipulates that campaigning be stopped 48 hours prior to polling day. For Indian states a pre-election is a must

Voting Day

Campaigning ends the day before the voting day. Government schools and colleges are chosen as polling stations. The Collector of each district is in charge of polling. Government employees are employed to many of the polling stations. Electronic Voting Machines (EVMs) are being increasingly used instead of ballot boxes to prevent election fraud via booth capturing, which is heavily prevalent in certain parts of India. An indelible ink manufactured by the Mysore Paints and Varnish Limited is applied usually on the left index finger of the voter as an indicator that the voter has cast his vote. This practice has been followed since the 1962 general elections to prevent bogus voting.

Post Elections

After the election day, the EVMs are stored in a strong room under heavy security. After the different phases of the elections are complete, a day is set to count the votes. The votes are tallied typically, the verdict is known within hours. The candidate who has mustered the most votes is declared the winner of the constituency. The party or coalition that has won the most seats is invited by the President to form the new government. The coalition or party must prove its majority in the floor of the house (Lok Sabha) in a vote of confidence by obtaining a simple majority (minimum 50%) of the votes in the house.

Voter Registration

For few cities in India, the voter registration forms can be generated online and submitted to the nearest electoral office. Some of the socially relevant websites like is good place to gather information on voter registration.

Absentee Voting

As of now, India does not have an absentee ballot system. Section 19 of The Representation of the People Act (RPA)-1950 allows a person to register to vote if he or she is above 18 years of age and is an 'ordinary resident' of the residing constituency i.e. living at the current address for 6 months or longer. Section 20 of the above Act disqualifies a non-resident Indian (NRI) from getting his/her name registered in the electoral rolls. Consequently, it also prevents a NRI from casting his/her vote in elections to the Parliament and to the State Legislatures.

The Representation of the People (Amendment) 2006 Bill was introduced in the Parliament by Shri Hanraj Bharadwaj, Minister of Law and Justice during February 2006 with an objective to amend Section 20 of the RPA-1950 to enable NRIs to vote. Despite the report submitted by the Parliamentary Standing Committee two years ago, the Government has so far failed to act on the recommendations. The Bill was reintroduced in the 2008 budget session of the Parliament to the Lok Sabha. But no action taken once again.

Several civic society organizations have urged the government to amend the RPA act to allow NRI's and people on the move to cast their vote through absentee ballot system.

9

Public Policy

Public policy can be generally defined as the course of action or inaction taken by governmental entities (the decisions of government) with regard to a particular issue or set of issues. Other scholars define it as a system of "courses of action, regulatory measures, laws, and funding priorities concerning a given topic promulgated by a governmental entity or its representatives." Public policy is commonly embodied "in constitutions, legislative acts, and judicial decisions." In the United States, this concept refers not only to the end result of policies, but more broadly to the decision-making and analysis of governmental decisions. Public policy is also considered an academic discipline, as it is studied by professors and students at public policy schools of major universities throughout the country. The American (United States of America) professional association of public policy practitioners, researchers, scholars, and students is the Association for Public Policy Analysis and Management.

GOVERNMENT ACTIONS

Shaping public policy is a complex and multifaceted process that involves the interplay of numerous individuals and interest groups competing and collaborating to influence policymakers to act in a particular way. These individuals and groups use a variety of tactics and tools to advance their aims, including advocating their positions publicly, attempting to educate supporters and opponents, and mobilizing allies on a particular issue. In this context, advocacy can be defined as attempting to influence public policy through education, lobbying, or political pressure. Advocacy groups "often attempt to educate the general public as well as public policy makers about the nature of problems, what legislation is needed to address problems, and the funding required to provide services or conduct research. Although advocacy is viewed as unseemly by some in the professional and research community, it is clear that public policy priorities are influenced by advocacy. Sound research data can be used to educate the public as well as policy makers, thereby improving the public policy process."

As an Academic Discipline

As an academic discipline, public policy brings in elements of many social science fields and concepts, including economics, sociology, political economy, program evaluation, policy analysis, and public management, all as applied to problems of governmental administration, management, and operations. At the same time, the study of public policy is distinct from political science or economics, in its focus on the application of theory to practice. While the majority of public policy degrees are master's and doctoral degrees, several universities also offer undergraduate education in public policy.

Different policy schools tackle policy analysis differently. The Harris School of Public Policy Studies at the University of Chicago has a more quantitative and economics approach to policy, the Heinz College at Carnegie Mellon uses computational and empirical methods, while the John F. Kennedy School of Government at Harvard University has a more political science and leadership based approach. The Indiana University School of Public and Environmental Affairs provides traditional public policy training with multidisciplinary concentrations available in the environmental sciences and non-profit management.

PUBLIC POLICY DOCTRINE (CONFLICT OF LAWS)

Public policy is the body of principles that underpin the operation of legal systems in each state. This addresses the social, moral and economic values that tie a society together: values that vary in different cultures and change over time. Law regulates behaviour either to reinforce existing social expectations or to encourage constructive change, and laws are most likely to be effective when they are consistent with the most generally accepted socialite norms and reflect the collective morality of the society. In performing this function, Cappalli has suggested that the critical values of any legal system include impartiality, neutrality, certainty, equality, openness, flexibility, and growth. This assumes that a state's courts function as *dispute resolution systems*, which avoid the violence that often otherwise accompanies private resolution of disputes. That is, citizens have to be encouraged to use the court system to resolve their disputes. The more certain and predictable the outcome of a court action, the less incentive there is to go to court where a loss is probable. But certainty must be subject to the needs of individual justice, hence the development of equity. A judge should always consider the underlying policies to determine whether a rule should be applied to a specific factual dispute. If laws are applied too strictly and mechanically, the law cannot keep pace with social innovation. Similarly, if there is an entirely new situation, a return to the policies forming the basic assumptions underpinning potentially relevant rules of law, identifies the best guidelines for resolving the immediate dispute. Over time, these policies evolve, becoming more clearly defined and more deeply embedded in the legal system.

FUNDAMENTAL PRINCIPLES

The fundamental policy in the operation of a legal system is that *ignorantia juris non excused* (*ignorance of the law is no excuse*). It would completely undermine the enforcement of any law if the person potentially at fault was able to raise as a successful defence that he or she had not been aware of the particular law. For this reason, all the main legislatures publish their laws freely whether in hard copy or on the Internet, while others offer them for sale to the public at affordable prices. Because everyone is entitled to access the laws as they affect their personal lives, all adults are assumed responsible enough to research the law before they act. If they fail to do so, they can hardly complain if their acts prove unlawful, no matter how transiently they may be within the jurisdiction. The only exception to this rule excuses those of reduced capacity, whether as infants or through mental illness (for example, see the principle of *doli incapax* which raises an irrebuttable presumption in criminal law that an infant is incapable of committing a crime).

Underpinning most social, moral and religious systems is the policy of *sanctity of life* (also culture of life). In criminal law, for example, duress is not allowed as a defence to murder because no threat is supposed to overcome a person's moral aversion to taking the life of another, Lord Jauncy in *R v Gotts* (1992) 2 AC 412 stated:

The reason why duress has for so long been stated not to be available as a defence to a murder charge is that the law regards the sanctity of human life and the protection thereof as of paramount importance... I can therefore see no justification in logic, morality or law in affording to an attempted murderer the defence which is withheld from a murderer.

In refusal of treatment and death with dignity/right to die situations, commission and omission by doctors and hospital authorities resulting in the death of patients has become of increasing significance as societies debate whether the duty to preserve life outweighs the right of the autonomous patient to choose death. More contentious are those situations in which the patient is unable to make the choice personally, e.g. because in a persistent vegetative state or *en ventre sa mere*, i.e. a child in gestation.

Similarly, in many branches of law, the Doctrine of Evasion prevents persons, both natural and artificial, from evading the application of obligations and liabilities already attaching to them. This represents a practical application of the policy that, as an outcome of the social contract, all persons owing allegiance to a state should be entitled to assume that everyone will receive fair and equal treatment before the law, i.e. there will be no favouritism or preferential treatment to any person by virtue of their rank or status within society. As such, this is an exception to the policy in the Law of Contract which usually allows the parties autonomy to enter into whatever agreement they want and which might otherwise be taken to permit the parties to exclude the normal operation of the law as between themselves.

There are policies specific to all the main branches of law. Hence, one of the policies in family law is *parens patriae*, i.e. that the state is the default parent for all those children within its jurisdiction and that, if it is necessary to protect the interests of the child, the state will usurp the rights of the natural parents and assert its own rights as every child's legal guardian. Within the EU, the right of the child to be heard in any proceedings is a fundamental right provided in Article 24 Charter of Fundamental Rights of the European Union. The views of the child shall be considered on matters which concern him in accordance with his age and maturity. It also provides that the child's best interest shall be the primary consideration in all actions relating to children, whether taken by public authorities or private institutions.

A policy which overlaps between family law and contract law is *favour matrimonii* which requires that any marriage entered into with a genuine commitment should be held valid unless there is some good reason to the contrary, matching contract law, where the preference is always to give effect to the genuine expectation of the parties.

Discussion

The policies adopted by states have come into being for several reasons. Some are aspects of the concept of sovereignty and reflect the essence of territoriality. Thus, public laws which either define the constitution of the state or regulate its powers can only apply within the boundaries agreed as a part of the process of *de jure* recognition of statehood by the international community. Other policies are aspects of the social contract, and they define and regulate the relationship between a state and those citizens who owe it allegiance. To that extent, these policies interact with (and sometimes overlap) civil rights and human rights. A number of these rights are defined at a supranational level and it will necessary for states to consider the extent to which international principles of law are to be allowed to influence the operation of law within their territories. Independently of the work of the international community to produce harmonised principles, the courts in one state may sometimes be faced with lawsuits which either seek to evade the operation of foreign laws through forum shopping or seek the enforcement of "foreign" laws. This is becoming increasingly common as people now move with reasonable freedom between states and international trade routinely services markets in different states. Such lawsuits will not be troublesome if the "foreign" law is the same as the forum law. But serious difficulties will arise if the application of the "foreign" law would produce a different result. These conflicts are resolved under the systems of law known as Conflict of Laws.

In Conflict cases, no court will apply a "foreign" law if the result of its application would be contrary to public policy. This is problematic because excluding the application of foreign laws would defeat the purpose of Conflict of Laws by giving automatic preference to the forum court's domestic law. Thus, for the most part, courts are slower to invoke public policy in cases involving a foreign element than when a domestic legal issue is involved. That said, in those countries that have adopted Treaty and Convention obligations involving human rights, (e.g. in the UK the Human Rights Act 1998 is now in operation) broader concepts of public policy may now apply. Thus, courts may have to consider the "justice" implicit in a law that allows a husband to divorce his wife, but not *vice versa*, as an aspect of sexual discrimination. Similarly, it would be possible to question the propriety of polygamous marriages, the *talaq* system of divorce which is available in some Islamic states, and Jewish divorce known as the *get*, but it is likely that the courts would be cautious to avoid any implication that they were discriminating against religions. Equally difficult are the Family Laws which regulate incestuous relationships and capacity. For example, it is probable that one state should not be too quick to condemn another because it allows a marriage between an uncle and a niece, or allows a marriage with a girl of 13 (e.g. as in Northern Nigeria), particularly if the parties are not proposing residence in the forum state.

OVERVIEW OF PUBLIC POLICY: THE PUBLIC AND ITS POLICIES

Public policy is an attempt by the government to address a public issue. The government, whether it is city, state, or federal, develops public policy in terms of laws, regulations, decisions, and actions. There are three parts to public policy-making: problems, players, and the policy.

The *problem* is the issue that needs to be addressed. The *player* is the individual or group that is influential in forming a plan to address the problem in question. *Policy* is the finalized course of action decided upon by the government. In most cases, policies are widely open to interpretation by non-governmental players, including those in the private sector. Public policy is also made by leaders of religious and cultural institutions.

Academics continue to contemplate the definition of public policy, since there is currently no consensus. The study of public policy began in 1922, when Charles Merriam, a political scientist, sought to build a link between political theory and its application to reality. Numerous issues are addressed by public policy, including crime, education, foreign policy, health, and social welfare.

In 1993, due to ineffective healthcare policies, the Clinton administration sought to implement a policy that would bring about a national healthcare system. As part of the policies being considered, the US federal government would protect the healthcare consumer's rights, consumers would be able to form alliances to obtain better healthcare prices, and caregivers would be required to provide fair healthcare packages. Players involved in the policy-making process included lobbying groups and politicians. While some changes were made to healthcare provisions by legislators, the policies advocated by the Clinton administration were not put into effect as result of political differences.

The rational model for the public policy-making process can be divided into three parts: agenda-setting, option-formulation, and implementation. Within the agenda-setting stage, the agencies and government officials meet to discuss the problem at hand. In the second stage, option-formulation, alternative solutions are considered and final decisions are made regarding the best policy. Consequently, the decided policy is implemented in the final stage. Implied within this model is the fact that the needs of the society are a priority for the players involved in the policy-making process. Also, it is believed that the government will follow through on all decisions made by the final policy.

Unfortunately, those who frame the issue to be addressed by policy often exert an enormous amount of influence over the entire process through their personalities, personal interests, political affiliations, and so on. The bias is extenuated by the players involved. The final outcome of the process, as well as its implementation, is therefore not as effective as that which could result from a purely rational process. Overall, however, public policy continues to be vital in addressing social concerns.

SOCIAL AND CULTURAL FACTORS: CONSTRAINING AND ENABLING

Changing Demographics

The postwar baby boomers are rapidly approaching the official age for retirement and yet are predicted to live even longer. But already it is estimated that 3m people between the age of 50 and 65 have been forced into premature retirement. All this generation will need pensions and medical services for many more years than the previous generations. Whilst the UK may well be less impacted than other western economies, the situation is already ringing alarm bells within Government and with large pension fund managers.

The birth rate continues to decline as many women make their career a higher priority.

- Government will shift retirement and medical risks to private sector who may come under pressure to accept all risks at normal rates.
- A shift to defined contribution pension schemes will highlight the need for companies to generate good returns on people's investments as well as to reduce administrative costs.
- Increase in market size will attract new players. Retailers with their strong brands are increasingly aggressive. Foreign companies are making investments in the UK. US companies have much lower costs.
- To supply increasing demand for private retirement, medical, accident, sickness and unemployment cover.
- Women will increasingly make their own insurance and investment provisions.

Individualism

The 80's and 90's have seen an increasing demand for individualism. Many factors may account for this: the majority have their basic needs met; there is an over supply of goods; lifestyles are more varied; and people are better educated and more informed.

- Consumers are becoming cynical with mass market advertising which promises much but often fails to deliver.
- A move away from standard products and services with a potential increase in development and operational costs for providers.
- To provide flexible products that can be tailored to people's individual needs, behaviours and personalities.

Changing Lifestyles

The increasing divorce rate, women being more independent and/or marrying later, an increase in the single elderly, are all creating more smaller households, though not necessarily a need for smaller houses. This is leading to higher demand for new houses (compounded by a large but aging stock of Victorian houses) which will no doubt fuel house prices.

- This situation may fuel another boom and bust with another future spell of consumer reaction in the light of negative equity and repossessions.
- Larger volumes of households to insure.
- Mortgage lending increases both in the volume and size of mortgages.

The changing employment patterns means many more people are working for themselves or working on a contract basis. People's income will fluctuate more widely.

- There is a possibility of a large segment of the population becoming relatively poor and unable to meet the cost of adequate risk protection. Thus the market could contract.
- Increasing need for private pensions and insurance risks.
- Increasing need for insurance for small business (contents, business interruption, professional indemnity, financial advise, etc.).

Lifestyles are becoming less predictable, more fragmented, and we have more active but riskier lives. Divorce, re-marriages, redundancy, 24 hour/7 day working, zero hour or low hour work contracts, work hard-play hard lifestyles, are just some of the drivers.

- Many people are so confused about pensions and the other more complex investment products that they are putting off making any decision or are buying inappropriate products.
- Many standard financial products are ill-suited to fluctuating incomes and circumstances but they continue to be sold. There is a likely backlash when consumers suspend or terminate such products and then realise the consequences.
- Need for more flexible products that can adapt to peoples circumstances.
- There is an increasing need for personalised financial planning with regular reviews (e.g. Clerical Medical with Provision, and Allied Dunbar).
- Need for insurance linked to leisure activities (e.g. accident, holiday, sport insurances).

Polarisation

Predictions for the coming years suggests a society that continues to be polarised. Will Hutton suggests a 40-30-30 society: 40% in permanent and generally well paid work; 30% on part-time or contract work, or self-employed; and 30% unemployed or living of basic state benefits. People may not be permanently within any category but could drift from one to another.

- Large segments of society may be unable to afford adequate protection, thus diminishing the market size.
- Social unrest may increase insurance claims.
- Premiums may rise or have tight exclusion clauses, thus again diminishing demand.
- This scenario is likely to give rise to ever more complex financial requirements, many of which will be of a short term nature.

POLITICAL MOVEMENT

A political movement is a social movement in the area of politics. A political movement may be organized around a single issue or set of issues, or around a set of shared concerns of a social group. In contrast with a political party, a political movement is not organized to elect members of the movement to government office; instead, a political movement aims to convince citizens and/or government officers to take action on the issues and concerns which are the focus of the movement.

Political movements are an expression of the struggle of a social group for the political space and benefits. The political movements are presented by non-state groups who are led by their elite. In fact the process of the construction of identities and reinforcing them is also a part of political movements.

A political movement may be local, regional, national, or international in scope. Some have aimed to change government policy, such as the anti-war movement, the Ecology movement, and the Anti-globalization movement. Many have aimed to establish or broaden the rights of subordinate groups, such as abolitionism, the women's suffrage movement, the Civil rights movement, feminism, men's rights movement, gay rights movement, the Disability rights movement, or the inclusive human rights movement. Some have represented class interests, such as the Labour movement, Socialism, and Communism, others have expressed national aspirations, such as anticolonialist movements, Ratana, Zionism, and Sinn Fein. Political movements can also involve struggles to decentralize or centralize state control, as in Anarchism, Fascism, and Nazism.

Some activists and scholars claim that along with globalization a new type of political movement emerges that is not merely international or single-issue focused, but is characterized with global approach. This has been termed a global citizens movement and debate continues over whether it has manifested or is still a latent potential.

Identification of Supporters

A difficulty for scholarship of movements is that for most of them, neither insiders to a movement nor outsiders apply consistent labels or even descriptive phrases. Unless there is a single leader who does that, or a formal system of membership agreements, activists will typically use diverse labels and descriptive phrases that require scholars to discern when they are referring to the same or similar ideas, declare similar goals, adopt similar programs of action, and use similar methods.

There can be great differences in the way that is done, to recognize who is and who is not a member or an allied group:

- Insiders: Often exaggerate the level of support by considering people supporters whose level of activity or support is weak, but also reject those that outsiders might consider supporters because they discredit the cause, or are even seen as adversaries.
- Outsiders: Those not supporters who may tend to either underestimate or overestimate the level or support or activity of elements of a movement, by including or excluding those that insiders would exclude or include.

It is often outsiders rather than insiders that apply the identifying labels for a movement, which the insiders then may or may not adopt and use to self-identify. For example, the label for the levellers political movement in 17th century England was applied to them by their antagonists, as a term of disparagement. Yet admirers of the movement and its aims later came to use the term, and it is the term by which they are known to history.

Caution must always be exercised in any discussion of amorphous phenomena such as movements to distinguish between the views of insiders and outsiders, supporters and antagonists, each of whom may have their own purposes and agendas in characterization or mischaracterization of it.

POLICY

A policy is typically described as a principle or rule to guide decisions and achieve rational outcome(s). The term is not normally used to denote what is actually done, this is normally referred to as either procedure or protocol. Where as a policy will contain the 'what' and the 'why', procedures or protocols contain the 'what', the 'how', the 'where', and the 'when'. Policies are generally adopted by the Board of or senior governance body within an organisation where as procedures or protocols would be developed and adopted by senior executive officers.

The term may apply to government, private sector organizations and groups, and individuals. Presidential executive orders, corporate privacy policies, and parliamentary rules of order are all examples of policy. Policy differs from rules or law. While law can compel or prohibit behaviours (e.g.

a law requiring the payment of taxes on income), policy merely guides actions toward those that are most likely to achieve a desired outcome.

Policy or policy study may also refer to the process of making important organizational decisions, including the identification of different alternatives such as programs or spending priorities, and choosing among them on the basis of the impact they will have. Policies can be understood as political, management, financial, and administrative mechanisms arranged to reach explicit goals.

IMPACT

Intended Effects

The intended effects of a policy vary widely according to the organization and the context in which they are made. Broadly, policies are typically instituted to avoid some negative effect that has been noticed in the organization, or to seek some positive benefit.

Corporate purchasing policies provide an example of how organizations attempt to avoid negative effects. Many large companies have policies that all purchases above a certain value must be performed through a purchasing process. By requiring this standard purchasing process through policy, the organization can limit waste and standardize the way purchasing is done.

The State of California provides an example of benefit-seeking policy. In recent years, the numbers of hybrid cars in California has increased dramatically, in part because of policy changes in Federal law that provided USD $1,500 in tax credits (since phased out) as well as the use of high-occupancy vehicle lanes to hybrid owners (no longer available for new hybrid vehicles). In this case, the organization (state and/or federal government) created an effect (increased ownership and use of hybrid vehicles) through policy (tax breaks, highway lanes).

Unintended Effects

Policies frequently have side effects or unintended consequences. Because the environments that policies seek to influence or manipulate are typically complex adaptive systems (e.g. governments, societies, large companies), making a policy change can have counterintuitive results.

For example, a government may make a policy decision to raise taxes, in hopes of increasing overall tax revenue. Depending on the size of the tax increase, this may have the overall effect of reducing tax revenue by causing capital flight or by creating a rate so high that citizens are deterred from earning the money that is taxed.

The policy formulation process typically includes an attempt to assess as many areas of potential policy impact as possible, to lessen the chances that a given policy will have unexpected or unintended consequences. Because of the nature of some complex adaptive systems such as societies and governments, it may not be possible to assess all possible impacts of a given policy.

POLICY CYCLE

In political science the policy cycle is a tool used for the analyzing of the development of a policy item. It can also be referred to as a "stagist approach". One standardized version includes the following stages:

1. Agenda setting (Problem identification)
2. Policy Formulation
3. Adoption
4. Implementation
5. Evaluation.

An eight step policy cycle is developed in detail in *The Australian Policy Handbook* by Peter Bridgman and Glyn Davis: (now with Catherine Althaus in its 4th edition)

1. Issue identification
2. Policy analysis
3. Policy instrument development
4. Consultation (which permeates the entire process)
5. Coordination
6. Decision
7. Implementation
8. Evaluation.

The Althaus, Bridgman & Davis model is heuristic and iterative. It is intentionally normative and not meant to be diagnostic or predictive. Policy cycles are typically characterized as adopting a classical approach. Accordingly some postmodern academics challenge cyclical models as unresponsive and unrealistic, preferring systemic and more complex models.

Content

Policies are typically promulgated through official written documents. Policy documents often come with the endorsement or signature of the executive powers within an organization to legitimize the policy and demonstrate that it is considered in force. Such documents often have standard formats that are particular to the organization issuing the policy. While such formats differ in form, policy documents usually contain certain standard components including:

- A purpose statement, outlining why the organization is issuing the policy, and what its desired effect or outcome of the policy should be.
- An applicability and scope statement, describing who the policy affects and which actions are impacted by the policy. The applicability and scope may expressly exclude certain people, organizations, or actions from the policy requirements. Applicability and scope is used to focus the policy on only the desired targets, and avoid unintended consequences where possible.
- An effective date which indicates when the policy comes into force. Retroactive policies are rare, but can be found.
- A responsibilities section, indicating which parties and organizations are responsible for carrying out individual policy statements. Many policies may require the establishment of some ongoing function or action. For example, a purchasing policy might specify that a purchasing office be created to process purchase requests, and that this office would be responsible for ongoing actions. Responsibilities often include identification of any relevant oversight and/or governance structures.
- Policy statements indicating the specific regulations, requirements, or modifications to organizational

behaviour that the policy is creating. Policy statements are extremely diverse depending on the organization and intent, and may take almost any form.

Some policies may contain additional sections, including:

- Background, indicating any reasons, history, and intent that led to the creation of the policy, which may be listed as motivating factors. This information is often quite valuable when policies must be evaluated or used in ambiguous situations, just as the intent of a law can be useful to a court when deciding a case that involves that law.
- Definitions, providing clear and unambiguous definitions for terms and concepts found in the policy document.

Typologies

Policy addresses the intent of the organization, whether government, business, professional, or voluntary. Policy is intended to affect the 'real' world, by guiding the decisions that are made. Whether they are formally written or not, most organizations have identified policies. Policies may be classified in many different ways. The following is a sample of several different types of policies broken down by their effect on members of the organization.

Distributive Policies

Distributive policies extend goods and services to members of an organization, as well as distributing the costs of the goods/services amongst the members of the organization. Examples include government policies that impact spending for welfare, public education, highways, and public safety, or a professional organization's.

Regulatory Policies

Regulatory policies, or mandates, limit the discretion of individuals and agencies, or otherwise compel certain types of behaviour. These policies are generally thought to be best applied when good behaviour can be easily defined and bad behaviour can be easily regulated and punished through fines or sanctions. An example of a fairly successful public regulatory policy is that of a speed limit.

Constituent Policies

Constituent policies create executive power entities, or deal with laws. Constituent policies also deal with Fiscal Policy in some circumstances.

Miscellaneous Policies

Policies are dynamic; they are not just static lists of goals or laws. Policy blueprints have to be implemented, often with unexpected results. Social policies are what happens 'on the ground' when they are implemented, as well as what happens at the decision making or legislative stage.

When the term policy is used, it may also refer to:

- Official government policy (legislation or guidelines that govern how laws should be put into operation)
- Broad ideas and goals in political manifestos and pamphlets
- A company or organization's policy on a particular topic. For example, the equal opportunity policy of a company shows that the company aims to treat all its staff equally.

The actions the organization actually takes may often vary significantly from stated policy. This difference is sometimes caused by political compromise over policy, while in other situations it is caused by lack of policy implementation and enforcement. Implementing policy may have unexpected results, stemming from a policy whose reach extends further than the problem it was originally crafted to address. Additionally, unpredictable results may arise from selective or idiosyncratic enforcement of policy.

Types of policy analysis include:

- Causal (resp. non-causal)
- Deterministic (resp. stochastic, randomized and sometimes non-deterministic)
- Index
- Memoryless (e.g. non-stationary)
- Opportunistic (resp. non-opportunistic)
- Stationary (resp. non-stationary).

These qualifiers can be combined, so for example you could have a stationary-memoryless-index policy.

Types

- Communications and Information Policy
- Defence policy
- Domestic policy
- Economic policy
- Education policy
- Energy policy
- Environmental Policy
- Foreign policy
- Health policy
- Housing policy
- Human resource policies
- Information policy
- Macroeconomic policy
- Monetary policy
- National defence policy
- Population policy
- Privacy policy
- Public policy in law
- Social policy
- Transportation policy
- Urban policy
- Water policy.

Other Uses of the Term

- In enterprise architecture for systems design, policy appliances are technical control and logging mechanisms to enforce or reconcile policy (systems use) rules and to ensure accountability in information systems.
- In insurance, policies are contracts between insurer and insured used to indemnify (protect) against potential loss from specified perils. While these documents are referred to as policies, they are in actuality a form of contract-see insurance contract.
- In gambling, policy is a form of an unsanctioned lottery, where players purport to purchase *insurance* against a

chosen number being picked by a legitimate lottery. Or can refer to an ordinary Numbers game

- In artificial intelligence planning and *reinforcement learning*, a policy prescribes a non-empty deliberation (sequence of actions) given a non-empty sequence of states.
- In debate, the term "policy" is slang for policy or cross-examination debate.

PROCESS OF POLICY-MAKING IN INDIA SINCE INDEPENDENCE

Policy process in India is done at many levels. The goals of the policy are determined by the vision of the leader of the political party in the ruling. Then these policies are detailed at the secretariat and passed down the ladder for the implementation. By the trickle down effect, these policies are reached to the grass root level. Following are the broad stages of the policy determination.

Policy Structure

Parliament is the supreme legislative body of a country. Our Parliament comprises of the President and the two Houses, Lok Sabha (House of the People) and Rajya Sabha (Council of States). The President has the power to summon and prorogue either House of Parliament or to dissolve Lok Sabha. The Constitution of India came into force on January 26, 1950. The first general elections under the new Constitution were held during the year 1951-52 and the first elected Parliament came into being in April, 1952. (India Net Zone)

But the Parliament has to follow certain procedure to decide any policy. The Fundamental Rights, Directive Principles of State Policy and Fundamental Duties are sections of the Constitution of India that prescribe the fundamental obligations of the State to its citizens and the duties of the citizens to the State.

These sections comprise a constitutional bill of rights and guidelines for government policy-making and the behaviour and conduct of citizens. These sections are considered vital elements of the constitution, which was developed between 1947 and 1949 by the Constituent Assembly of India.

The Directive Principles of State Policy are guidelines for the framing of laws by the government. These provisions are not enforceable by the courts, but the principles on which they are based are fundamental guidelines for governance that the State is expected to apply in framing and passing laws. The Fundamental Duties are defined as the moral obligations of all citizens to help promote a spirit of patriotism and to uphold the unity of India. These duties concern individuals and the nation. Like the Directive Principles, they are not legally enforceable.

Economical Policy

Nehru was fascinated by Soviet Union's Piatiletka or 5-year plan and tried implementing the same for the Indian Economy. He wanted India to have the best combination of Socialism and Capitalism and tried to implement Democratic Socialism in India. He wanted the state to be a principal entrepreneur and all its citizens to be equal share holders. He strengthened the democratic pillars of nation immensely by creating proper wealth distribution systems at all levels.

Nehru's economic policies are often confused by critics with those of his daughter, Indira Gandhi, who was more left-wing. Nehru's economics of state intervention and investment were conceived at a time when transfers of capital and technology important to India were not easily forthcoming from the developed world (which incidentally also had plenty of state-sponsored capital controls.) Nehru is often criticised by ill-informed commentators of the present-day, when transfers of capital are unhindered, easily channelled by recipient nations, and even encouraged for their high returns in emerging markets.

The Soviet Union was the only major power to allow India to develop independent capabilities in many spheres of heavy industry, engineering, and cutting-edge technologies. India's combination of internal political freedom, economic and political independence throughout its existence can be favourably compared with many client-states of the United States and the Soviet Union.

Till 1991, India followed more or less the same policy, and then it followed the policy of the liberalisation. This opened up the economy and brought in more FDI.

Foreign Policy

The foundations of India's foreign policy were laid during the freedom movement when our leaders, even when fighting for independence, were engaged with the great causes of the time. The principles of India's foreign policy, that emerged then, have stood the test of time: a belief in friendly relations with all countries of the world, the resolution of conflicts by peaceful means, the sovereign equality of all states, independence of thought and action as manifested in the principles of Non-alignment, and equity in the conduct of international relations. Under the leadership of Jawaharlal Nehru, India was the founder member of the Non-aligned Movement. India has also been in the forefront of the world community in the struggle against colonialism. A notable feature of Indian foreign policy has been its strong advocacy of general and complete disarmament, with nuclear disarmament being accorded the highest priority. As a founder member of the United Nations, India has been firmly committed to the purposes and principles of the United Nations and has made significant contributions to its various activities, including peace-keeping operations. India's foreign policy has always regarded the concept of neighbourhood as one of widening concentric circles, around a central axis of historical and cultural communalities. From this point of view, it has always given due priority to the development of relations with South East Asia.

Development Policy

The social problems of contemporary India are the result of a complex nexus between the factors of exclusion and inclusion rooted in history, values, and cultural ethos. Many of these problems based on the policy of segregation have not been addressed by the development strategy launched since Independence. Recent policies of globalization have further undermined the role of larger socialite norms as well as the state apparatus that could counter exclusionary forces. The agenda of social development has remained unfinished, keeping social tensions simmering. Today, however, in the policy debate, orthodox economic liberalism is giving way to concerns regarding social consequences of globalization, as it affects the poorest and the marginalized sections of the population. Thus, a number of highly important and far-reaching social policy measures have been brought on to the development agenda, in the form of the Right to Information Act, Rural Employment Guarantee Act, the Rural Health Mission among others. This unique volume argues the need to harness the energy of the nation to ensure their effective implementation through an overview of trends and patterns of development along with policies and programmes. It identifies key concerns and proposes measures of possible intervention. (Oxford)

Conclusion

Issues of sustainable livelihood and social and political participation of the vulnerable groups exists as the major problem in the India. They have least participation and access in the social, economic, political and cultural sector. They have been marginalized from the mainstream State system and the development process. Governments have failed to guarantee people's rights in the implementation level. People of the vulnerable groups are unable to acquire and use their rights. This has caused very insignificant access of this groups in the State system and the resources. They do not have adequate access to justice and equity. Though the States have incorporated equality in their policy, the vulnerable groups have not been able to feel it in reality. They have been facing many challenges in enjoying their right to sustainable livelihood and social and political participation due to lack of priority of the States in protection and promotion of the interests of the vulnerable groups. Governments and elites of the region back up State terrorism and militarization in the name of national or internal security, resulting in violation of the civil and political rights of those who struggle for economic, social and cultural rights.

Human rights violation is supported by the unjust structure of society. There are many structures in the Indian societies that have to dismantled – unjust economic social and cultural structures. We can take the case of peasants for instance. If the peasants do not own and control the productive resources such as land, financial capital and technology, we cannot imagine human rights for them. As long as workers are laid off, or if they receive unjust, very low wages because of policies dictated by the International Monetary Fund (IMF), World Bank and

World Trade Organization (WTO) and carried out by respective governments, there will never be improvement in economic, social and cultural rights or the right to development, nor will there be improvement in the realization of the civil and political rights of our peoples. This arises because the policies of such international organizations always influence the policies of India. To conclude, the government has to retrospect the basic policy making process which it is using for the last 60 years. This will help greatly in the development of the people.

POLICY ANALYSIS

Policy analysis is "determining which of various alternative policies will most achieve a given set of goals in light of the relations between the policies and the goals". However, policy analysis can be divided into two major fields. Analysis of policy is analytical and descriptive—i.e., it attempts to explain policies and their development. Analysis for policy is prescriptive—i.e., it is involved with formulating policies and proposals (e.g., to improve social welfare). The area of interest and the purpose of analysis determines what type of analysis is conducted. A combination of policy analysis together with program evaluation would be defined as Policy studies.

Policy Analysis is frequently deployed in the public sector, but is equally applicable to other kinds of organizations. Policy analysis has its roots in systems analysis as instituted by United States Secretary of Defence Robert McNamara during the Vietnam War.

Approaches

Although various approaches to policy analysis exist, three general approaches can be distinguished: the analycentric, the policy process, and the meta-policy approach. The analycentric approach focuses on individual problems and its solutions; its scope is the micro-scale and its problem interpretation is usually of a technical nature. The primary aim is to identify the most effective and efficient solution in technical and economic terms (e.g. the most efficient allocation of resources). The policy process approach puts its focal point onto political processes and involved stakeholders; its scope is the meso-scale and its problem interpretation is usually of a political nature. It aims at determining what processes and means are used and tries to explain the role and influence of stakeholders within the policy process. By changing the relative power and influence of certain groups (e.g., enhancing public participation and consultation), solutions to problems may be identified.

The meta-policy approach is a systems and context approach; i.e., its scope is the macro-scale and its problem interpretation is usually of a structural nature. It aims at explaining the contextual factors of the policy process; i.e., what are the political, economic and socio-cultural factors influencing it. As problems may result because of structural factors (e.g., a certain economic system or political institution), solutions may entail changing the structure itself.

Methodology

Policy analysis is methodologically diverse using both qualitative methods and quantitative methods, including case studies, survey research, statistical analysis, and model building among others. One common methodology is to define the problem and evaluation criteria; identify all alternatives; evaluate them; and recommend the best policy agenda per favour.

Models

Many models exist to analyze the creation and application of public policy. Analysts use these models to identify important aspects of policy, as well as explain and predict policy and its consequences.

Some models are:

Institutional Model

Public policy is determined by political institutions, which give policy legitimacy. Government universally applies policy to all citizens of society and monopolizes the use of force in applying policy.

Process Model

Policy creation is a process following these steps:

- Identification of a problem and demand for government action.
- Formulation of policy proposals by various parties (e.g., congressional committees, think tanks, interest groups).

- Selection and enactment of policy; this is known as Policy Legitimation.
- Evaluation of policy.

This model, however, has been criticized for being overly linear and simplistic. In reality, stages of the policy process may overlap or never happen. Also, this model fails to take the multiple actors attempting the process itself as well as each other, and the complexity this entails.

Rational Model

Policy is intended to achieve *maximum social gain.* Rationally, the policy that maximizes benefits while minimizing costs is the best policy. It is a part of rational choice theory. This is step by step mode of analysis. It has its own limitations. The thinking procedure implied is linear and can face difficulties in extra ordinary problems or chaotic problems which has no sequences of happenings.

Incremental Model

Policy is a continuation of previous government activity, with minimal changes made to previous policy. The goal is a systematic periodic review.

Group Model

The political system's role is to establish and enforce compromise between various, conflicting interests in society.

Elite Model

Policy is a reflection of the interests of those individuals within a society that have the most power, rather than the demands of the mass.

Six-step Model

1. Verify, define and detail the problem
2. Establish evaluation criteria
3. Identify alternative policies
4. Evaluate alternative policies
5. Display and distinguish among alternative policies
6. Monitor the implemented policy.

10

Indian Public and Political Administration

Public administration can be broadly described as the study and implementation of policy. As a moral endeavour, public administration is linked to pursuing the public good through the creation of civil society and social justice. The adjective 'public' often denotes 'government', though it increasingly encompasses Non-governmental organizations such as those of civil society or any entity and its management not specifically acting in self-interest. The term public administration sometimes is taken to refer to bureaucracy (as in Federal Administration). Although used negatively, bureaucracy is needed to perform day-to-day functions of government. In truth, public administration and bureaucracy are in a sense, the same thing.

THE PRE-GENERATION

The pre-generation includes thinkers such as Plato, Aristotle and Machiavelli. Until the birth of the national state, the emphasis lay principally on the problems of moral and political nature, and on the organization of the public administration. The operation of this administration was a less urgent problem. Machiavelli wrote the book The Prince, which offered a guideline for European rulers. The operation of the administration, and not only the organization, also profited from the attention it received in this book. From the 16th century, the national state was the reigning model of the administrative organization in Western Europe. These states needed an organization for the implementation of law and order and for setting up a defensive structure. The need for expert civil servants, with knowledge about taxes, statistics, administration and the military organization grew. In the 18th century the need for administrative expertise grew even further.

Therefore king Frederick William I of Prussia established professorates in Cameralism, an economic and social school of thought within 18th century Prussia to reform society, at the universities of Frankfurt an her Oder and Halle. The most well know professor of Cameralism was Johann Heinrich Gottlob Justi (1717-1771), who linked Cameralism and the idea of natural law with each other, but the leading Public Administration scholar at that time was Christian Wolff, who was not a Cameralist. Cameralism is a predecessor of the modern science of public administration.

The First Generation

Lorenz von Stein, since 1855 professor in Vienna, is considered the founder of the science of public administration. In the time of Von Stein the science of public administration was considered to be a form of administrative law, but Von Stein thought that opinion was too restrictive. His opinions were innovative in several respects:

- He considered the science of public administration a melting pot of several disciplines, like sociology, political sciences, administrative law and public finance. In the opinion of Von Stein the science of public administration was an integrating science.
- According to Von Stein the science of public administration was an interaction between theory and practice. He considered the public administration as leading practically, but the theory had to form the base.
- Von Stein thought that the science of public administration should strive to adopt a scientific method.

In the United States Woodrow Wilson was the first to consider the science of public administration important. Wilson was more influential to the science of public administration than Von Stein, primarily due to an article Wilson wrote in 1887 in which he argued in favour of four concepts:

- Separation between politics and the public administration.
- Consideration of the government from a commercial perspective.
- Comparative analysis between political and private organizations and political schemes.
- Reaching effective management by training civil servants and assess their quality.

The separation between politics and the public administration, which Wilson argued, has been the subject of fierce debates for a long time, and the different points of view on this subject differentiate periods in the science of public administration.

The Second Generation

The discussion about the separation between politics and the public administration as argued by Wilson continued to play an important role up to 1945. Luther Gulick and Lyndall Urwick were the founders of the Science of Administration. They integrated the ideas of earlier theorists like Henri Fayol into a comprehensive theory of administration. Gulick and Urwick believed that the thoughts of Fayol offered a systematic treatment of management, which was unique at that time. They believed that this could be applied as well for the management of companies as for administrative sciences. They did not want to separate the two disciplines, but believed a single Science of Administration, which exceeds the borders between the private and the public sector, could exist. Later on the Science of Administration would focus primarily on governmental organizations. The reasoning of the Science of Administration was largely borrowed from the fourteen principles of organization of Fayol.

The Third Generation

After 1945 the third generation arose which questioned the ideas of Wilson and the second generation. Initially the distinction between politics and the public administration was strongly relativized by the third generation, but the discussion would continue. Because of the unsuccessful American intervention in Vietnam and the Watergate scandal politics got discredited and in the eighties there was again a plea in favour of bureaucracy, especially in the United States. The public administration had to detach itself from politics. After Louis Brownlow from the University of Chicago chaired the Hoover Commission on the Reorganization of Government, he founded Public Administration Service on the University of Chicago campus (at 1313 E. 60th Street). From 193 until the late 1970s PAS provided consulting services to governments at all levels: cities counties, states, the federal government and many foreign countries.

How Can Public Administration and Policy be Most Effectively Taught?

The question of what teaching methods would best serve adult learners has long been debated in universities and in the specialist literature on pedagogy. One form this challenge takes for teachers of policy and administration is how to prepare students for the complexities of a public sector environment, in which ethical dilemmas, conflicting notions of the "public interest," and multiple accountability pressures are all common.

The generic answer in many professional schools has been to promote problem-based learning in various forms. It arises from a long-standing critique-much in vogue in university centres devoted to teaching methods, and given a new interpretation in Steven Aufrecht and Xie Ming's chapter-of hierarchical, lecture-based methods. These methods take various forms. Faculties of medicine perhaps have the most plausible application: rigorous, closely supervised clinical education to accompany theoretical learning. Yet the subjects of policy analysis and administration are rather unlike the controlled environment of hospital examination rooms. Business schools have developed a more applicable model, emphasizing group work, internships, and applied case analysis. An important point to note is that none of these methods is free of controversy or practical challenge.

Take the use of case studies. They are widely employed in both business and public administration classrooms, and are widely thought to provide the opportunity to integrate political, economic, and organizational analysis for "real-life" problem-solving and to stimulate the development of managerial "wisdom." Yet typical public policy cases have also been criticized as portraying the policy world in terms of "high-level, lone protagonists beset by hostile political forces," and of de-emphasizing the institutional and historical contexts of policy action. If the critique rings true for American policy contexts, it may have even greater traction when case studies "cooked" in Western contexts are served to current or future public managers from developing or non-Western country settings.

Several chapters look beyond case analysis for problem-based learning methods. Carole Comerton-Forde and her colleagues from the University of Sydney explore group work in public policy programs, while Richard Hayllar offers a detailed description of the use of extended role-plays "to develop policy and decision-making skills in cases where interpretations of what is in the 'best public interest' are strongly contested," as he puts it in his evocative title. While no chapter focuses on e-learning methods, there is little doubt that this new technology will be increasingly important in the years to come, and an important way to provide distance education and in-service training to public sector personnel in a wide catchment area.

Does it Matter?

This is a third type of question that can be asked of policy education. Put differently, what impact does training in public policy and administration have on the practice of governance or the quality of governmental decision-making? The question may sit uncomfortably for educators; indeed, only one of the chapters in this section-that by Mangahas on the potential impact on Millennium Development Goal attainment-addresses this type of issue. The reluctance stems largely from the general difficulty of quantifying the impact of higher education in any field-except on the subsequent wages of graduates, a measure which is decidedly unhelpful for the public sector. The question may also be uncomfortable for university administrators. After all, policy and administration schools-particularly those catering to students from developing countries-probably have among the highest percentages of students whose tuition is paid by third parties among all the professional schools. Are these generous funders, whether donors or governments, getting their money's worth?

In this regard one might recall Chambers' (1983) evocative (if simplistic) description of the cultural and attitudinal gulf separating "positive practitioners"-for whom every problem is solvable with the right mix of resources and skills-and "negative academics"-annoyingly insisting on the profound structural constraints on effective policy intervention. Professional schools of public administration and policy everywhere straddle, even embody, this divide. But it is a tension that can border on "schizophrenia" when the context is policy education in less developed settings.

We know that the productivity and "room for maneuver" for individual public managers depends heavily on how facilitative their work environments are: on the incentives, resources, information, and public authority that these managers can mobilize.

If all such incentives and resources are weak to the breaking point in many developing country settings (as many "negative academics" might contend), what will a better grasp of benefitcost analysis bring our well-trained public servant? To put the question more strongly, how tenuous is the link-for it must be tenuous-between the short exposure of mid-career managers to expensive, short-duration executive education programs and the quality of policy outputs emerging from the systems in which they must operate?

There may be good answers to this question. Indeed, some aspects of developing country environments may enhance managerial discretion and, by extension, the importance of its sensitive application (Grindle and Thomas 1991). But to ask the question underlines the difficulties of moving the pedagogical discussion from one based (to use public management-speak) on the "process and outputs" to the "outcomes and impacts" of policy education. Ultimately, educators of the "guardians" of once and future Republics can always fall back onto Oscar Wilde's famous dictum: "If you think education is expensive, try ignorance." But perhaps we can do better than this. Examining the impact of policy education in producing not just more capable, but more effective public managers is an important future arena for discussion-one the chapters point toward without directly addressing.

ENHANCING THE ROLE OF PUBLIC ADMINISTRATION EDUCATION

The Millennium Development Goals (MDGs) establish targets for reducing poverty, improving health care and education, promoting economic growth, empowering women, and creating an enabling environment for sustainable development (UNDP 2003). The magnitude of the challenge for achieving the MDGs is formidable. Unless drastic and concerted actions are undertaken at all levels-from global to local-it is unlikely that the desired results and outcomes will be significantly realized (DFID 2003). The attainment of the MDGs requires collective action and commitment of international, national, and subnational institutions involving governments, civil society, and the private sector. Addressing the enduring problems of poverty and environment degradation is predicated on the successful implementation of governance reforms to rectify the policy and institutional frameworks that discriminate against the historically disadvantaged and marginalized sectors. The MDGs are expected to be resisted, since new concepts and paradigms must be introduced to the policy arena, together with new administrative systems that challenge strongly held views and practices. Any effort to promote citizen-centred policies and pro-poor change will understandably be opposed by well-organized and influential groups that benefit from the status quo.

Critical to the achievement of the MDGs is the promotion of institutional and organizational development, which requires the learning of new skills, strategies, approaches, and tools. Building capacity for identifying and responding to citizens' needs, particularly those of the poor, is an imperative for most developing countries. Functional skills in cooperating with others, managing stakeholders, and establishing networks and partnerships should be improved. Measuring and reporting performance to enhance efficacy and promote accountability of public officials are also necessary. To meet the MDGs, public administration education must play a key role. Despite the global interest in and broad support for work toward realizing the MDGs, they are yet to be formally introduced in the teaching and learning processes of many schools of public administration in the Philippines. This paper seeks to suggest what such schools can and should do to support actions toward fulfilment of the MDGs. It also aims to examine how the academic curricula for teaching public administration may be strengthened to develop competencies for institutional and organizational development looking toward the MDGs.

This chapter begins with a brief discussion of what will it take to achieve the MDGs. This is followed by a description of the agenda for promoting good governance and its link to reaching the MDGs. The paper then explains a framework for promoting institutional and organizational development. A discussion of perspectives in effective curriculum design follows. Next, the paper provides some general observations on academic curricula in public administration. The paper concludes with recommendations to strengthen programs of instruction and educative roles to help achieve the MDGs.

PROVIDING AN ENABLING ENVIRONMENT FOR ACHIEVING

Targeting poverty reduction, women's empowerment, and environmental sustainability require substantial changes in political, economic, and social systems (Brinkerhoff 2004). The enduring problems that the MDGs seek to address are the consequence of decades of policies and practices at international and national levels. As such, significant improvements in living conditions in developing countries will be realized through specific reform measures at the national and subnational levels, matched with focused interventions from the international community.

International and national instruments are the key to reaching the MDGs. International instruments involve effective debt reduction, trade-related policies, reform of the Bretton Woods Institutions and the World Trade Organization, and increased quantity and better quality of international aid (GFID 2002). National instruments include improving the delivery of basic services, particularly to the poor; a more equitable and transparent taxation system; and a guarantee of peace and order (GFID 2002). Public policies are too often insufficiently focused around issues related to poverty, health care, education, gender, and environment. Likewise, administrative capacities are inadequately prepared and resources are scarce for promoting change and pursuing pro-poor development. Although the attainment of the MDGs is not the sole responsibility of governments, governments actually play a critical role in making services work for the people and raising the quality of life. Governments perform thousands of functions, but in essence, they perform four major types of activities that affect almost every aspect of living:

(i) They formulate and monitor policies;
(ii) They raise revenues to implement policies;
(iii) They implement policies, some through provision of goods and services; and
(iv) They provide an enabling environment for private sector growth and social development.

The reduced or nonexistent capacity for good governance has nonetheless weighed down government performance. Good governance or sound development management is therefore a sine qua non for achieving the MDGs.

Governance is broadly defined as the sound exercise of political, economic, and administrative authority to manage a country's resources for development. It involves the institutionalization of a system through which citizens, institutions, organizations, and groups in the society articulate their interests, exercise their rights, and mediate their differences in pursuit of the collective good (ADB 1995).

It embraces not only the affairs of government, but also the proactive role of the private sector and civil society in national development. Governance is, thus, not the sole province of government. Instead, its functions are delegated to, or assumed by, other institutions and organizations in the business sector and civil society (UNDP 1997). Its concern with the sound exercise of authority underscores its ethical moorings. Thus, its basic elements are accountability, participation, predictability, and transparency, which are also the key principles of sound development management (ADB 2003). The basic elements of governance, its key dimensions, and specific areas of action. Promoting good governance poses opportunities as well as challenges as it brings together the public sector, civil society, the private sector, and communities in the tasks of evolving policies, programs, organizational and operational mechanisms, and institutional arrangements that can effectively respond to the needs of the people, ensure the judicious and transparent use of public funds, encourage growth of the private sector, promote effective delivery of public services, and uphold the rule of law.

Mainstreaming good governance not only requires capacitating individuals and institutions, but also providing the appropriate policy environment to institutionalize reforms (ADB 2005). At the individual level, capacity building for good governance focuses on the process of equipping civil servants and stakeholders with the understanding; skills; and access to information, knowledge, and training that enable them to work together and perform effectively. At the organizational level, governance reforms involve the elaboration and establishment of enabling management systems, structures, processes, and procedures, not only within organizations but also in the management of relationships between and among the different organizations and sectors. At the institutional level, capacity building includes making legal and regulatory changes to enable organizations, institutions, and agencies at all levels and in all sectors to enhance their capacity.

Sound development management identifies the roles of the state as:

- Creating a conducive economic environment,
- Protecting the vulnerable,
- Improving government efficiency and responsiveness,
- Empowering people and democratizing the political system,
- Decentralizing the administrative system,
- Reducing gaps between rich and poor,
- Encouraging cultural diversity and social integration, and
- Protecting the environment.

POLITICAL ADMINISTRATION OF INDIA

India is a democracy. Before its independence its future leaders chose the liberal democratic system as the administration system of India. On 26/01/1950, India declared itself as Republic. On this day the Constitution of India came into force. Today India is a federation of 28 states and 7 union territories and formally this federation is known as a Union.

Nominally the head of the country is the President in whom all executive powers are vested, but the real administrator of the country is the Prime Minister. After the national elections are held the President calls the most suitable candidate to form a government, known as the central government. Normally this candidate is the head of the largest party in the parliament. In case the government resigns because of any reason, the President can call the other candidate to form the government. The President can also declare, according to government advice, on new elections and if necessary an emergency state. The President has the right to be updated about crucial government matters and other rights like giving amnesty to prisoners etc.

rding to the Constitution, elections are to be held once in every five years, unless the parliament dissolves earlier or on the other hand, emergency is declared and in such a case parliament can continue another year.

The Indian Parliament consists of two houses. The Lower House called the Lok Sabha and the Upper House called the Rajya Sabha. In the national elections candidates are chosen for the Lower House. The candidates are elected in territorial constituencies. There are 543 territorial constituencies. Two members from the Anglo-Indian community are nominated to the Lower House by the President. The law, which obliges Government office to reserve 15% from the Scheduled Castes and 7% from the Scheduled Tribes, also exists in the Parliament. At least 22% of the Indian Parliament members belong to these two communities. In the past few years there is an attempt to oblige a law to allow about 33% women as Parliament members. The Upper House, Rajya Sabha, consists of up to 250 members. Of these members 230 are elected by state legislatures and about 15 are nominated by the President. Unlike the Lower House, the Upper House cannot be dissolved, but one third of its members resign every two years.

Most of the parliamentary activities, passing laws, no-confidence votes, budget bills, take place in the Lower House. The Upper House together with the Lower House amends the Constitution. These two Houses together with the state legislatures also elect the President. The states have their own legislatures. Some states have two Houses and some only one House. The Lower House where most of the legislature activities happen is called the Vidhan Sabha. The state elections are held every five years unless the state government is dissolved earlier. In these elections members for the Lower House are elected.

Head of a state is called Chief Minister, who is member of the Lower House. Constitutionally the figurehead of the state is the Governor, who is appointed by the President according to the advice of the national government. After the state elections the governor calls for the suitable candidate to form the government. In general the governor has more legislative rights at state level than the President has at national level. The governor can call on early elections in the state, or fire the government if he thinks that the government has failed or is unstable.

In the federal relations between the state and central government, the central government has more authority on state matters than the state government. For example the central government has the right to redistribute the state borders without consulting the state governments on this matter. If the political conditions in any state are not stable, the national government can call on the President to declare President's rule in that specific state. And so the government in that state is dissolved, which means an emergency rule is declared and sometimes if necessary the army is put to work in that state.

Even though the Constitution determinates the rights of the different authorities in the administration process, there can be other pressures like strong lobbies or strong political parties, which, sometimes determinate the real administration process. Sometimes the authority implemented by the President is questioned by the government or by political parties as deviation from his constitutional rights as the nominal head of the Union.

RESERVATION IN INDIA

Indian Government now Indian law provides for a quota system whereby a percentage of posts are reserved in employment in Government and in the public sector units, and in all public and private educational institutions, except in the religious/linguistic minority educational institutions, in order to mitigate backwardness of the socially and educationally backward communities and the Scheduled Castes and Tribes who do not have adequate representation in these services and institutions. The reservation policy is also extended to the Scheduled Castes and Scheduled Tribes for representation in the Parliament of India. The central government of India reserves 27% of higher education, and individual states may legislate further reservations. Reservation cannot be exceeded 50%, as per the rulings given by the supreme court, but certain Indian states like Rajasthan have proposed a 68 % reservation which includes a 14% reservation for forward castes.

Reservations are intended to increase the social diversity in campuses and workplaces by lowering the entry criteria for certain identifiable groups that are grossly under-represented in proportion to their numbers in the general population. Caste is the most used criteria to identify under-represented groups. However there are other identifiable criteria for under-representation—gender (women are under represented), state of domicile (North Eastern States, as Bihar and Uttar Pradesh are under-represented), rural people, etc. — as revealed by the Government of India sponsored National Family Health and National Sample surveys.

The underlying theory is that the under-representation of the identifiable groups is a legacy of the Indian caste system. After India gained independence, the Constitution of India listed some erstwhile groups as Scheduled Castes (SC) and Scheduled Tribes (ST). The framers of the Constitution believed that, due to the caste system, SCs and the STs were historically oppressed and denied respect and equal opportunity in Indian society and were thus under-represented in nation-building activities. The Constitution laid down 15% and 7.5% of vacancies to government aided educational institutes and for jobs in the government/public sector, as reserved quota for the SC and ST candidates respectively for a period of five years, after which the situation was to be reviewed. This period was routinely extended by the succeeding governments.

Later, reservations were introduced for other sections as well. The Supreme Court ruling that reservations cannot exceed 50% (which it judged would violate equal access guaranteed by the Constitution) has put a cap on reservations. However, there are state laws that exceed this 50% limit and these are under litigation in the Supreme Court. For example, the caste-based reservation fraction stands at 69% and is applicable to about 87% of the population in the state of Tamil Nadu.

HISTORY OF THE PRACTICE

Reservations in favour of Backward Classes (BCs) were introduced long before Independence in a large area, comprising the Presidency areas and the Princely States south of the Vindhyas. Chatrapati Sahuji Maharaj, Maharaja of Kolhapur in Maharashtra introduced reservation in favour of backward classes as early as 1902 to eradicate poverty from amongst them and to give them their due share in the State administration. The notification of 1902 created 50% reservation in services for backward classes/communities in the State of Kolhapur. This notification is the first Government Order providing for reservation for the welfare of depressed classes in India.

The concept of untouchability was not practiced uniformly throughout the country, the identification of oppressed classes is not an easy task. What is more, the practice of segregation and untouchability prevailed more in the southern parts of India and was more diffused in Northern India. An additional complexity is that there are certain castes/communities, which are considered as untouchables in one province but not in other provinces. Some castes, based on traditional occupations, find place in both Hindu and non-Hindu communities. Listing of castes has had a long history, starting from the earliest period of our history with Manu. Medieval chronicles contain description of communities located in various parts of the country. During the British colonial period, listings were undertaken after 1806, on an extensive scale. The process gathered momentum in course of the censuses from 1881 to 1931.

The Backward Classes movement also first gathered momentum in South India particularly in Tamil Nadu. The continuous efforts of some of the social reformers of the country viz. Rettamalai srinivasa Paraiyar, Ayothidas Pandithar www.paraiyar.webs.com, Jyotiba Phule, Babasaheb Ambedkar,

Chhatrapati Sahu ji Maharaj and others, completely demolished the wall created by the upper classes between them and the untouchables.

India is divided into many endogamous groups, or castes and sub-castes, as a result of centuries of practicing a form of social hierarchy called the caste system. Proponents of reservation policy says that the traditional caste system, as it is practised, leads to severe oppression and segregation of the lower castes and limited their access to various freedoms, including education. Caste, according to ancient scriptures such as "Manu Smriti", is "Varnasrama Dharma", which translates to "offices given according to class or occupation". "Varna" in Varnasrama (Varna + Ashrama) is not to be confused with the same word meaning 'colour'. The practice of caste in India followed this rule.

- 1882-Hunter Commission appointed. Mahatma Jyotirao Phule made a demand of free and compulsory education for all along with proportionate reservation/ representation in government jobs.
- 1891-The demand for reservation of government jobs was made as early as 1891 with an agitation in the princely State of Travancore against the recruitment of non-natives into public service overlooking qualified native people.
- 1901-Reservations were introduced in Maharashtra in the Princely State of Kolhapur by Shahu Maharaj. Reservations in the princely states of Baroda and Mysore were already in force.
- 1908-Reservations were introduced in favour of a number of castes and communities that had little share in the administration by the British.
- 1909-Provisions were made in the Government of India Act 1909
- 1919-Montagu-Chelmsford Reforms introduced.
- 1919-Provisions were made in the Government of India Act 1919
- 1921-Madras Presidency introduces Communal G O in which reservation of 44 per cent for non-Brahmins, 16 per cent for Brahmins, 16 per cent for Muslims, 16 per

cent for Anglo-Indians/Christians and eight per cent for Scheduled Castes.

- 1935-Indian national congress passes resolution called Poona Pact to allocate separate electoral constituencies for depressed classes.
- 1935-Provisions in Government of India Act 1935.
- 1942-B.R. Ambedkar established the All India Depressed Classes federation to support the advancement of the scheduled castes. He also demanded reservations for the Scheduled castes in government services and education.
- 1946-1946 Cabinet Mission to India proposes proportionate representation with several other recommendations.
- 1947-India obtained Independence. Dr. Ambedkar was appointed chairman of the drafting committee for Indian Constitution. The Indian constitution prohibits discrimination on the grounds only of religion, race, caste, sex and place of birth. While providing equality of opportunity for all citizens, the constitution contains special clauses "for the advancement of any socially and educationally backward classes of citizens or for the Scheduled Castes and the Scheduled Tribes". Separate constituencies allocated to Scheduled Castes and Tribes to ensure their political representation for 10 years.(These were subsequently extended for every 10 years through constitutional amendments).
- 1947-1950-Debates of the Constituent Assembly.
- 26/01/1950-The Constitution of India came in force.
- 1953-Kalelkar Commission was established to assess the situation of the socially and educationally backward class. The report was accepted as far as Scheduled Castes and Scheduled Tribes were concerned. The recommendations for OBC's were rejected.
- 1956-Schedules amended as per Kaka Kalelkar report.
- 1976-Schedules amended.
- 1979-Mandal Commission was established to assess the situation of the socially and educationally backward. The commission didn't have exact figures for a sub-

caste, known as the Other Backward Class(OBC), and used the 1930 census data, further classifying 1,257 communities as backward, to estimate the OBC population at 52%.

- o 1980-the commission submitted a report, and recommended changes to the existing quotas, increasing them from 22% to 49.5%.As of 2006 number of castes in Backward class list went up to 2297 which is the increase of 60% from community list prepared by Mandal commission.
- o 1990-Mandal commission recommendations were implemented in Government Jobs by Vishwanath Pratap Singh. Student Organisations launched nationwide agitations. Rajiv Goswami Delhi university student attempted self-immolation. Many students followed suit.
- o 1991-Narasimha Rao Government introduced 10% separate reservation for Poor Among Forward Castes.
- o 1992-Supreme court upheld reservations to Other backward classes in Indira Sawhney Case.
- o 1995-Parliament by 77th Constitutional amendment inserted Art 16(4) (A) permitting reservation in promotions to the Schedule Castes and Schedule Tribes. Later it was further amended to include consequential seniority by 85th amendment.
- o 1998-Central Government conducted large nationwide survey for the first time to estimate economical and educational status of various social groups.. The National Sample Survey puts the figure at 32%. There is substantial debate over the exact number of OBC's in India, with census data compromised by partisan politics. It is generally estimated to be sizable, but lower than the figures quoted by either the Mandal Commission or and national Sample Survey. Mandal commission has been criticised of fabricating the data. National surveys indicated that status of OBC is comparable to Forward castes in many areas.
- o 2005 August 12-The Supreme Court delivered a unanimous judgement by 7 judges on 12 August 2005 in the case of P.A. Inamdar & Ors. vs. State of

Maharashtra & Ors. declaring that the State can't impose its reservation policy on minority and non-minority unaided private colleges, including professional colleges.

- o 2005-93rd Constitutional amendment brought for ensuring reservations to other backward classes and Scheduled castes and Tribes in Private Educational institutions. This effectively reversed the 2005 August Supreme Court judgement.
- o 2006-The Constitution Bench of the Supreme Court in M. Nagraj & Ors Vs. Union of India & Ors upheld the constitutional validity of Art 16(4) (A), 16(4) (B) and proviso to Art 335.
- o 2006-Reservations introduced for Other backward classes in Central Government Educational Institutions. Total Reservation went up to 49.5%.
- o 2007-Supreme Court give stayed on OBC reservation in Central Government Educational Institutions.
- o 2008—The Supreme Court of India on 10 April 2008, upheld the Government's move for initiating 27% OBC quotas in Government funded institutions. The Court has categorically reiterated its prior stand that "Creamy Layer" should be excluded from the ambit of reservation policy. The Supreme Court avoided answering the question whether reservations can be made in private institutions, stating that the question will be decided only as and when a law is made making reservations in private institutions. The verdict produced mixed reactions from supporting and opposing quarters.

Several criteria to identify creamy layer has been recommended, which are as follows: Those with family income above Rs 250,000 a year should be in creamy layer, and excluded from the reservation quota. Also, children of doctors, engineers, chartered accountants, actors, consultants, media professionals, writers, bureaucrats, defence officers of colonel and equivalent rank or higher, high court and Supreme Court judges, all central and state government Class A and B officials. The court has requested Parliament to exclude MPs' and MLAs' children, too.

Reservations and Judiciary

Indian Judiciary has pronounced some Judgments upholding reservations and some judgments for fine tuning its implementations. Lot of judgments regarding reservations have been modified subsequently by Indian parliament through constitutional amendments. Some judgments of Indian judiciary has been flouted by state and central Governments.

LEADERSHIP IN PUBLIC ADMINISTRATION

The importance of public administration for poverty alleviation and development was recognized in the NAPSIPAG region more than 50 years ago, when colleges and institutes of public administration were started and later, when the Eastern Regional Organization for Public Administration organized annual conferences and seminars where major issues of poverty and development were discussed. Several academic experts from the West, especially from the United States, came to the region with technical assistance programs and made recommendations for the reorganization of governmental machinery. Paul Appleby's report on public administration in India was accepted by the then Government of India with acclaim in 1953 and it led to the inauguration of the Indian Institute of Public Administration by Prime Minister Nehru, who continued to be its President till his death in 1964.

Postgraduate studies in public administration that started in university departments and colleges in India, South Korea, the Philippines, and Thailand were largely influenced by the "theories" of public administration taught in American universities. This was because it was in the United States that the subject was developed as an academic discipline, though often in departments of political science. Conceptually, much was borrowed from terminologies developed in the armed forces and applied to business management situations in the West. Asian scholars who wrote textbooks on public administration were largely influenced by these concepts and terminologies in describing their own systems of administration.

A mainly descriptive structural approach was followed, with very little consideration for behavioural aspects of relevance to their own societies. Subjects like leadership were neglected in their curricula until recently. Perhaps this was due to the prevailing notion that it was a subject to be dealt with in political science; the closest discussion of the subject came under the rubric of "POSDCORB," described as the "Functions of the Executive" by Gulick and Urwick. As is well known, the acronym stood for Planning, Organizing, Staffing, Directing, Coordinating, Reporting and Budgeting. These functions implied scope for leadership, yet critics found the model mechanical and without concern for the ground realities of situations under which bureaucracies operated.

The exposure to administrative situations in Asian countries helped American scholars like Fred Riggs, Ferrel Heady and William Siffin realize the need to understand the history and background of administrative systems in Thailand, the Philippines and other countries, before ideas and institutions developed in the United States were applied.

Fred Riggs in particular emphasized through his lectures on the ecology of public administration the need to describe administrative ecology before considering prescriptions for reform. His Prismatic Model further attempted to provide hypothetical characteristics of administrative environment in developing societies. Influenced by such innovations in the thinking and study of public administration, many Asian scholars like Hahn-Been Lee and Jose Abueva came out with analytical propositions based on field research in their respective countries. Research done by this author in India and the Philippines (Valsan 1970) helped in developing a conceptual framework applicable to development administration beyond the POSDCORB criteria, which are universally relevant.

Later experience and observations in Bangladesh, Egypt, and Sri Lanka all the more convinced the author that development administrators, while discharging the functions of POSDCORB, needed to be aware of the importance of the "Five 'I's"— Information, Inspiration, Innovation, Introjection, and Integration. Development administrators found an awareness of these dynamic elements valuable in helping them perform well in the leadership roles often required for development administration. For the sake of clarity and for emphasizing their contemporary relevance, an elaboration of each concept is attempted below:

INFORMATION

Unlike the 1960s, when this conceptual formulation was identified, the importance of information for leadership in public administration is easier to understand today. The information revolution that the world has witnessed during the last few decades has made data and ideas from anywhere in the world available to the leadership. It has also helped make field research and feedback information essential for decision making by administrators. It has helped attempts to replicate successful projects in countries far away with locally relevant modifications. A famous example is the Grameen Bank concept originated in Bangladesh under the dynamic leadership of Muhammad Yunus, which has spread all over the developing world, helping rural women through micro-credit projects. Information technology (IT) initiatives in E-government have spread out to several countries with varying degrees of success, but definitely influencing the thinking and functioning of leaders and administrators. The availability of information windows at the village level has expedited the process of applying for benefits and services available to common citizens, and for their speedy delivery.

Under the POSDCORB formulation, information as a function was included under reporting, which was more in an upward direction in a hierarchical organization. Reporting back to the people or subordinates was unknown in such a dispensation. Today, information as a dynamic element in development administration can be accessed and passed on from any direction and utilized for accomplishing the goals of the organization. Awareness of its importance and familiarity, if not mastery of its computer utilization, has become an essential qualification for dynamic leadership.

For developing democracies of the Asia–Pacific region, political parties and representatives find IT useful to collect and analyse information and to project popular demands more meaningfully in parliaments and public forums, thus influencing policy formulation. For instance, in Kerala, India, the Marxist Communist Party, which had in the early days opposed the introduction of computers on grounds of its leading to massive unemployment, is reported to have equipped its own offices with modern computers. Rajiv Gandhi was a modernizer in this respect, inviting technically competent Indians from abroad to introduce a revolution in the field of telecommunications using IT. In short, awareness of the importance of information with all its technological implications is a must for development leadership. It is equally important for coordinating all activities concerned with the plight of the poor, thus avoiding the duplication of efforts and funding that often occurs because of development partner contributions or scarce budgetary allocations of governments.

INSPIRATION

Mechanical models of administration and theoretical analyses of leadership have neglected the importance of inspiration, whereas it can be one of the mobilizing forces for development administration and poverty alleviation activities. Inspiration here is being looked at both as an individual experience and as a collective requirement for successful administration, contributing to development as well as in tackling the problems of acute poverty.

This writer was impressed by its role in community development programs of the 1950s and 1960s in Bangladesh, India, and the Philippines. Leaders like S. K. Dey, who was the first community development minister in India; Akhtar Hameed Khan, who resigned from the prestigious Indian Civil Service and followed Gandhian idealism in launching a community development program in Comilla in East Pakistan (now Bangladesh); and Ramon Magsaysay, who established the Presidential Assistant for Community Development in the Philippines, were all inspired by the desire to serve their respective communities or nations by tackling the problems of the rural masses. They in turn were able to inspire hundreds of their countrymen to join these movements, imbibing the spirit of public service.

One example is that of Muhammad Yunus, who started the Grameen banks. As a student at the Comilla Academy, he was inspired by the leadership of Akhtar Hameed Khan. Similarly, Jimmy Yen, who launched the Philippine Rural Reconstruction Movement (PRRM) in order to uplift the living conditions of the rural population, was able to inspire people like Dr. Juan Flavier, who later took over the mantle of PRRM. Hence, the relevance of the "chain of inspiration" concept for development, which is to be seen as a parallel with the "chain of command" concept in the mechanical model of management. That inspiration is equally important in the alleviation of poverty is clearly demonstrated in the life and contributions of Mother Teresa. Apart from her claim of divine inspiration, which is not part of our analysis, it was a fact that the poverty and misery of the sick and the dying inspired her to take care of those mortals. In turn, she was able to inspire a large number of young Sisters of Charity, who continue to serve the poor in several countries, even since her passing from the scene. The fact that they survive based on donations by private individuals belonging to all religions and institutions who are inspired by the message of the Mother and the service of her followers is equally important for the purpose of this analysis.

Looking at more productive projects for reducing poverty using the potentials of the healthy among the poor, one finds the livelihood programs of PRRM and the Kudumbasree projects of Kerala, meant for augmenting the income of women in need of support, succeeding wherever political, social, or bureaucratic leadership is inspiring. Here, it is important to emphasize that bureaucratic leadership is possible wherever there is ideal political leadership. Good examples of commitment set by political leaders or ministers can inspire civil servants and civil society volunteers to contribute to the success of development programs. Conversely, corrupt, greedy, and incompetent political bosses can kill the enthusiasm of even the most honest and competent subordinates. In short, it is only the inspired who can inspire.

The above discussion naturally leads to the question of the *sources of inspiration*. In the original work mentioned earlier, this writer attempted to compare the concept of charisma with that of inspiration and, among other points of comparison, mentioned that whereas charisma is supposed to have only one supernatural source, inspiration can have a multiplicity of sources.

For instance, even when one's boss is corrupt and uninspiring, the goals of the organization and the needs of the poor or the clientele, as well as the dedication of one's own subordinates, can sometimes sustain one's inspiration to serve.

Charisma as a concept can be even anti-development, or go against the interest of poverty alleviation programs. For instance, those who attribute charisma to Mother Teresa sometimes withdraw from the movement, saying that the Mother was charismatic, which they are not, and they cannot be expected to serve the way she did.

The same is applicable to the discussion of Gandhi, who was also considered charismatic and thus even worshipped, but seldom followed by his so-called followers. On the contrary, if they can draw inspiration from the causes for which Mother Teresa or Mahatma Gandhi worked, more success will be achieved in attaining the goals they shared with their leaders. A rational understanding of the concept of inspiration and attempts to instill it in organizations and administrative systems can lead to attaining organizational goals for human development. A caveat must be added, however, that our analysis excludes the role of what may be called negative inspiration for destructive activities commonly reported in the media in the new millennium.

INNOVATION

Another dynamic element in this conceptual model is innovation. Bureaucracy in general and public administration in particular are well known for routine and blind following of established practices. Awareness of the need for innovative thinking on the part of administrators was considered essential in order to achieve the development goals that could not wait for slow and incremental methods at the expense of suffering masses. Especially in the case of programs for alleviating poverty, bureaucratic excuses and corrupt practices have to be met with innovative initiatives. IT, as mentioned earlier, has opened avenues for more innovative approaches to decision making and service delivery. Also, as indicated earlier, information about other successful programs can be utilized for introducing innovative activities in a new setting. India's green revolution introduced many innovations in agriculture, leading to higher productivity, but the distribution system did not match the success of the scientists and the farmers, with the result that poverty and malnutrition continue to haunt rural areas in some states. Political leadership in such situations also did not come up with innovative solutions for bureaucracies to implement. In tackling abject poverty and facing natural calamities like floods, drought, cyclones, and earthquakes, bureaucracies and social and political workers are challenged to introduce quick and effective innovations and makeshift arrangements. An awareness of the importance of innovation in such critical situations is important in the training of civil servants for administrative leadership. Innovative approaches in communicating with the masses are important for implementing sensitive activities like family planning. The successful utilization of local political leadership for canvassing and mobilizing the masses for attending male sterilization camps in Kerala, India, in the 1970s introduced many innovative incentives to the participants and their families (Valsan 1977). Literacy campaigns also try out incentives and innovative methods of teaching in order to attract women and elderly illiterates.

INTROJECTION

During the last 3 decades, public administration and management sciences have seen major innovations and terminologies like Total Quality Management, New Public Management, and Human Resources Development. The concept of introjection suggested by Fred W. Riggs is important in the context of trying to introduce innovations successfully implemented in the West to Asian, Pacific, African, and Latin American countries. Borrowing from psychology, which calls for the selective internalization of values, Riggs implies here accepting reforms or innovations that can work in a society, and rejecting those that are not suitable or may even cause disturbance to the polity.

The concept can be applied even while trying to imitate in one part of a country a policy or practice that has proved successful in another part. A typical example was the attempt to introduce male sterilization in North India, copying successful innovative methods adopted in Kerala mentioned earlier. Kerala being a highly literate state, it was possible to mobilize the masses for the family planning program. In Uttar Pradesh, with poor literacy rates, on the other hand, the bureaucrats and politicians who wanted similar results even used force, thereby causing political damage to the ruling Congress Party in the election that followed and making family planning an untouchable subject even for the federal Government, thereby causing the increase of the national population beyond a billion. Had they been aware of the importance of introjection, such a situation could have been avoided. The failure of many programs for poverty alleviation is also traceable to the inability of bureaucrats and social workers to take into account the sociocultural background of the population and the special conditions of poverty prevailing in each society. In short, awareness of the concept of introjection is important for leaders trying to introduce reforms simply because of their success elsewhere.

INTEGRATION

Closely related to the concept of introjection is integration, which is most important for the stability of any society. As modernization is supposed to be accompanied by differentiation of functions, developing countries in their urge for development through modernization imitate developed countries in introducing institutions and structures that are expected to function in the same way as in the West.

However, the proliferation of institutions and agencies without sufficient coordination leads to chaotic situations, causing administrative breakdown or political instability. In this connection, it is worth remembering the Riggsian addition to his revision of the prismatic model, in which he emphasized the role of integration for diffracted societies. Prismatic conditions prevail where no integration of differentiated functions occurs.

Awareness of the importance of introjection helps in understanding the need for integrating the departments and institutions created. Reforms that are likely to tear the society apart due to lack of information should be kept in abeyance until objections to their implementation are explained and public acceptance obtained. In short, by taking into account ecological factors affecting development in a society, leaders can introduce reforms without disturbing the integration and the integrity of the society concerned. The dynamic model of development administration suggested by the above analysis does not ignore the role of POSDCORB executive functions, but urges the awareness of the importance of the "Five I's"—Information, Inspiration, Innovation, Introjection, and Integration—for performing a leadership role in the society. Extensive discussions on the model were held during graduate seminars with participants from different countries, many of whom supported its validity as a supplement to POSDCORB. However, in the context of poverty and problems faced by the weaker sections of society, leaders involved in alleviating misery, pain, and humiliation of those sections of the population, to be effective, need to call on some special attributes that they may have or that can be consciously cultivated.

EMPATHY

Here again, Mother Teresa's example is unique. Inspiration for undertaking the task of picking up the old, sick, and needy from the streets of Calcutta and treating, feeding, and housing them could have been effective only because of her capacity to empathize with their lot. It is one thing to feel sympathy and to donate some amount, food, or clothes as many of us do, but another experience to put oneself in their situation and to cater to their felt needs. Empathy is equally important for those involved in crisis management situations tackling natural calamities. Other instances of exemplary capacity for empathy can be cited, but other attributes of equal importance need our attention.

ENTHUSIASM

Any movement involving mobilization of people needs leaders who are not only inspired by its goals, but are enthusiastic about achieving them. Their commitment, the way they articulate goals, methods, and details, and their electrifying influence over their followers reflect that enthusiasm. It is an attribute that is important for fund-raising for noble causes.

Juan Flavier of PRRM, who later became a cabinet secretary in the Philippines and is now a Senator, is an example that comes to one's mind. Watching him in the early years of PRRM, making inspirational talks full of ideas, wit, and humour to enthuse the volunteers going to the barrios, was a pleasure.

EFFICIENCY

Lest it be felt that all our talk of inspiration, empathy, and enthusiasm in leadership is devoid of concern for practical aspects of running organizations, it is important to emphasize the attribute of efficiency, without which no leadership in public service or administration is possible. Akhtar Hameed Khan, who was trained in the erstwhile Indian Civil Service, was conscious of this at Comilla. He attached considerable importance to bookkeeping and training volunteers in financial management. Especially for organizations depending upon donations or government subsidies, accountability depends upon the efficiency of the leadership. Many organizations begun with good intentions for public service did not survive beyond the lifetime of their founders, because no mechanism was built in for continuation of an efficient system of management. Punctuality, dependability, and fairness in the treatment of clientele, colleagues, and subordinates constitute this important attribute essential for public service. Unfortunately, very often institutions for charitable purposes run by governments lack efficient leadership.

ENTREPRENEURSHIP

Normally considered a business management concept, entrepreneurship as an attribute for leadership in public administration and poverty alleviation activities is increasingly becoming important due to the challenges faced by modern organizations. Closely related to the concept of innovation suggested earlier, success in achieving organizational goals, especially in commercial organizations run by governments, largely depends upon this attribute. An example from India would be the Managing Director of Kochi International Airport Authority, V. J. Kurian, who is a member of the Indian Administrative Service. Though building the airport was a political decision, the financing of it through public contributions and donations, which were later converted into shares in the commercially constituted airport company, were all achieved to a large measure due to the entrepreneurship of this government officer.

The story of the successful operation and continuing development of this airport is itself worth a case study in leadership. Mother Teresa, in addition to all her inspiring qualities, was also considered during her lifetime as an entrepreneur who was able to start branches of her Missionaries of Charity in several countries. The Grameen Bank concept in Bangladesh is another example of encouraging the spirit of entrepreneurship among rural women by providing micro-credit for starting small commercial activities.

ETHICS

When all the qualities and attributes of leadership for public administration are discussed, one cannot ignore the importance of ethics. A universal outcry against corruption in government organizations has occurred during the last decade. This implies unethical practices and deals between individuals serving in public and private enterprises at the expense of the taxpayers of the countries concerned. Even charitable activities and relief operations are not immune to allegations of corruption.

Private greed getting accommodated in public organizations is despised, but such practices seem to continue to multiply. This is a challenge to the leadership of all countries and from it arises the need to identify honest men and women in administration and to assign them to leadership positions, giving necessary training in other attributes required in performing leadership tasks. Negative reporting in the media and casual description of all bureaucrats and politicians as corrupt does not solve the problem. A positive approach to cultivating ethical attributes among civil servants and politicians and giving prominent recognition to men and women of integrity can go a long way in generating leadership in public organizations.

A natural question that may be raised while discussing the attributes of leadership mentioned above is that of the cultivability of these qualities among political and bureaucratic personnel. A general answer will be that it is possible, not only through training programs designed for human development, but through exemplary leadership of eminent individuals who should be assigned the task of mentoring their colleagues and subordinates.

Watching the efficiency, enthusiasm, entrepreneurship, capacity for empathy, and ethical attributes of a leader can inspire those around him or her to perform better and to prepare themselves to wear the mantle. Delegation of responsibilities is important under such a dispensation, so that the leaders can make sure about the capabilities of their colleagues and subordinates who are one day going to be in charge. Concentration of all authority in one person's hands can be detrimental to the creation of leadership capabilities in organizations.

Conclusion: While suggesting the inadequacy of the POSDCORB model for leadership in development and charitable activities for poverty alleviation, the foregoing analysis has tried to emphasize the utility of the model, but also the need to supplement it with an awareness on the part of those in leadership positions of the importance of Information, Inspiration, Innovation, Introjection, and Integration and of cultivating the leadership attributes of Empathy, Enthusiasm, Efficiency, Entrepreneurship, and Ethics. In addition, it is suggested that one of the functions of leaders is to produce leaders, monitoring and setting personal examples as role models to be followed. Assignments to responsible positions in public administration need also to be based on this important leadership role of the incumbents.

11

Sociological Aspects of Administrative Ethics

Moral attributes such as honesty, being devoted to one's social duty and principles, responsibility for one's words and action are very important for civil servants. Morality as a basis for personnel management and the moral features of civil servants are of special value, especially during the deep political, social and economic reforms taking place in Russia. Global social changes are extremely rapid in all spheres of society. This means a transition from totalitarianism to democracy in political life; a transition from a command to a market economy; and each individual becoming actively involved into political and social processes. These changes in society, economy, lifestyle, are accompanied by social tension and conflict. The role of moral factors in the regulation of public relations is becoming more and more important for modern society, just as the role of legal, political and other regulatory instruments becomes more crucial. This is of special importance for civil servants. Public opinion justly links the prestige of a civil servant, first of all, with decency, honesty and responsibility.

The above-mentioned shows that there is a need to take moral factors seriously into account in developing governmental personnel management policy and in daily work with civil servants. At the same time, serious difficulties arise if the analysis of morality problems is applied to government personnel management and senior government managers. On the one hand, at the ordinary level it can be reduced to general considerations about a strong sense of duty and serving people, democracy, promoting public concerns, the principle of no corruption and not using one's position for mercenary purposes. On the other hand, spiritual and moral problems are complicated, disunified, and are so hardly formalized that it is almost impossible to concretise recommendations or to work out any unified rules.

Public administration development in the Russian Federation depends to a large extent on the staff of governmental institutions, on the personal and professional features of civil servants. Currently moral factors have a higher importance, since the role of professionalism, competence, and management culture is growing. The level of responsibility and independence in making decisions is increasing. In these circumstances, special social and moral requirements are imposed on the civil servants. The aim of the paper is to analyse the morality and moral behaviour of the modern Russian civil servant and the role of moral factors in the field of public administration. The analysis is based on the results of a representative regional survey conducted in Sverdlovskaja Oblast', one of the units of the Russian Federation, containing 73 municipalities and 44 towns. Besides the analysis of governmental staff statistics, the survey included:

- a two-stage quote representative sample interview with 450 civil servants;
- a sample survey of 710 individuals involved with different aspects of the professional activities of civil servants, aimed at capturing the image of civil servants held by the public.

The purpose of the survey is to investigate moral culture in the area of public administration, the efficiency of the moral regulation of employee behaviour and the role of moral factors in duty performance of those employed in the area of public administration.

PROFESSIONAL ETHICS AND FEATURES OF ADMINISTRATIVE ETHICS

Most civil servant activities involve communicating with the public and having constant daily personal contact with many people. Besides legal and other regulatory systems, morality is another important instrument of normative individual activity and behaviour regulation in any sphere of life. Labour morality usually includes professional ethics that determine moral principles and individual behaviour standards for any sphere of labour activity.

Professional ethics are a set of norms that determines an individual position towards professional duties, professional relations with other employees and, finally, towards society as a whole. Professional ethics reflects the specifics of morality, personal interrelationships and behaviour coming from professional activities. It is common practice to distinguish professional ethics for activities related to direct communications with people, such as medicine, journalism, legal science, general sciences, etc. Activities dealing with special public duties like military service, police service, sports or public and political activities and others are also characterized by special moral codes.

Professional ethics can be considered as a concrete expression of general ethical norms caused not only by the specifics of relations between professional groups and public, but the specifics of personal relations within a professional group. It is the existence of special personal relations within professional groups that results in special moral norms regulating these relations. Professional ethics include: first, behavioural codes defining certain types of moral relations between individuals who consider these codes optimal for the performance of a professional duty; second, the ground for these codes, the social and psychological interpretation of cultural and humanistic purposes of the profession, its epos. Professional ethics studies:

- the position of a professional group and its members towards society and other groups, and their concerns;
- the personal moral features of a specialist that provide the highest level of his/her professional duty performance;
- specifics of moral relations between specialists and individuals to whom a specialist's activities are directed;
- relationships within professional groups and special professional moral standards expressing these relationships;

- professional activity as a personal moral feature and professional activity values;
- specifics, goals and techniques of professional education.

Moral aspects of personal labour relations suggest that the goal of a professional activity, its motivations, moral statements, ways to achieve goals, evaluation system of labour results and their social value are clearly identified. Professional morality exists not only in the field of theoretical principles and statements but in everyday notions and individual professional behaviour patterns for different professional activities. Since special professional duties and tasks, as well as conditions of their performance, form the basis of professional ethics, they can strongly affect its content. A special moral relationship arises between people during a labour process. First of all, it includes personal attitudes towards labour and the participants of the labour process, as well as the moral relations that result from an interception of the interests of a professional group and society, not to mention the interests of different professional groups. Professional ethics both reflects the development of moral relation components mentioned above and presupposes that new unique components expressing qualitative attributes of a given profession can arise.

Professional ethics should not be considered a consequence of inequality between professional groups. However, society requires a very high morality level from certain professions. Labour activities in certain professional areas are based on a high level of coordination between participants, which causes increasing needs for cooperative behaviour. Special attention is paid to the moral features of individuals, such as having the right to make decisions in the areas of human life, high valued assets, health service, education and management, with public administration as a part. It is extremely difficult to formalize, regulate and put these activities into instruction. These activities are creative by their nature. The specifics of certain professional group labour activities makes moral relations much more complicated. A new component is added to them: the relationship with people to whom an activity is directed. Since management means an 'invasion' into the personal internal world, moral responsibility is a priority in this case. To determine the level of confidence in a civil servant, society takes into account both his/her educational level or amount of special knowledge and skills, and his/her moral features—one of the most important components of civil servant professional fitness. General moral norms are specified in the course of a civil servant's professional activities, taking into account labour features and the structure of moral relations typical for a given profession.

The responsibility is higher for professions based on personal contacts with other people. For these professions the value of initiative and independence in making decisions and resolving conflicts is increased. Therefore, the availability of highly developed and qualitatively special personal moral features is considered by society as the most important component of the professional fitness of an individual involved in such a profession. What professional features should the civil servant possess?

The requirement to look after the interests of society and the state is a basis for administrative ethics, which must serve the maintenance of law and human rights. Under the conditions of command and bureaucratic management techniques, administrative ethics were deformed, with dangerous consequences for social morality. This change was caused by making all parts of social life state-controlled, with an extremely high level of management centralization; unlimited power for a hierarchically structured administrative; bureaucratic machinery that promoted the separation of practical morality from what was declared; propagation of departmental (corporate) interpreting of professional behaviour codes; disciplinary diligence; imitations of assiduity and servility. This ethics was highly formalized and ritualised. Civil service ethics is a set of principles, norms and rules of behaviour, moral values and moral requirements. These are applicable to individuals that act as professional managers in the field of public administration. Considering morality as a universal regulator of personal relations is extremely important nowadays, during a time of profound change in all spheres of society, including personal moral values. Moral standards and rules of behaviour are of special significance for employees communicating daily with people. Furthermore, the moral prestige of civil servants and senior and top managers, as well as the quality of the moral and psychological atmosphere, is important for effective government. There are many definitions of administrative ethics. Normally it is stressed that governmental employees set up ethical standards for managerial decisions, analyse these standards and bear personal and professional responsibility for the decisions made. Civil service ethics is considered as 'a set of moral norms and requirements for those in public administration to aim their professional activity at attainment of common wealth and effective use of moral values'. The goal of civil service ethics is to keep the essence and content of professional activities that are socially approved. Its tasks are to regulate employee relations by means of norms, behaviour and actions, and to form an ethical component in the consciousness of public administration employees.

Civil service ethics is based upon moral norms (the Latin word 'norm' means rule, pattern; this is one of the simplest forms of moral requirement, which is used as a component of moral relations and as a form of moral consciousness). These norms are approved by society, in its role as an important regulator of collective activities and existence as well as upon professional values, which are closely connected to public administration. The ethical approach to employees' professional activity allows the recovery of original imperative meanings of ethical norms that were ignored for a long time, an increase in the individual and collective responsibility of specialists for their actions, and an improvement in the significance and prestige of the professional activities of every employee.

Administrative ethics studies all moral aspects of public administration employees' and senior managers' activities. It includes three basic components.

- Values: individual, group and social statements, opinions and attitudes towards concepts like freedom, justice, honesty, loyalty, neutrality, responsibility, etc.
- Standards and norms: the principles that guidethe actions of people and employees and help lead and control their behaviour (laws, codes, rules).
- Behaviour: different forms of employee activity limited by certain standards and norms corresponding with social values.

The style and norms of professional relations vary, depending on the type of activity. This, in turn, determines the atmosphere within the professional group. The features of the public administrator group depend on civil servant duties. This means, first of all, direct participation in preparing, making and putting into reality different governmental decisions; second, rights and opportunities to sometimes act on the behalf of the state; third, a combination of formal and procedure subjected duty regulation and wide opportunities to make authoritarian and subjective decisions; fourth, involvement in a very special professional status group of individuals working as part of the government machinery. These features mean that this group has more opportunities to influence society and social development and, consequently, bears higher responsibility for these processes than any other citizen does.

All this forms the basis for special features of mortality and psychology. For most employees, they give rise to a higher social responsibility, a prospective analytical way of thinking, and the ability to take consequences into account when making decisions. The theory and methodology of administrative ethics have been intensively studied in the United States since the 1960 and 1970s, when the government machinery of the US underwent several big scandals involving top officials. The first nationwide conference on 'Governmental ethics', in Washington in 1989, had more than 700 participants.

The abilities of the authorities to defend the interests of ordinary people, to honour citizens' self-respect and to provide social protection are the most important criteria for evaluating its activities. Such an evaluation of a civil servant is based on moral features such as honesty, decency and responsibility. The moral features of civil servants and moral factors in their activities were key points of the discussion at the international conference on administrative ethics problems that took place in the US in 1994. The participants of the conference mentioned that the development of democracy and a market economy to a large extent depends on the level of confidence citizens place in public authorities and civil servants. The problem of professional, administrative and leadership ethics has also been studied in Russia in recent years, with primary attention being paid to the principles and norms of leaders' moral behaviour, and the need to consider one's rights and activities as professional duty. Aspects of primary importance in this kind of analysis also include socially dangerous features like abusing a position of power, an unfair attitude to colleagues and bribery.

An ethical analysis of civil service problems allows us to develop recommendations and to provide professional public administrators with the necessary ethical knowledge. From the practical point of view, civil service ethics is a system of ethical knowledge and practical recommendations for professional managers. It is a generalization of moral experience in the field of management. From this point of view, ethics is an essential component of an employee's competence. Experience demonstrates that employees, especially top officials, take a great interest in the practical recommendations, behaviour standards and ethical codes that promote the effective growth of a career.

SPECIAL ETHICAL REQUIREMENTS FOR THE CIVIL SERVICE

Being a special type of professional activity, the civil service is characterized by a unique set of ideals and values that have arisen as a result of professional principles and the development of behaviour standards. There are several ways to determine ethical requirements for civil servants. First, they reflect the concept and goals of the civil service as well as special tasks of different governmental institutions. Second, these principles are influenced by a conception of an ideal or target public administration model adopted in society. 'The source of administrative ethics is a civil society, since its needs, concerns and expectations are expressed in ethical norms and requirements.'

To define ethical requirements for civil servants it is necessary, first of all, to understand clearly the aim of the civil service and the mission of the civil servant. Unfortunately, this idea has not been expressed clearly in the ongoing discussion about the concept of civil service. We support the opinion that the main function of the state is 'to serve the society, state and citizens, to put into practice the principles of democracy, to extend conditions for civil society development, to stimulate self-government development by means of professional management techniques, to delegate to public institutions and citizens as many administrative functions as possible...to develop and support their easy activities by means of both law and those moral principles and values that are crucial for public consciousness.'

This means that administrative ethics should perform the following basic tasks:

- to participate in the regulation of the relationship between government and citizens;
- to promote public and state concerns in government activities as much as possible;
- to provide public administration staff with certain behavioural standards based on morality.

The main task of administrative ethics is participation in the regulation of the relationship between government and the people. A system of ethical standards and requirements should assist:

1. In putting into practice social constitutional values, such as freedom, social justice, equal opportunities, essential civil rights;
2. In overcoming differences between public groups by means of development and performing reasonable and constructive policies, compromising ethics and social integration; ethical aspects of working out and making decisions in the area of public administration are of primary importance in this case;
3. In distributing public wealth, goods, benefits and compensations made by governmental bodies; furthermore, in the course of governmental institutions performing these tasks, the problems of justice, equality, etc. arise;
4. In increasing authority prestige, since any state and regional government institution employee represents power in general, and ordinary people consider his/her activities as actions of the state; this imposes a special responsibility for those employed in the area of public administration. The importance of administrative ethics tasks means an increasing need to define ethical criteria

for every public servant, and to impose responsibility for his/her professional activities. This requires developing a unified approach to set up easily interpreted moral principles and standards and to work out a unified system of values and ideals.

It is possible to use social and state concerns as criteria and an ultimate aim for civil servants' professional activity. Professional ethics for the civil service suppose that one should search for and use all possible resources, including the social and personal resources of both civil servants and service customers. However, this can only be done to achieve socially and professionally approved goals, and never for narrow corporate or personal mercenary goals.

Professional civil service ethics is not an exclusive regulator of servant behaviour, and does not contradict any other technique. Its standards and principles correspond to the same goals as do the requirements of public administration legislative and instructive bases. Moreover, civil servant ethics requires professional groups and specialists working for these groups to serve social, professional, group and single customer concerns.

Special ethical requirements for civil servants are necessary in order to realize in society such constitutional values as freedom, social justice, equal opportunities and essential human rights. Therefore, there is a strong relationship between ethical requirements and constitutional values. Special requirements for civil servant should cover the following standards: requirements (how professional morality directs civil servant behaviour in certain conditions); prohibitions (what is prohibited in professional behaviour); recommendations (how civil servants should behave in certain moral conditions).

Civil servants have no right to place public concerns below individual or group concerns, or to wittingly, systematically promote the concerns of an independent social group if this is harmful for society and the state. The servant must act to serve national interests and to increase public wealth in Russia. The actions, proposals and decisions made by a civil servant should not undermine the prestige of authority. His/her duties should not depend on his/her private concerns, and a servant should not evade personal responsibility.

One of the features of civil service ethics is a special moral standard. This standard allows civil servant not to follow or even to ignore any order or instruction that contradicts seriously to Constitution of Russian Federation or violates basic human rights even if this order or instruction has legal administrative or normative basis.

It is extremely important to develop high moral responsibility for public administration employees who are dealing with individuals representing different social groups. It should be mentioned that from the citizen, professional group or institution point of view it is public administration employee who represents the state and acts on behalf or according to the order of the government body. His/her behaviour, style of work, ways to resolve problems and to talk to ordinary people finally forms the impression upon government machinery. All mentioned above oblige to develop measures to improve style of ministries and departments work as well as to control the performance of government administrative machinery. It is necessary to pay attention to high responsibility for one's duties in the employee education, to inculcate in servant the features like efficiency, orderliness, irreproachable and honest duty performance as well as ability to foresee and to work prospectively. The features like energy in getting things done, effectiveness, accuracy, disciplinary, organizational culture, ability to plan personal efforts and link them with prospective goals, readiness to bear risks, aspiration to continuing self-education and rising qualification skills.

The moral responsibility of civil servants is increasing: many have power and the right to apply compulsory measures. They should use these rights rationally. It is well known that any managerial process is more successful if the participants of the process perform their tasks believing that this performance is vital, and when they understand their global task. Individuals with an organic combination of personal and social attitudes, who do not separate professional duties from what comes from the heart, intellect and will, usually have high prestige among both the public and their colleagues. The responsibility of top government officials is extremely important. They should manifest a pattern of adequate labour discipline, making and carrying out effective decisions. Public opinion evaluates their actions from the point of view of both material and moral results, as well as examining the influence of these actions on public morality. Government officials should possess both the ability to effectively guide production processes and devote themselves to high moral standards (such as modesty, self-control, principled behaviour, tact and kindness in personal contacts with people). Ethical aspects arise at all levels for civil servants—when problems are defined that inherently involve public concern; during conscientious and objective data collection; in making detailed analyses of possible consequences; regarding the proportion between common wealth and the personal goals of a decisionmaker; in selecting techniques to perform decisions; and so on. Civil servant duties presuppose that the civil servant possess features like neutrality, competency, impartiality, succession and 'transparency'. In the opposite case, a threat to basic human rights may arise. The key features of for a civil servant are a high level of competency as well as personal features, civic attitudes, high morality and the ability to serve his or her country, to follow the law, and to keep national and international moral and spiritual values.

MORAL CULTURE OF CIVIL SERVANTS

Moral culture is an artificial integral indicator of personality moral development. Moral culture shows itself in the ability of individuals to deliberately and voluntary follow moral standards and to execute purposeoriented behaviour that is characterized by the harmonic combination of personal and public concerns. Moral freedom is represented by the ability of a personality to independently express his/her will while selecting a way of action within the framework of predetermined alternatives as well as his/her ability to control his/her own behaviour and to take responsibility for its result. The most important core components of personal moral freedom are:

- recognizing the requirements of moral standards;
- recognizing these standards as an internal need;
- making decisions in accordance with internal statements, without any external (legal or arbitrary) pressure;
- making strong-willed efforts and having self-control in terms of decision performance, feeling emotional satisfaction with the results achieved;

- taking responsibility for causes and consequences of actions.

Moral culture is a qualitative measure of moral development and the moral maturity of a personality. Personal moral culture can be reduced neither to external ethics nor to moral self-reflexes. Moral culture is not limited by learning basic moral requirements and features like conscientiousness, honesty and disinterestedness, although it can not exist without these truisms. Personal values and ideals, objectively historically determined personal goals, attitudes and ideals are all of crucial importance. Each civil servant has certain duties depending on his/her position. The combination of these duties forms the concept of professional duty. The moral aspects of a civil servant's professional duty are strongly recognized internal atements towards voluntary willingness to conscientiously perform his/her duties, to understand vital necessities of his/her job. Faultless professional duty performance by a civil servant is a matter of honour. Deep understanding and conscientious professional duty performance determines public acknowledgement of a civil servant and, at the end, predetermines such components of honour as recognition of self-respect.

Civil servants are given extraordinary rights, opportunities to act on behalf of the state and participate in preparing, making and performing decisions that can result in serious social and economic consequences for the majority of the population. Therefore, there must be higher requirements in terms of both their professional and moral features. For example, in France the key ethical feature is a requirement of integrity; i.e., it is not only honesty, incorruptibility and moral innocence as well as high level of morality that completely prevents bribery. Civil servant moral culture is expressed in actions, behaviour, relationships with others, and even in the appearance of a civil servant. As D. Carnegi mentioned, there are four types of personal contacts: our image is based on what we do, how we look, what we say and how we say that.

What are the personal features of those employed in the area of public administration? According to survey responses, the principal features of the civil servants are professionalism and competency (this was mentioned by 85.1% of respondents), responsibility (45.8% of respondents) and assiduity (30.2% of respondents). Other features made reference to were respect for the law, organizational abilities, initiative, ability to understand local problems.

The Civil Service Law of the Russian Federation stresses that each servant is obliged to strictly follow social moral and ethical standards both at the workplace and in ordinary life, to prevent the offence of public order and community rules. In recent years, there have been serious changes in executive governments tasks, social roles and staff. New people became civil servants. Most of them are young and full of energy, but have no professional experience. They introduced a number of new components into the style of work of executive governments. But along with positive changes, the activity of executive governments is characterized by several negative social and ethical phenomena.

MORAL ASPECTS OF CORRUPTION

Corruption is the most dangerous 'functional' or 'professional' form of criminal behaviour by civil servants. The socially dangerous consequences of corruption are familiar to everybody. The VIII Congress of the UN, which took place in Havana in 1990, stressed the necessity of developing a conduct code for officials. It was recognized that the problem of corruption is urgent all around the world, that corruption severely damages the economy, undermines governmental decisions, reduces morality, decreases citizen confidence in the government and destroys the principle of impartial justice. Bribery is the core component of corruption. However, this phenomenon is not mentioned in criminal statistics annuals issued in the developed countries. Governments are very unwillingly prosecute 'their own' corrupted officials. According to UN data, in 1970-1990 the proportion of bribery was less than 1% of the total 10-12 crime types collected by the international community. In 1986-1990, this rate rose to 8% all around the world. The upward trend is continuing.

Corruption cannot be reduced simply bribery, especially in conditions of a market economy, free trade and democracy. New phenomena—lobbying, favouritism, protectionism, contributions for political needs, budget investments to commercial enterprises, assignation of state property to joint stock ventures, use of contacts with criminals—are not indicated by official criminal statistics, except a few very simple cases. Corruption is usually defined as a social phenomenon characterized by the fact that bribable governmental officials and other servants use official duties and advantages as well as prestige and other opportunities to promote their personal and narrow group or corporate concerns. There are several different explanations of the origination of corruption. Some people argue that the reason for corruption is bad legislation that leads to moral degradation. Others state that legislation does not matter, and bribery is nothing else but the reflection of age-old vices, confirmed by the quotations from Tsitseron speeches, Old Russian chronicles, etc. Other specialists consider the increasing number of officials, bureaucratisation of public life, and unwarranted extensions of the government role as the main reasons for corruption. Corruption often arises if government tries to regulate the market with help of non-market techniques. This is the second explanation for the reasons of tremendous widespread of corruption.

The third approach states that the main reasons of corruption are economic. First of all, this is any form of monopolization. Another reason is that a rapid market evolution leads to large amounts of money being transferred out of control. The complication of organizational business rules lead to increasing roles for mediators. A large number of people, having no basic market culture and able only to 'make money' but not to earn money, became entrepreneurs. More and more specialists recognize that reasons of this third type are the most important. These include the development of market relations and the related inevitable disparity between new public practices and existing legal norms, which should be either supported or adjusted appropriately if they became obsolete. Legal regulation is not always effective in Russia. There is a lot of space for personal discretion and arbitrariness. Sometimes making requirements not uniform is itself considered as bribe extortion and provokes bribery.

There are three forms of civil servant corruption. The first one is receiving immunity from prosecution and punishment. The second is avoiding local government penalties for the violation of different norms and instructions. The third is obtaining licenses, contracts and permissions. Corruption in Russia, first of all, is a mean of appropriate performance of legal services and the achievement of socially approved goals. Western research on corruption considers bribes in the USSR as a 'universal lubricating action' in the economy and a typical way to attract a boss's attention. A special feature is that businessmen use their personal contacts with public administration employees rather than legal and organized lobbying through numerous political parties, entrepreneurial unions or associations. This means that businessmen in Russia prefer non-institutional lobbying (91.3% of interviewed participants of the First Russian Congress of Entrepreneurs in 1996 agreed with this statement).

Traditional forms of bribery among civil servants include giving priority to a foreign company that gave a bribe but had no competitive advantages; entering into contracts unprofitable for the country; promoting product distribution; mediating in trade deals; not punishing foreign companies breaking delivery contracts, etc. New forms of criminal activity are also becoming widespread. For example, the entire industry of unofficial services rendered for bribes by participants in intergovernmental economic relations has arisen because of the lack of official commercial information. Bribery for controlling 'start' currency funds is practiced in banking by enterprises and institutions making foreign contracts.

Bribery has always been the most latent crime. Many researchers states that undiscovered bribery makes up 98% of total bribery. Criminal cases are instituted against only 70% of the total number of bribe-takers. And only 19% of them go to prison. The number of people who were convicted is only some tens. The problem of official corruption is extremely large.

Fighting corruption is not effective in most cases. The dynamics of corruption acts made by Russian officials at all levels in the difficult period of perestroika and reform reflect the slackening anti-corruption measures of the 1990s, rather than a real decrease in corruption. Organizational and legal anti-corruption measures underway at the moment should bring more positive results. The Eighth UN Congress on preventing criminal activity and treating offenders adopted a resolution on corruption in public administration. It states that corrupted civil servant activity can destroy the potential effectiveness of any type of governmental program and is especially dangerous for weak economies.

Unfortunately, the efforts undertaken to stop corruption are not effectively linked with the measures aimed at economic stabilization. Furthermore, economic and social reforms do not include measures for reducing the criminal effects of transition period collateral phenomena. At the same time, in developed countries the economic administration system and the entire civil service is—to a certain extent—protected from corruption and power abuse by a system of administrative and regulatory measures. These include, on the one hand, accounting, effective disciplinary and other measures aimed at civil servants, and measures for their social protection; on the other hand, appropriate banking and financial instructions prohibit large illegal money transactions.

Important measures in the fight against corruption are legal stability and clear normative regulation of property relations. Diminishing corruption is only possible if these matters are absolutely clarified. According to public opinion, the level of corruption among officials is extremely high. Nowadays, the problem of corruption is becoming universal. One of the reasons for this phenomenon is the fact that the history of human beings, as Shpengler stressed, has entered the stage of civilization when all problems are becoming global, and market relations are available everywhere around the world. Market orientation suggests that people manipulate each other, and every individual acts as a means (not as a purpose) and considers himself a good.

To investigate public opinion on corruption among civil servants we interviewed earlier 710 individuals. Most of the respondents (85.5%) stated that corruption exists in governmental institutions. It should be pointed out that the level of corruption perceived by the general public seems too high. Many respondents link the wide corruption among civil servants with general moral degradation (38.6%), the personal features of a civil servant (27.5%), and low salaries (48.5%). Taking these results into consideration, it is possible to conclude that the general public does not know how bureaucracy as a social institute performs. Therefore, they indicate subjective factors (like personal features, greed, avidity) as key reasons for corruption. As far as objective factors, they indicate only global reasons, such as moral degradation or economic difficulties.

The respondents considered that the most widespread phenomena among civil servants are power abuse (46.3%), bribe extortion and corruption (31.3%), and ignoring laws (25.8%). At the same time, 34.2% of the interviewed believe that bribes facilitate problem solving. In terms of legality, only 40% of the respondents are of the opinion that it is necessary to carry out the letter of the law; others prefer just to follow a law (26.5%) or instruction (31.0%). This is evidence of legal nihilism. Every second respondent thinks that it is possible to evade the law or to use it to attain personal goals.

What is the most efficient way to fight corruption in Russia? Most of the respondents (61,7%)—regardless of their educational level, or social or economic position—believe it is prosecution. Improving legislation (36.5%) was the second choice and political will of the government (30.0%) was third. But none of these measures are exhaustive.

Government military forces can do nothing about criminality without having extraordinary rights. Suppose society provided them with these rights. Will society then be able to control how these extraordinary rights are used? The criminal net is so closely connected to the system of legal relations (economic, social, including contacts with law-enforcement agencies) that no one direct anti-criminal measure can have an effect unless it is supported by a system of laws that classifies any activity as legal or illegal.

The most important anti-corruption measure is legal stabilization and improved legislation. Another aspect is openness in official activity, transforming the civil service into a 'public service' that would serve the people.

EMPLOYEES' MORAL STANDARDS

The basic condition of civil servant effectiveness at any level of power is his/her image combined with a positive public image of the civil service. Therefore, identifying opinions held by the public about civil servants is a necessary condition, together with analysing the results. This can be an important way to increase the effectiveness of personnel management policy.

While conducting the survey, we were interested in the extent to which, according to public opinion, personal and moral features of civil servants developed because these features influence the effectiveness of duties performed by a civil servant. The respondents said that the most important civil servant personal features are efficiency, assiduity and competency. Organizational abilities, ability to compromise and understanding local problems were also mentioned. It is evident that low morality to a large extent determines the quality of governmental institution performance. Moreover, the authorities do not always have the necessary resources to perform their duties.

REASONS FOR CONFLICTS AND THEIR IMPACT ON MORALITY AND GOVERNMENT EMPLOYEE ACTIVITY

The activities of authorities as well as public administration usually entail conflicts. It is a legal basis that is used as the main regulator of conflicts between the authorities and the people, conflicts between servants of public administration bodies. However, the role of morality and moral culture in preventing and regulating conflicts is extremely high. The higher the moral culture, the more effective moral regulation of conflicts becomes. To successfully regulate the conflict it is necessary to identify its reasons. A number of reasons are directly related to civil servants violating social moral standards.

All types of conflict behaviour (fights, games, disputes and others) are typical in the area of public administration. However, most conflicts in this area are caused, first of all, by the difference between various units, groups and persons in status and concerns: i.e., by 'natural' factors that arise from professional role distinctions and are subjected to regulation by legal and moral standards and rules. The dominating role of different types of conflict behaviour in the area of public administration means that the principal task is to prevent, regulate and ease conflict, or exclude its acute forms. This is more important than completely resolving or eliminating it.

Different techniques can be used to settle conflicts. These are different forms of conciliation commissions and procedures that work out compromises; professional codes and organizational culture norms; and strong limitations or even direct prohibitions on certain protest forms (for example, strikes).

In other words, conflict regulation in the area of public administration is made, first of all, with help of techniques based on a set of peaceful measures—from simple compromise to finding ways of cooperation. The use of force or threats to use force are rather exclusive and non-typical ways of regulation in this case.

The key problem here is what causes conflicts. One of the most popular reasons, especially for the conflict between a boss and a subordinate, is the difference of moral values. For example, the subordinate may consider that he/she has a right to always state his/her opinion.

At the same time, the boss may consider that the subordinate has a right to express his/her opinion only if he/she was asked, and that the subordinate must follow a superior's orders. These conflicts often arise between managers striving for efficiency and subordinates. Conflicts are caused by differences in behaviour as well as individual personal features (for example, high levels of aggression and hostility).

Inadequate communications and bad information distribution can be both the reason and the consequence of conflict. Preventing civil servants or a professional group from understanding each other may work as a catalyst for conflict. Research has shown that inadequate information causes conflict between bosses and subordinates.

These conflicts result from the inability of the boss to correctly distribute duties and tasks, and the necessity to perform tasks that are not included in the list of duties of a given civil servant. These problems can arise or be enforced if the boss is unable to develop a clear list of duties for subordinates. The survey results have shown that conflicts rarely arise in public administration institutions. This was espoused by 57.3% of the civil servants interviewed. Only 2% of the respondents thought that conflicts arise in their organizations rather often. But 19.3% of the respondents consider that there are no conflicts in their organizations at all. Conflicts with bosses are frequently caused by enlisting subordinates to perform tasks that are not part of their direct duties; because of leadership style; and low salaries. Inadequate organization of labour can become a reason for conflict both between bosses and subordinates and between colleagues. According to the survey, 42.4% of the interviewed civil servants think that it is much better to have no conflicts; 30.4% of respondents mentioned that conflicts prevent work; 5.8% of respondents considered that conflicts neither help nor hinder work; 8% of the respondents were of the opinion that conflicts help to solve problems and speed up decision making.

12

The Historical Development of the State

The earliest forms of the state emerged whenever it became possible to centralize power in a durable way. Agriculture and writing are almost everywhere associated with this process: agriculture because it allowed for the emergence of a class of people who did not have to spend most of their time providing for their own subsistence, and writing (or the equivalent of writing, like Inca quipus) because it made possible the centralization of vital information.

The State in Classical Antiquity

The history of the state in the West usually begins with classical antiquity. During that period, the state took a variety of forms, none of them very much like the modern state. There were monarchies whose power (like that of the Egyptian Pharaoh) was based on the religious function of the king and his control of a centralized army. There were also large, quasi-bureaucratized empires, like the Roman empire, which depended less on the religious function of the ruler and more on effective military and legal organizations and the cohesiveness of an aristocracy.

Perhaps the most important political innovations of classical antiquity came from the Greek city-states and the Roman Republic. The Greek city-states before the 4th century granted citizenship rights to their free population, and in Athens these rights were combined with a directly democratic form of government that was to have a long afterlife in political thought and history. In contrast, Rome developed from a monarchy into a republic, governed by a senate dominated by the Roman aristocracy. The Roman political system contributed to the development of law, constitutionalism and to the distinction between the private and the public spheres.

From the Feudal State to the Modern State in the West

The story of the development of the specifically modern state in the West typically begins with the dissolution of the western Roman empire. This led to the fragmentation of the imperial state into the hands of private lords whose political, judicial, and military roles corresponded to the organization of economic production. In these conditions, according to Marxists, the economic unit of society was the state. The state-system of feudal Europe was an unstable configuration of suzerains and anointed kings. A monarch, formally at the head of a hierarchy of sovereigns, was not an absolute power who could rule at will; instead, relations between lords and monarchs were mediated by varying degrees of mutual dependence, which was ensured by the absence of a centralized system of taxation. This reality ensured that each ruler needed to obtain the 'consent' of each estate in the realm. This was not quite a 'state' in the Weberian sense of the term, since the king did not monopolize either the power of lawmaking (which was shared with the church) or the means of violence (which were shared with the nobles). The formalization of the struggles over taxation between the monarch and other elements of society (especially the nobility and the cities) gave rise to what is now called the Standestaat, or the state of Estates, characterized by parliaments in which key social groups negotiated with the king about legal and economic matters. These estates of the realm sometimes evolved in the direction of fully-fledged parliaments, but sometimes lost out in their struggles with the monarch, leading to greater centralization of lawmaking and coercive (chiefly military) power in his hands. Beginning in the 15th century, this centralizing process gives rise to the absolutist state.

The Modern State

The rise of the modern state as a public power constituting

the supreme political authority within a defined territory is associated with western Europe's gradual institutional development beginning in earnest in the late 15th century, culminating in the rise of absolutism and capitalism.

As Europe's dynastic states--England under the Tudors, Spain under the Habsburgs, and France under the Bourbons—embarked on a variety of programs designed to increase centralized political and economic control, they increasingly exhibited many of the features that now define sovereign states. This centralization of power involved the delineation of political boundaries, as European monarchs gradually defeated or co-opted other sources of power, such as the Church and lesser nobility. In place of the fragmented system of feudal rule, with its often indistinct territorial claims, large, unitary states with extensive control over definite territories emerged. This process gave rise to the highly centralized and increasingly bureaucratic forms of absolute monarchical rule of the 17th and 18th centuries, when the principal features of the contemporary state system took form, including the introduction of a standing army, a central taxation system, diplomatic relations with permanent embassies, and the development of state economic policy—mercantilism.

Cultural and national homogenization figured prominently in the rise of the modern state system. Since the absolutist period, states have largely been organized on a national basis. The concept of a national state, however, is not synonymous with nation state. Even in the most ethnically homogeneous societies there is not always a complete correspondence between state and nation, hence the active role often taken by the state to promote nationalism through emphasis on shared symbols and national identity.

It is in this period that the term "state" is first introduced into political discourse in more or less its current meaning. Although Niccolò Machiavelli is often credited with first using the term to refer to a territorial sovereign government in the modern sense in *The Prince*, published in 1532, it is not until the time of the British thinkers Thomas Hobbes and John Locke and the French thinker Jean Bodin that the concept in its current meaning is fully developed. Today, most Western states more or less fit the influential definition of the state in

Max Weber's *Politics as a Vocation.* According to Weber, the modern state monopolizes the means of legitimate physical violence over a well-defined territory. Moreover, the legitimacy of this monopoly itself is of a very special kind, "rational-legal" legitimacy, based on impersonal rules that constrain the power of state elites.

However, in other parts of the world not all states fit Weber's definition. They may not have a complete monopoly over the means of legitimate physical violence over a definite territory, or their legitimacy may not be adequately described as rational-legal. But they are still recognizably distinct from feudal and absolutist states in the extent of their bureaucratization and their reliance on nationalism as a principle of legitimation. Since Weber, an extensive literature on the processes by which the sovereign state emerged from the feudal state has been generated. Marxist scholars, for example, assert that the formation of modern states can be explained primarily in terms of the interests and struggles of social classes.

Scholars working in the broad Weberian tradition, by contrast, have often emphasized the institution-building effects of war. For example, Charles Tilly has argued that the revenue-gathering imperatives forced on nascent states by geopolitical competition and constant warfare were mostly responsible for the development of the centralized, territorial bureaucracies that characterize sovereign states in Europe. States that were able to develop centralized tax-gathering bureaucracies and to field mass armies survived into the modern era; states that were not able to do so did not.

KINDS OF STATES

Sovereign States

A Sovereign state is a state with a defined territory on which it exercises internal and external sovereignty, a permanent population, a government, independence from other states and powers, and the capacity to enter into relations with other sovereign states. It is also normally understood to be a state which is not dependent on, or subject to any other power or state. While in abstract terms a sovereign state can exist without being recognised by other sovereign states, unrecognised states will often find it hard to exercise full treaty-making powers and engage in diplomatic relations with other sovereign states.

History

Since the late 19th century, virtually the entirety of the world's inhabitable land has been parceled up into areas with more or less definite borders claimed by various states. Earlier, quite large land areas had been either unclaimed or uninhabited, or inhabited by nomadic peoples who were not organized as states. However, even within present-day states there are vast areas of wilderness, like the Amazon Rainforest, which are uninhabited or inhabited solely or mostly by indigenous people (and some of them remain uncontacted). Also, there are states which do not hold *de facto* control over all of their claimed territory or where this control is challenged (as in the 2006 civil war in Somalia).

Currently the international community comprises more than 200 sovereign states, the vast majority of which are represented in the United Nations. These states form what international relations theorists call a system, where each state takes into account the behaviour of other states when making their own calculations. From this point of view, states embedded in an international system face internal and external security and legitimation dilemmas. Recently the notion of an international community has been developed to refer to a group of states who have established rules, procedures, and institutions for the conduct of their relations. In this way the foundation has been laid for international law, diplomacy, formal regimes, and organizations.

Definition

Sovereignty is a term that is frequently misused. Lassa Oppenheim said "There exists perhaps no conception the meaning of which is more controversial than that of sovereignty. It is an indisputable fact that this conception, from the moment when it was introduced into political science until the present day, has never had a meaning which was universally agreed upon." In the opinion of Justice Evatt of the High Court of Australia "sovereignty is neither a question of fact, nor a question of law, but a question that does not arise at all."

In casual usage, the terms "country", "nation", and "state" are often used as if they were synonymous; but in a more strict usage they can be distinguished:

- *Nation* denotes a people who are believed to or deemed to share common customs, origins, and history. However, the adjectives *national* and *international* are frequently used to refer to matters pertaining to what are strictly *sovereign states*, as in *national capital*, *international law*.
- *State* refers to the set of governing and supportive institutions that have sovereignty over a definite territory and population.

Recognition

State recognition signifies the decision of a sovereign state to treat another entity as also being a sovereign state. Recognition can be either express or implied and is usually retroactive in its effects. It doesn't necessarily signify a desire to establish or maintain diplomatic relations.

There is no definition that is binding on all the members of the community of nations on the criteria for statehood. In actual practice, the criteria are mainly political, not legal. L.C. Green cited the recognition of the unborn Polish and Czech states in World War I and explained that "recognition of statehood is a matter of discretion, it is open to any existing state to accept as a state any entity it wishes, regardless of the existence of territory or an established government."

In international law, however, there are several theories of when a state should be recognized as sovereign.

Constitutive Theory

The constitutive theory of statehood defines a state as a person of international law if, and only if, it is recognized as sovereign by other states. This theory of recognition, was developed in the 19th century. Under it, a state was sovereign if another sovereign state recognized it as such. Because of this, new states could not immediately become part of the international community or be bound by international law, and recognized nations did not have to respect international law in their dealings with them. In 1815 at the Congress of Vienna the Final Act only recognised 39 sovereign states in the European diplomatic system, and as a result it was firmly established that in future new states would have to be recognized by other states, and that meant in practice recognition by one or more of the great powers.

One of the major criticisms of this law is the confusion caused when some states recognize a new entity, but other states do not. Hersch Lauterpacht, one of the theory's main proponents, suggested that it is a state's duty to grant recognition as a possible solution. However, a state may use any criteria when judging if they should give recognition and they have no obligation to use such criteria. Many states may only recognize another state if it is to their advantage.

In 1912, L. F. L. Oppenheim had the following to say on constitutive theory:...International Law does not say that a State is not in existence as long as it is not recognised, but it takes no notice of it before its recognition. Through recognition only and exclusively a State becomes an International Person and a subject of International Law.

Declarative Theory

By contrast, the "declarative" theory defines a state as a person in international law if it meets the following criteria: 1) a defined territory; 2) a permanent population; 3) a government and 4) a capacity to enter into relations with other states. According to declarative theory, an entity's statehood is independent of its recognition by other states. The declarative model was most famously expressed in the 1933 Montevideo Convention.

Article 3 of the Convention declares that statehood is independent of recognition by other states. In contrast, recognition is considered a requirement for statehood by the constitutive theory of statehood.

A similar opinion about "the conditions on which an entity constitutes a state" is expressed by the European Economic Community *Opinions of the Badinter Arbitration Committee*. The Badinter Arbitration Committee found that a state was defined by having a territory, a population, and a political authority.

State Practice

State practice relating the recognition states typically falls somewhere between the declaratory and constitutive approaches. International law does not require a state to recognise other states. Recognition is often withheld when a new state is seen as illegitimate or has come about in breach of international law. Almost universal non-recognition by the international community of Rhodesia and the *Turkish Republic of North Cyprus* are good examples of this. In the former case, recognition was widely withheld when the White minority seized power and attempted to form a state along the lines of Apartheid South Africa. A move which the United Nations Security Council described as the creation of an "illegal racist minority regime". In the latter case recognition was wildly withheld from a state created in Northern Cyprus on land which was illegally invaded by Turkey in 1974.

De facto *and* De Jure *States*

Most sovereign states are states *de jure* and *de facto* (i.e. they exist both in law and in reality). However, sometimes states exist only as *de jure* states in that an organisation is recognised as having sovereignty over and being the legitimate government of a territory over which they have no actual control.

Many continental European states maintained governments-in-exile during the Second World War which continued to enjoy diplomatic relations with the Allies, notwithstanding that their countries were under Nazi occupation.

A present day example is the Sovereign Military Order of Malta, which is a United Nations observer, has bi-lateral diplomatic relations with 104 states, while having no territory and possessing only extraterritorial areas (i.e. embassies and consulates). Other states may have sovereignty over a territory but lack international recognition, these are *de facto* states only. Somaliland is commonly considered to be such a state. For a list of entities that wish to be universally recognized as sovereign states, but do not have complete worldwide diplomatic recognition, see the list of states with limited recognition.

NATION STATES

The nation-state is a state that self-identifies as deriving its political legitimacy from serving as a sovereign entity for a country as a sovereign territorial unit. The state is a political and geopolitical entity; the nation is a cultural and/or ethnic entity. The term "nation-state" implies that the two geographically coincide, and this distinguishes the nation state from the other types of state, which historically preceded it.

History and Origins

The origins and early history of nation-states are disputed. A major theoretical issue is: "which came first — the nation or the nation state?" For nationalists themselves, the answer is that the nation existed first, nationalist movements arose to present its legitimate demand for sovereignty, and the nation-state met that demand. Some "modernisation theories" of nationalism see the national identity largely as a product of government policy, to unify and modernise an already existing state. Most theories see the nation state as a 19th-century European phenomenon, facilitated by developments such as mass literacy and the early mass media. However, historians also note the early emergence of a relatively unified state, and a sense of common identity, in Portugal and the Dutch Republic.

In France, Eric Hobsbawm argues the French state preceded the formation of the French people. Hobsbawm considers that the state made the French nation, and not French nationalism, which emerged at the end of the 19th century, the time of the Dreyfus Affair. At the time of the 1789 French Revolution, only half of the French people spoke some French, and between 12 percent to 13 percent spoke it "fairly", according to Hobsbawm. During Italian unification, the number of people speaking the Italian language was even lower. The French state promoted the unification of various dialects and languages into the French language. The introduction of conscription and the Third Republic's 1880s laws on public instruction, facilitated the creation of a national identity, under this theory.

The theorist Benedict Anderson argues that nations are "imagined communities" (the members cannot possibly know each other), and that the main causes of nationalism and the creation of an imagined community are the reduction of privileged access to particular script languages (e.g. Latin), the movement to abolish the ideas of divine rule and monarchy, as well as the emergence of the printing press under a system of capitalism (or, as Anderson calls it, *print-capitalism*). The "state-driven" theories of the origin of nation-states tend to emphasise a few specific states, such as England and its rival France. These states expanded from core regions, and developed a national consciousness and sense of national identity ("Englishness" and "Frenchness"). Both assimilated peripheral regions (Wales, Cornubia, Brittany, Occitania); these areas experienced a revival of interest in the regional culture in the 19th century, leading to the creation of autonomist movements in the 20th century.

Some nation-states, such as Germany or Italy, came into existence at least partly as a result of political campaigns by nationalists, during the 19th century. In both cases, the territory was previously divided among other states, some of them very small. The sense of common identity was at first a cultural movement, such as in the *Völkisch movement* in German-speaking states, which rapidly acquired a political significance. In these cases, the nationalist sentiment and the nationalist movement clearly precede the unification of the German and Italian nation-states.

Historians Hans Kohn, Liah Greenfeld, Philip White and others have classified nations such as Germany or Italy, where cultural unification preceded state unification, as *ethnic nations* or *ethnic nationalities*. Whereas 'state-driven' national unifications, such as in France, England or China, are more likely to flourish in multiethnic societies, producing a traditional national heritage of *civic nations*, or *territory-based nationalities*.

The idea of a nation-state is associated with the rise of the modern system of states, often called the "Westphalian system" in reference to the Treaty of Westphalia (1648). The balance of power, which characterises that system, depends for its effectiveness upon clearly defined, centrally controlled, independent entities, whether empires or nation states, which recognise each other's sovereignty and territory. The Westphalian system did not create the nation-state, but the nation-state meets the criteria for its component states (assuming that there is no disputed territory).

The nation-state received a philosophical underpinning in the era of Romanticism, at first as the 'natural' expression of the individual peoples. The increasing emphasis during the 19th century on the ethnic and racial origins of the nation, led to a redefinition of the nation-state in these terms. Racism, which in Boulainvilliers's theories was inherently antipatriotic and antinationalist, joined itself with colonialist imperialism and "continental imperialism", most notably in pan-Germanic and pan-Slavic movements. This relation between racism and ethnic nationalism reached its height in the fascist and Nazi movements of the 20th century. The specific combination of 'nation' ('people') and 'state' expressed in such terms as the *Völkische Staat* and implemented in laws such as the 1935 Nuremberg laws made fascist states such as early Nazi Germany qualitatively different from non-fascist nation-states. Obviously, minorities, who are not part of the *Volk*, have no authentic or legitimate role in such a state. In Germany, neither Jews nor the Roma were considered part of the *Volk*, and were specifically targeted for persecution. However German nationality law defined 'German' on the basis of German ancestry, excluding *all* non-Germans from the 'Volk'. In recent years the nation-state's claim to absolute sovereignty within its borders has been much criticised. A global political system based on international agreements and supra-national blocs characterized the post-war era. Non-state actors, such as international corporations and non-governmental organizations, are widely seen as eroding the economic and political power of nation-states, potentially leading to their eventual disappearance.

Before Nation-states

In Europe, in the 18th century, the classic non-national states were the *multi-ethnic* empires, (the Austro-Hungarian Empire, the Russian Empire, the Ottoman Empire, the British Empire) and smaller states at what would now be called sub-national level. The multi-ethnic empire was a monarchy ruled by a king, emperor or sultan. The population belonged to many ethnic groups, and they spoke many languages. The empire was dominated by one ethnic group, and their language was usually the language of public administration. The ruling dynasty was usually, but not always, from that group. This type of state is not specifically European: such empires existed on all continents. Some of the smaller European states were not so ethnically diverse, but were also dynastic states, ruled by a royal house. Their territory could expand by royal intermarriage or merge with another state when the dynasty merged. In some parts of Europe, notably Germany, very small territorial units existed. They were recognised by their neighbours as independent, and had their own government and laws. Some were ruled by princes or other hereditary rulers, some were governed by bishops or abbots. Because they were so small, however, they had no separate language or culture: the inhabitants shared the language of the surrounding region.

In some cases these states were simply overthrown by nationalist uprisings in the 19th century. Liberal ideas of free trade played a role in German unification, which was preceded by a customs union, the Zollverein. However, the Austro-Prussian War, and the German alliances in the Franco-Prussian War, were decisive in the unification. The Austro-Hungarian Empire and the Ottoman Empire broke up after the First World War and the Russian Empire became the Soviet Union, after the long Russian Civil War.

Some of the smaller states survived: the independent principalities of Liechtenstein, Andorra, Monaco, and the republic of San Marino. (Vatican City is different. Although there was a larger Papal State, it was created in its present form by the 1929 Lateran treaties between Italy and the Roman Catholic Church.)

Characteristics of the Nation-state

Nation-states have their own characteristics, differing from those of the pre-national states. For a start, they have a different attitude to their territory, compared to the dynastic monarchies: it is semi-sacred, and non-transferable. No nation would swap territory with other states simply, for example, because the king's daughter got married. They have a different type of border, in principle defined only by the area of settlement of the national group, although many nation states also sought natural borders (rivers, mountain ranges).

The most noticeable characteristic is the degree to which nation-states use the state as an instrument of national unity, in economic, social and cultural life.

The nation-state promoted economic unity, first by abolishing internal customs and tolls. In Germany this process, the creation of the Zollverein, preceded formal national unity. Nation-states typically have a policy to create and maintain a national transportation infrastructure, facilitating trade and travel. In 19th-century Europe, the expansion of the rail transport networks was at first largely a matter for private railway companies, but gradually came under control of the national governments. The French rail network, with its main lines radiating from Paris to all corners of France, is often seen as a reflection of the centralised French nation-state, which directed its construction. Nation states continue to build, for instance, specifically national motorway networks. Specifically trans-national infrastructure programmes, such as the Trans-European Networks, are a recent innovation. The nation-states typically had a more centralised and uniform public administration than its imperial predecessors: they were smaller, and the population less diverse. (The internal diversity of, for instance, the Ottoman Empire was very great.) After the 19th-century triumph of the nation-state in Europe, regional identity was subordinate to national identity, in regions such as Alsace-Lorraine, Catalonia, Brittany, Sicily, Sardinia and Corsica. In many cases, the regional administration was also subordinated to central (national) government. This process was partially reversed from the 1970s onward, with the introduction of various forms of regional autonomy, in formerly centralised states such as France.

The most obvious impact of the nation-state, as compared to its non-national predecessors, is the creation of a uniform national culture, through state policy. The model of the nation-state implies that its population constitutes a nation, united by a common descent, a common language and many forms of shared culture.

When the implied unity was absent, the nation-state often tried to create it. It promoted a uniform national language, through language policy. The creation of national systems of compulsory primary education and a relatively uniform curriculum in secondary schools, was the most effective instrument in the spread of the national languages. The schools also taught the national history, often in a propagandistic and mythologised version, and (especially during conflicts) some nation-states still teach this kind of history. Language and cultural policy was sometimes negative, aimed at the suppression of non-national elements. Language prohibitions were sometimes used to accelerate the adoption of national languages, and the decline of minority languages. In some cases these policies triggered bitter conflicts and further ethnic separatism. But where it worked, the cultural uniformity and homogeneity of the population increased. Conversely, the cultural divergence at the border became sharper: in theory, a uniform French identity extends from the Atlantic coast to the Rhine, and on the other bank of the Rhine, a uniform German identity begins. To enforce that model, both sides have divergent language policy and educational systems, although the linguistic boundary is in fact well inside France, and the Alsace region changed hands four times between 1870 and 1945.

THE SOVEREIGN STATE IN MODERN POLITICAL THOUGHT

The rise of the modern state system was closely related to changes in political thought, especially concerning the changing understanding of legitimate state power. Early modern defenders of absolutism such as Thomas Hobbes and Jean Bodin undermined the doctrine of the divine right of kings by arguing that the power of kings should be justified by reference to the people. Hobbes in particular went further and argued that political power should be justified with reference to the individual, not just to the people understood collectively. Both Hobbes and Bodin thought they were defending the power of kings, not advocating democracy, but their arguments about the nature of sovereignty were fiercely resisted by more traditional defenders of the power of kings, like Sir Robert Filmer in England, who thought that such defenses ultimately opened the way to more democratic claims.

These and other early thinkers introduced two important concepts in order to justify sovereign power: the idea of a state of nature and the idea of a social contract. The first concept describes an imagined situation in which the state-understood as a centralized, coercive power-does not exist, and human beings have all their natural rights and powers; the second describes the conditions under which a voluntary agreement could take human beings out of the state of nature and into a state of civil society. Depending on what they understood human nature to be and the natural rights they thought human beings had in that state, various writers were able to justify more or less extensive forms of the state as a remedy for the problems of the state of nature. Thus, for example, Hobbes, who described the state of nature as a "war of every man, against every man," argued that sovereign power should be almost absolute since almost all sovereign power would be better than such a war, whereas John Locke, who understood the state of nature in more positive terms, thought that state power should be strictly limited. Both of them nevertheless understood the powers of the state to be limited by what rational individuals would agree to in a hypothetical or actual social contract.

The idea of the social contract lent itself to more democratic interpretations than Hobbes or Locke would have wanted. Jean-Jacques Rousseau, for example, argued that the only valid social contract would be one were individuals would be subject to laws that only themselves had made and assented to, as in a small direct democracy. Today the tradition of social contract reasoning is alive in the work of John Rawls and his intellectual heirs, though in a very abstract form.

Rawls argued that rational individuals would only agree to social institutions specifying a set of inviolable basic liberties and a certain amount of redistribution to alleviate inequalities for the benefit of the worst off.

Lockean state of nature reasoning, by contrast, is more common in the libertarian tradition of political thought represented by the work of Robert Nozick. Nozick argued that given the natural rights that human beings would have in a state of nature, the only state that could be justified would be a minimal state whose sole functions would be to provide protection and enforce agreements. Murray Rothbard, another prominent libertarian, suggests that these protection and enforcement functions of government lead to a definition of the state as any entity that has a monopoly on crime in a given area.

Some contemporary thinkers, such as Michel Foucault, have argued that political theory needs to get away from the notion of the state: "We need to cut off the king's head. In political theory that has still to be done." By this he meant that power in the modern world is much more decentralized and uses different instruments than power in the early modern era, so that the notion of a sovereign, centralized state is increasingly out of date.

FEDERATED STATES

A federation (Latin: *foedus, foederis*, 'covenant'), also known as a federal state, is a type of sovereign state characterized by a union of partially self-governing states or regions united by a central (federal) government. In a federation, the self-governing status of the component states is typically constitutionally entrenched and may not be altered by a unilateral decision of the central government. The form of government or constitutional structure found in a federation is known as federalism. It can be considered the opposite of another system, the unitary state. The government of Germany with sixteen federated *Länder* is an example of a federation, whereas neighboring Austria and its *Bundesländer* was a unitary state with administrative divisions that became federated, and neighboring France by contrast has always been unitary. Federations may be multi-ethnic, or cover a large area of territory, although neither is necessarily the case. Federations are most often founded on an original agreement between a number of sovereign states based on mutual concerns or interests. The initial agreements create a stability that encourages other common interests, brings the disparate territories closer, and gives them all even more common ground. At some time this is recognized and a movement is organized to merge more closely. Other times, especially when common cultural factors are at play such as ethnicity and language, some of these steps in this pattern are expedited and compressed. The international council for federal countries, the Forum of Federations, is based in Ottawa, Canada. It helps share best practices among countries with federal systems of government, and currently includes nine countries as partner governments.

Bibliography

Ashraf, A.: *Political Sociology : A New Grammar of Politics*, Universities Press, Delhi, 1983.

Balveer Singh: *Medical Sociology of Tribal Community*, Himanshu, Delhi, 1992.

Carl, J. Friedrich: *Constitutional Government and Democracy*, Boston, Ginn, 1950.

Chandra, Suresh : *Understanding Political Sociology*, Jnanada Prakashan, Delhi, 2011.

Diwan, Jagmohan : *Fundamentals of Rural Sociology*, Cyber Tech Pub, Delhi, 2009.

Engineer, Asghar Ali: *Mandal Commission Controversy*, Delhi, Ajanta Publications, 1991.

Eysenck, Hans : *Psychoticism as a Dimension of Personality*, Pergamon, Elsevier Science Inc, Amsterdam, 1997.

Fran Tonkiss: *Contemporary Economic Sociology: Globalization, Production, Inequality*, Manohar, Delhi, 2008.

Gurukal, Rajan: *The Formation of Caste Society in Kerala*, Rawat Publications, New Delhi, 1994.

James, L. Brierly: *The Law of Nations,* New York, Oxford University Press, 1955 .

Jeff Hass: *Economic Sociology: An Introduction*, Manohar, Delhi, 2008.

Khan, Masood Ali : *Cultural Sociology of India*, Arise Pub, Delhi, 2006.

Kramer, Laura : *The Sociology of Gender : A Brief Introduction*, Rawat, Delhi, 2004.

Laura Kramer: *The Sociology of Gender : A Brief Introduction*, Rawat, Delhi, 2004.

Louis, Prakash : *The Political Sociology of Dalit Assertion*, Gyan, Delhi, 2003.

Masood Ali Khan: *Cultural Sociology of India*, Arise Pub, Delhi, 2006.

Michael Stewart: *Modern Forms of Government: A Comparative Study*, New York, Frederick A. Praeger, 1961.

Ramesh, G. S. : *Philosophy of Indian Sociology*, Global Vision, Delhi, 2005.

Rao, M. S. A.: *Social Movement and Social Transformation: A Study of Backward Class Movement*, New Delhi, Macmillian Press, 1978.

Rathod, P B : *Fundamentals of Political Sociology*, ABD, Delhi, 2005.

Ruhela, S.P. : *Research Tools in Sociology of Education*, Indian, Delhi, 2001.

Samuel H. Beer : *Patterns of Government: The Major Political Systems of Europe*, New York, Random House, 1958.

Silverberg, James: *Social Mobility in the Caste System in India*, Mouton Publishers, The Hague, 1968.

Stephen K. Bailey: *Congress Makes a Law*, New York, Columbia University Press, 1950.

Sujatha, V. : *Health by the People : Sociology of Medical Lore*, Rawat, Delhi, 2003.

Thomas R. : *Elements of Government*, New York, Random House, 1960.

Tyagi, S.P. : *Sociology and Social Conflict*, Sublime, Delhi, 2006.

Verma, R.P. : *Dynamics of Political Sociology*, Rajat, Delhi, 2001.

Weinberg, R. : *Women Anthropologists*, Westport, CT: Greenwood, 1988.

Yogendra Singh: *Ideology and Theory in Indian Sociology*, Rawat, Delhi, 2004.

Index

R

S

T

W